OXFORD ENGLISH MONOGRAPHS

Victorian Poetry and the Culture of the Heart

KIRSTIE BLAIR

CLARENDON PRESS · OXFORD

OXFORD

UNIVERSITY PRESS

Great Clarendon Street, Oxford OX2 6DP

Oxford University Press is a department of the University of Oxford.
It furthers the University's objective of excellence in research, scholarship,
and education by publishing worldwide in

Oxford New York

Auckland Cape Town Dar es Salaam Hong Kong Karachi
Kuala Lumpur Madrid Melbourne Mexico City Nairobi
New Delhi Shanghai Taipei Toronto

With offices in

Argentina Austria Brazil Chile Czech Republic France Greece
Guatemala Hungary Italy Japan Poland Portugal Singapore
South Korea Switzerland Thailand Turkey Ukraine Vietnam

Oxford is a registered trademark of Oxford University Press
in the UK and in certain other countries

Published in the United States
by Oxford University Press Inc., New York

British Library Cataloguing in Publication Data
Data available

Library of Congress Cataloging in Publication Data
Blair, Kirstie.
Victorian poetry and the culture of the heart / Kirstie Blair.
p. cm.—(Oxford English monographs)
Includes bibliographical references and index.
ISBN-13: 978–0–19–927394–2 (alk. paper)
ISBN-10: 0–19–927394–4 (alk. paper)
1. English poetry—19th century—History and criticism. 2. Heart in literature.
3. Body, Human, in literature. 4. Emotions in literature. I. Title. II. Series.
PR591B53 2006
821′.8093561—dc22   2006000900

Typeset by Laserwords Private Limited, Chennai, India
Printed in Great Britain
on acid-free paper by
Biddles Ltd., King's Lynn, Norfolk

ISBN 0–19–927394–4   978–0–19–927394–2

Acknowledgements

Many people have helped in the writing of this book. Particular thanks are due to my D.Phil. supervisor, Matthew Reynolds, examiners Robert Douglas-Fairhurst and Matthew Campbell, and the readers for Oxford University Press for their helpful comments and encouragement. I am also grateful to Tom Perridge at OUP for his help in the preparation of the manuscript. Colleagues and former colleagues and friends at Oxford, particularly Mina Gorji, Anthony Bale, Alex Gillespie, Timothy Phillips, Marion Turner, Elliot Kendall, Muireann O'Cinneide, Julia Reid, Isobel Hurst, and Stefano Evangelista, have always been on hand for advice and support. Jason Rudy and Matthew Bevis kindly read and commented on chapters of this work: their suggestions were extremely useful. Catherine Robson shared her unpublished work (which deals with similar themes) with me, and reading it has undoubtedly contributed to this book. I have also benefited greatly from conversations with Kate Flint, Tricia Lootens, Emma Mason, and Mary Arseneau, among others. With regard to the medical history content, George Rousseau, Steve Sturdy, and Lorna Campbell provided invaluable help. Feedback I received at various conferences in the past few years, in particular those hosted by the Tennyson Society, the British Association for Victorian Studies, the 'Framing and Imagining Disease' workshop, and the Victorians Institute, was also very helpful in shaping my work. In addition, I would not have started working on Victorian literature or continued to work on it were it not for my undergraduate tutor, Mark Wormald, who first interested me in this topic.

In producing this book I have used several libraries extensively. Thanks are particularly due to the staff of the Upper Reading Room in the Bodleian Library, the English Faculty Library, and the Radcliffe Science Library in Oxford, and the Wellcome Library for the History of Medicine in London. Earlier versions of the argument and material contained in this book have been published elsewhere. Part of Chapter 1 appeared as ' "Proved on the Pulses": Heart Disease in Victorian Culture, 1830–1860' in George Rousseau with Miranda Gill, David Haycock, and Malte Herwig (eds.), *Framing and Imagining Disease in Cultural History* (Houndmills: Palgrave, 2003), 285–302 and a section from Chapter 2 is included in 'Spasmodic Affections: Poetry, Pathology and the Spasmodic Hero', *Victorian Poetry*, 42 (2004), Special Issue: Spasmodic Poetry and Poetics, ed. Jason Rudy and Charles LaPorte, 473–90. Some material from Chapter 4 also appeared in 'Touching Hearts: Queen Victoria and the Curative Powers of *In Memoriam*', *Tennyson Research Bulletin*, 7 (2001), 246–55. I am grateful to Palgrave Macmillan and to the editors of *Victorian Poetry* and the *Tennyson Research Bulletin* for permission to reprint.

Finally, my greatest debt is to Matthew Creasy, who was there from the outset and has been an immense support throughout.

K.B.

Contents

Abbreviations

Allott and Super	*Matthew Arnold: A Critical Edition of the Major Works*, ed. Miriam Allott and R. H. Super (Oxford: Oxford University Press, 1986)
Collected Works	*The Collected Works of Samuel Taylor Coleridge*, ed. Kathleen Coburn et al., 16 vols. (London: Routledge, 1971–2001)
Cook and Wedderburn	*The Works of John Ruskin*, ed. E. T. Cook and Alexander Wedderburn, 39 vols. (London: George Allen, 1909)
EBB	Elizabeth Barrett Browning
Kelley and Lewis	*The Brownings' Correspondence*, ed. Philip Kelley and Scott Lewis, 13 vols. (Winfield, Kan.: Wedgstone Press, 1992–)
Lang	*The Letters of Matthew Arnold*, ed. Cecil Y. Lang, 6 vols. (Charlottesville: University Press of Virginia, 1996–2001)
Lang and Shannon	*The Letters of Alfred Lord Tennyson*, ed. Cecil Y. Lang and Edgar F. Shannon, 3 vols. (Oxford: Clarendon Press, 1982)
Mabbott	Edgar Allan Poe, *Collected Works*, ed. Thomas Ollive Mabbott, 3 vols. (Cambridge, Mass: Harvard University Press, 1969)
Memoir	Hallam Tennyson, *Alfred Lord Tennyson: A Memoir*, 2 vols. (London: Macmillan, 1897)
RB	Robert Browning
Sermons	*The Sermons and Devotional Writings of Gerard Manley Hopkins*, ed. Christopher Devlin (London: Oxford University Press, 1959)

Introduction

In 1841, *The Times* reported an inquest on Honoria Brien, a young woman who died unexpectedly in a state of poverty and starvation. The cause of her death was recorded as heart disease: largely, it seems, due to a witness who reported that Honoria told her, 'my heart is so compressed, and I am sure it is breaking'.[1] While a sense of 'compression' in the chest does have some authority as a symptom of cardiac illness, the chief weight of the witness statement clearly lay in the theory of heartbreak. The inquest was able to interpret a figurative expression as a physical reality. This would have been supported by contemporary medical authority. 'Violent feelings not only agitate, but may kill the heart in a moment; in short, broken hearts are medical facts,' as James Garth Wilkinson, philosopher and physiologist, observed in 1851.[2] Rather than ascribing Honoria's death purely to physical factors such as malnourishment, or attributing it to social or economic factors like poverty and deprivation, those involved in the inquest chose to perceive it in terms of emotional collapse.

In considering the heart in Victorian literature, the reader repeatedly encounters such moments, slippages between the metaphorical and the literal. Conceptions of the heart, whether in literature, medical textbooks, or the formal language of an inquest, oscillate

---

[1] *The Times*, 15 Jan. 1841, p. 5.
[2] James John Garth Wilkinson, *The Human Body and its Connexion with Man* (London: Chapman and Hall, 1851), 219.

uneasily between the primary physical sense of the organ within the breast and traditional associations of the heart with romantic love, spirituality, and the play of the emotions and passions. The heart, unlike more free-floating concepts such as 'soul' or even 'mind', is ultimately always embodied, tied to a specific location within the breast. In the nineteenth century, I suggest throughout this book, the rapid rise of physiological and medical explanations of bodily processes meant that the embodied heart assumed a vital role in culture and literature. References to the heart in the literature of this period take on more literal meanings, as figurative uses of the heart start to attract medical implications. Conversely, as actual heart disease comes to be read as a metaphor for cultural and social problems—loss of faith, for instance, or anxieties about appropriate gendered behaviour—references to the physical heart and to heart disease have significance beyond the purely literal. Franco Moretti argues that:

> Taking the figurative sense literally means considering the metaphor as an *element of reality*. It means, in other words, that a particular intellectual construction—the metaphor and the ideology expressed within it—really has become a 'material force', an independent entity, that escapes the rational control of its user.[3]

This formulation is more complicated in relation to the heart because heart metaphors already tend to be rooted in a 'material force', the physical heart. But Moretti's suggestive account does hint at how heart-based metaphors might shape physical reality and 'escape control' by carrying implications not foreseen by the user. The broken heart is a good example: if the loss of love is felt as a physical pain at the heart, is this because the metaphorical term 'heartbreak' has taken on materiality, or does the metaphor of heartbreak itself stem from the bodily location of this pain?[4]

---

[3] Franco Moretti, 'Dialectic of Fear', in *Signs Taken for Wonders: Essays in the Sociology of Literary Forms*, trans. Susan Fischer et al., 2nd edn. (London: Verso, 1988), 83–108 (p. 106).

[4] Mark Johnson has argued that all metaphors have their origins in the human body, though he is more concerned with actions than with sensations. *The Body in the Mind:*

To take one nineteenth-century example of metaphors acting on the body, in Robert Browning's 'The Flight of the Duchess' the narrator apparently feels the commonplace 'to make a clean breast' coming true:

> I always wanted to make a clean breast of it:
> And now it is made—why, my heart's blood, that went trickle,
> Trickle, but anon, in such muddy driblets,
> Is pumped up brisk now, through the main ventricle,
> And genially floats me about the giblets.[5]

'[T]rickle, | Trickle, but anon' breaks with the alternating iambic and anapaestic feet, introducing irregularity and uncertainty into the metre. The deliberate clumsiness of 'went trickle' and the enjambement slow down these lines and give a sense of stumbling, an uncertain pulse. In the succeeding line, Browning represents the 'briskness' of pulse and circulation through the return to a regulated rhythm, speeded on by the dactyls of 'thróugh thĕ maĭn véntrĭclĕ'. The narrator is tongue in cheek, but he is also expressing the medical commonplace that performing good acts and relieving the burden of guilty secrets would reduce tension within the body and thus might literally heal the heart. The phrase 'to make a clean breast' is performative, in that stating it already begins a physical process of cleansing.

In this study I am interested in precisely such conjunctions of the metaphorical and the literal, in the inevitable presence of the physical heart in poetic usage and in the way in which that presence is embodied in form and metre. What was at stake for poets in writing of and from the heart? What kind of culture of the heart existed in the Victorian period—what was known or surmised about its workings—and how did this impinge upon poetry? Considering

The Bodily Basis of Meaning, Imagination and Reason (Chicago: University of Chicago Press, 1987).

[5] Robert Browning, 'The Flight of the Duchess', XVII. 848–52. *Robert Browning: The Poems*, ed. John Pettigrew and Thomas Collins, 3 vols. (Harmondsworth: Penguin, 1981), vol. i. All further references are to this edition and will be given in the text.

this 'culture of the heart' implies studying the cultivation of the heart, analysing and representing its workings within the individual, and engaging with a wider interest in the heart as metaphor for society's communal problems or successes. The sheer number of references to the heart and to the related actions of pulse and circulation in Victorian literature, and its constant deployment in different discourses, suggests that during this period the culture of the heart often became a cult. The heart is both material and spiritual, public and private, active and passive; the most intimate part of an individual yet the most detached, in the sense that its actions cannot necessarily be controlled. Poetry provides the clearest instance of these negotiations. It was (and is) the literary genre most associated with personal and emotional revelations—writing of and from the heart—and was hence popularly perceived as the most affective. Victorian poetry constantly and self-consciously plays with metaphors of the heart, and the extent to which this play participates in and comments on the culture of the heart needs to be considered if we are to assess what nineteenth-century poetry was trying to do in terms of affect and whether it was successful.

The heart has of course been a vital literary image in English since the medieval period, and its consequence in earlier centuries as '*the single most important word referring both to the body and the mind*', as Robert Erickson puts it, has been ably assessed by a number of critics.[6] Eric Jäger's significant work on the heart in medieval literature concentrates on the image of the heart as text.[7] Also on medieval literature, Mihad Doueihi focuses on the particular set of metaphors surrounding the concept of eating or consuming the heart, using a theoretical perspective to assess their significance, and Jacques Le Goff considers the politicization of the metaphor of heart as king.[8] Scott Manning Stevens and Thomas Fuchs have recently

---

[6] Robert Erickson, *The Language of the Heart, 1600–1750* (Philadelphia: University of Pennsylvania Press, 1997), 11.

[7] Eric Jäger, *The Book of the Heart* (Chicago: University of Chicago Press, 2000).

[8] Mihad Doueihi, *A Perverse History of the Human Heart* (Cambridge, Mass.: Harvard University Press, 1997). Jacques Le Goff, 'Head or Heart? The Political Use of Bodily

examined from different perspectives the shifts in heart-centred metaphor immediately preceding and following William Harvey's *De Motu Cordis* (1628; first translated 1653).[9] Harvey's hugely influential work, which was still widely read in the nineteenth century, established the tendency to describe physiological actions of the heart in metaphorical terms, and to give its physical behaviour spiritual significance:

> So is the heart the first principle of life and the sun of the microcosm . . . by whose virtue and pulsation the blood is moved, made perfect, quickened and preserved from corruption and lumpiness, and this familiar household god performs his office for the whole body by nourishing, cherishing and quickening, being the foundation of life and the author of all things.[10]

The heart here possesses its own agency, and is associated with religion and morality as well as strength and nourishment. 'Virtue' sums this up in its pun on the Latin sense of 'virtus' as strength or courage and the related English sense of moral goodness: 'virtue' could be a physical attribute but is tilted towards spiritual significance. Erickson considers this passage and others as instances of Harvey thinking about the heart in gendered terms as well as relating its actions to biblical rhetoric. The heart 'like a husband, does his duty to the body'.[11] This kind of rhetoric, in Erickson's argument,

---

Metaphors in the Middle Ages', in Michel Feher et al. (eds.), *Fragments for a History of the Human Body*, 3 vols. (New York: Zone, 1989), iii. 12–27.

[9] Scott Manning Stevens, 'Sacred Heart and Secular Brain', in David Hillman and Carla Mazzio (eds.), *The Body in Parts: Fantasies of Corporeality in Early Modern Europe* (London: Routledge, 1997), 263–84. Thomas Fuchs specifically considers how the heart came to be seen as a mechanism in the 17th century (*The Mechanization of the Heart: Harvey and Descartes*, trans. Marjorie Grene (Rochester, NY: University of Rochester Press, 2001)).

[10] William Harvey, *An Anatomical Disputation Concerning the Movement of the Heart and the Blood in Living Creatures*, trans. and introd. Gweneth Whitteridge (Oxford: Blackwell, 1976), 76. Renewed interest in the heart in 19th-century medicine, Whitteridge notes, led to the republication of Harvey's treatise in the *London Medical and Surgical Journal* (1832–3), and then in a new translation in 1847 (p. ix).

[11] Erickson, 83.

inaugurates an enduring theme of the heart as masculine and phallic. He convincingly traces this and related metaphors of the heart as book or text in texts from *Paradise Lost* to *Clarissa*, noting the ways in which imagery of the heart is sexualized and used to represent desire. Erickson's study (which along with Jäger's is the most significant work on the literary heart) stops just before the advent of the age of sensibility in the 1790s. The story is taken up from here by John Beer's excellent *Wordsworth and the Human Heart*, which provides an exemplary account of the heart's significance for a particular writer and demonstrates how the heart came to be an index for poetic sympathy.[12] While there is no general study of the heart image in Romanticism, a number of studies from the last decade also touch upon this in their considerations of the role of sensibility, emotion, and enthusiasm in literature of this period.[13]

Victorian poetry evidently relies heavily upon these earlier uses of the heart in literature, but it also presents a renewed concentration of interest in heart-centred imagery and, crucially, a shift in focus towards the pathological. Romantic poets had ensured that poetry would be the discourse most associated with the sympathetic heart, written from the poet's heart to speak directly to that of the reader, based on principles of affect and communication. The influential image of the poet fostered in the first decades of the nineteenth century by Keats, Shelley, and Byron and their female contemporaries Letitia Landon and Felicia Hemans, among others, was of a man or woman more alert to the nuances of feeling, more conscious of the heart's demands. The fetishization of the poet's heart—shown literally in the case of Shelley's preserved heart—became commonplace.[14] Victorian poetry, however, frequently transforms this image

---

[12] John Beer, *Wordsworth and the Human Heart* (London: Macmillan, 1978).

[13] See for example Adela Pinch, *Strange Fits of Passion: Epistemologies of Emotion, Hume to Austen* (Stanford, Calif.: Stanford University Press, 1996); Jerome McGann, *The Poetics of Sensibility* (Oxford: Clarendon Press, 1996); Jon Mee, *Romanticism, Enthusiasm and Regulation: Poetics and the Policing of Culture in the Romantic Period* (Oxford: Oxford University Press, 2003).

[14] On Shelley's heart, see Eric O. Clarke, 'Shelley's Heart: Sexual Politics and Cultural Value', *Yale Journal of Criticism*, 8 (1995), 187–208. Charles Angell Bradford, in *Heart*

of the poet and the positive associations of writing from the heart into something darker and more dubious. Although the power of poetry as an agent in forming morality and positive emotions remained a commonplace of critical discourse in this period, poetry as a pursuit was also supposed to engender the kind of sensitivity and susceptibility which endangered health—and the heart was perceived as the organ most liable to suffer damage, both from reading and by writing poetry. Traditional associations of the heart with love, romance, spirituality, and altruism retain their force in Victorian poetry, but the heart is frequently represented as diseased and alienated, fallen away from these positive aspirations.

While assigning causes for this shift necessarily involves speculation, it does fit with general trends. If the period succeeding the French Revolution represented (on the Continent and in England) a point at which emotions were taken seriously as political operants and the heart's feelings were hence considered central to political and moral beliefs and actions, the consensus is that this brand of sentimentality rapidly lost credibility in England from the early nineteenth century onward and came to be perceived as politically and morally suspect.[15] Wordsworth's 'Lines Written above Tintern Abbey', to take a classic example, celebrates the 'sensations sweet | Felt in the blood and felt along the heart' as restorative and calming. 'Felt along the heart', a curious phrase which seems to substitute 'along' for the more common and easily imagined 'within', links heart and circulation by implying that these sensations run throughout the body, moving in each vein.[16] As the nineteenth century

---

Burial (London: Allen & Unwin, 1933), observes that the preservation of the hearts of famous figures became increasingly common at the start of the 19th century.

[15] For the strongest argument along these lines, see William Reddy, *The Navigation of Feeling: A Framework for the History of the Emotions* (Cambridge: Cambridge University Press, 2001). Janet Todd's short account of sensibility (*Sensibility: An Introduction* (London: Methuen, 1976)) also emphasizes the decline of sensibility in the first decades of the 19th century.

[16] 'Lines written a few miles above Tintern Abbey', lines 28–9. *Lyrical Ballads*, ed. R. L. Brett and A. R. Jones, 2nd edn. (London: Routledge, 1991). Further references to poems from this edition will be given in the text.

progressed, however, such Wordsworthian emphasis on healthful feeling and sympathy created through physical as well as mental identification became increasingly pathologized, as 'feeling' itself began to seem problematic and sympathy was discussed in terms which suggested the communication of disease as much as positive identification. When Arthur Hallam returns to Wordsworth's line in the late 1820s, in the opening of a gloomy poem about his misery and inability to write with feeling, he reworks it as 'When grief is felt along the blood'; a moment of despairing sadness, a rush of suffering along the veins instead of joy.[17] Hallam and his Cambridge contemporaries took instead for their model Coleridge's comment in *Aids to Reflection* on why men fear to interrogate their feelings:

> There is an aching hollowness in the bosom, a dark cold speck at the heart, an obscure and boding sense of a somewhat, that must be kept *out of sight* of the conscience; some secret lodger, whom they can neither resolve to eject or retain.[18]

Coleridge's use of 'at' (rather than 'in' or 'on') gives a vaguer sense of something near or around the heart, and also hints at the phrase 'at heart', meaning inwardly or secretly ('he was sick at heart'). This passage is alluded to in at least two letters between members of the Cambridge Apostles of Hallam and Tennyson's generation, and may lurk behind some of Tennyson's darker pronouncements on the heart in *Poems, Chiefly Lyrical* (1830). Michael Wheeler, noting that in Romanticism 'the heart and feeling are apotheosized as the inner or internal authority in both theology and literature', remarks on the number of times that Coleridge mentions the heart in *Aids to Reflection*.[19] Yet while Coleridge constantly invokes it, it is now less a reliable authority than an untrustworthy and decaying prop. 'Sensibility', he claims at one point, 'is not even a sure pledge

---

[17] 'A Farewell to Glenarbach', line 1. *The Writings of Arthur Hallam*, ed. T. H. Vail Motter (London: Oxford University Press, 1943).

[18] *Aids to Reflection*, ed. John Beer, 24, in *Collected Works*, vol. ix.

[19] Michael Wheeler, 'Tennyson, Newman and the Question of Authority', in David Jasper (ed.), *The Interpretation of Belief: Coleridge, Schleiermacher and Romanticism* (London: Macmillan, 1986), 185–201 (p. 187).

of a GOOD HEART.'[20] If the acuteness of feeling associated with sensibility can no longer guarantee a 'good' heart, where 'good' refers ambiguously to both moral worth and physical soundness, then the heart is compromised. Without a good heart the curative properties of affective literature are in doubt.

By the 1850s, the decade on which this study is centred, this brand of post-Romantic poetic despair can seem entrenched. Matthew Arnold's poetry, discussed in detail in Chapter 4, provides another instance. In 'The Buried Life' he also reworks a familiar exhortation from Wordsworth, 'That we have all of us one human heart' ('The Old Cumberland Beggar', 146), into 'The same heart beats in every human breast!'[21] In Wordsworth's line, 'one' is emphasized because it takes a rhythmical stress and thus slows down the iambic metre, effectively stressing that everyone participates in a general humanity, the hearts of poet and readers beating as one in sympathy and mutual support. In the context of 'The Old Cumberland Beggar', moreover, the heart's humanity is a valued asset. Arnold is not so sure. 'The same heart beats in every human breast!' is much more specific about the heart's location and its action, meaning that it is pinned down to the physical 'human' organ, frail and mortal, not a diffusive spiritual presence. An exclamation mark (as opposed to Wordsworth's full stop) suggests surprise and the line is immediately succeeded by 'But'. Since the primary focus of 'The Buried Life' is on a heart that is unknowable and inaccessible, saying that everyone has a similar heart becomes an image of isolation rather than community. Only the individual can hope to know his or her own heart, and that in very rare moments of grace. Sympathetic contact and affect in Arnold between poet and reader, poem and reader, or the poet and his own self, his 'buried life', is compromised.

Victorian poems frequently contain an intense and oddly patho-logical concentration on the heart, an interrogation or attempted

---

[20] *Aids to Reflection*, 57–8.

[21] 'The Buried Life', line 23. *Matthew Arnold: A Critical Edition of the Major Works*, ed. Miriam Allott and R. H. Super (Oxford: Oxford University Press, 1986). All further references are to this edition and are given in the text.

interrogation of its actions and feelings. I argue here that instances of this are particularly significant in their relation to three major discourses besides poetics: medicine, religion, and gender, all of which are explored in later chapters. I have concentrated on these discourses because each uses the heart to negotiate with various problems or questions raised by nineteenth-century culture. In terms of religion, the heart has of course always been an essential Christian symbol and its presence in the Bible informs much literary imagery. At the start of the nineteenth century, the rise of the Evangelical movement, with its concentration on a personal relationship with Christ, privileged the heart's feelings and gave them intense spiritual significance.[22] This inaugurated a debate over the function of feeling in religious faith; but the more that feeling was valued and presented as essential, the more doubts arose about the correct means to access and express it. By the 1850s poets like Arnold and his contemporaries were calling into question the validity of trusting individual feelings as a guide to faith and the security of God's presence in the heart. Religious faith itself, moreover, gradually became less of an established certainty throughout the period. Arnold's vision of an inaccessible heart sums up some of the Victorian culture of doubt in which he was a participant, whether willing or unwilling. A lack of trust in the heart and a tendency to present it as unreliable was also, I argue, strongly related to new medical and physiological investigations into heart, pulse, and circulation, which inevitably meant that the materiality of the heart came to the forefront of discussion. It is often in Victorian medical texts that the relation between literal and metaphorical, the 'real' heart and the heart sanctified by literary associations, is most marked. Cultural and religious representations of heartsickness by Coleridge and others may have influenced the medical establishment in its increased emphasis on heart disease, but equally medical interest in actual heart disease doubtless contributed to cultural perceptions of the heart as decayed and incapable of healthy feeling. As we

---

[22] Evangelical links to the heart are nicely expressed in the title as well as the content of Elisabeth Jay's study, *The Religion of the Heart: Anglican Evangelicalism and the Nineteenth-Century Novel* (Oxford: Clarendon Press, 1979).

will see, cardiac disease was associated with emotional sensitivity, which meant that it also had gendered implications and tended to be linked to peculiarly feminine complaints. Young men (like Arnold) who believed themselves to be sufferers risked being considered effeminate. The culture of the phallic heart explored by Erickson in eighteenth-century literature persists in much Victorian literature, but correspondingly the notion of the 'woman's heart'—emotional, acutely responsive, and sympathetic—began to gain ground.

The uneasy power attached to the heart in many Victorian texts is also so emphatic because the heart seemed to be *losing* much of its traditional resonance, being displaced by new theories and beliefs. The fact that, from the late eighteenth century onwards, an imaginative shift occurred in relation to bodily processes, by which the nervous system and/or the brain came to displace the heart as the central agent within the body, suggests that the focus on the heart in Victorian poetry and poetics might be less a sign of dominance than of imminent displacement. At the period when the heart was about to be superseded as a potent presence in literature and medicine, it clamours for notice. In effect, the fear displayed by many Victorian poets is that the heart is on the verge of becoming a cliché, a dead metaphor. As John Beer observes:

> Since Wordsworth's day, the tendency to refer to the heart vaguely and diffusely has increased to such an extent that the sensibility of the intelligent reader has become largely anaesthetized to any mention of it. For that reason such a reader may hardly respond to its presence in Wordsworth's pages either.[23]

While Beer has twentieth-century readers in mind, Victorian poets anticipate and fear this anaesthesia and lack of response, in themselves as much as their readers. The extreme actions frequently attributed to the heart in Victorian poetry—throbbings, palpitations, attacks, and shocks—are attention-seeking, in the sense that they simultaneously announce the poet's ability to experience intense feeling and aim to

---

[23] John Beer, 3.

make the reader forcibly notice and experience the heart's actions. From this perspective, moreover, the heart sums up a more general nineteenth-century poetic anxiety about affect, the power to convey feeling and emotion from poet to reader through the medium of the text. Laments that the nineteenth century was an 'unpoetic' age can be read through metaphors of heartsickness. If the heart, perceived by Victorian poets and critics as an essential poetic image linked to the process of writing and the sympathy of reading, ceased to be meaningful as a concept, then how could poetic affect be described and imagined?

It is in relation to this question that the culture of the heart in the nineteenth century becomes most important. The last two decades have seen a renewed cross-disciplinary interest in the study of affect, how emotion is created and transferred, evident in the fields of anthropology, philosophy, sociology, and literary criticism, among others. In this work, emotions are defined as a complex combination of physiological feeling or sensation and rational thought.[24] Emotional experience is broadly perceived as a product of its context in the sense that emotions may not exist as such before they are named and classified. Emotion is thus the product of 'embodied sociality' rather than or as well as an individual event.[25] As Ronald De Sousa puts it in his influential 1987 study *The Rationality of Emotion*:

> We would not *notice* emotional phenomena unless they had a public name ... This kind of social dependency of emotions has something to do with people's tendency to imitate and follow fashions, to 'be conventional' in the sense in which being conventional contrasts with being eccentric.[26]

---

[24] Martha Nussbaum, *Upheavals of Thought: The Intelligence of Emotions* (Cambridge: Cambridge University Press, 2001), 25. Isobel Armstrong also argues that affect should not be excluded from rationality in *The Radical Aesthetic* (Oxford: Blackwell, 2000), 87.

[25] M. L. Lyon and J. M. Barbalet, 'Society's Body: Emotion and the "Somatization" of Social Theory', in Thomas J. Csordas (ed.), *Embodiment and Experience: The Existential Ground of Culture and Self* (Cambridge: Cambridge University Press, 1995), 48–68 (p. 48).

[26] Ronald De Sousa, *The Rationality of Emotion* (Cambridge, Mass.: MIT Press, 1987), 249.

The primary physiological basis of emotion is shaped through language into an expressible experience of that emotion, and it is only then that it is identified as such. This suggests that rather than emotions being transhistorical and instantly recognizable, they might be shaped by a particular culture. Different societies will have different 'corporal maps' which are used to recognize or locate feelings.[27] Heartsickness, I suggest, exemplifies these ideas in that it was a fashionable Victorian ailment, but one which has now ceased to have much medical or social meaning. The condition it described has been reclassified under names such as 'stress' or 'depression' and is imagined differently once it is no longer envisaged as stemming from the heart. Symptoms which Victorian writers immediately attributed to cardiac disease might now be read as signs of a different condition or sickness. The way in which emotions are conceived and expressed, moreover, impacts not only upon mental perceptions but also upon physical behaviour. M. L. Lyon and J. M. Barbalet argue that:

> The body is intercommunicative and active, and it is so through emotion ... Emotion activates distinct dispositions, postures and movements which are not exactly attitudinal but also physical, involving the way in which individual bodies together with others articulate a common purpose, design or order.[28]

Teresa Brennan's recent study *The Transmission of Affect* extends Lyon and Barbalet's argument as she suggests that communication between individual bodies does not simply operate on a physical but on a physiological level: feeling another's heartbeat quicken might induce our own pulse to beat faster, for instance.[29] The heart's actions can be both read from the interior of the body (as in much poetry) and

---

[27] 'To feel is most often to recognize, localize or identify some phenomena in relation to corporal maps established from biological and cultural data.' Severine Pilloud and Micheline Louis-Courvoisier, 'The Intimate Experience of the Body in the Eighteenth Century: Between Interiority and Exteriority', *Medical History*, 47 (2003), 451–72 (p. 452).

[28] Lyon and Barbalet, 48.

[29] Teresa Brennan, *The Transmission of Affect* (Ithaca, NY: Cornell University Press, 2004), *passim*.

perceived in 'dispositions, postures and movements', gestures such as pressing a hand to the heart or external signifiers such as the blush.

Considering how Victorian poets perceived the heart immediately raises questions about what Brennan describes as the 'transmission' of affect, the process by which 'the emotions and affects of one person, and the enhancing or depressing energies these affects entail, can enter into another'.[30] Brennan argues that Western philosophy, in focusing on the self-contained individual and praising the mind at the expense of the body, has created difficulties in understanding 'that the senses and the flesh embody a logic that moves far faster than thought'.[31] Her work hence calls for a more nuanced understanding of the influence of one person's sensations upon another or the way in which an atmosphere might be created or enhanced by a group of people responding to each other. While her perspective, largely drawn from psychoanalytic discourse, concentrates more on the biological similarities of emotion across cultures and periods than on social constructivist views, it agrees with the concept of the body as 'intercommunicative'. *The Transmission of Affect* is heavily premissed on new neurological and biological investigations into the effects of sensory transmitters such as pheromones, but, as Brennan notes, science now appears to be confirming ideas that have been a staple of commonplaces and folk wisdom for centuries. Her study as well as recent medical research confirms that twenty-first-century medicine is to some extent enacting a return to ideas current in the nineteenth century and before—to take one example, the growing consensus that heart attacks (as well as many other illnesses) might have a more complex relation to stress and other emotional factors than has been assumed.

There are clear parallels between recent accounts of the emotional body and the nineteenth-century emphasis on the physical force of emotions. Feeling was seen as a performative act that had consequences for the body; as I examine in the first chapter, doctors believed that concentrating upon emotions of pain or grief—or

---

[30] Brennan, 3.   [31] Ibid. 136.

alternatively emotions of intense pleasure—might eventually lead to organic heart disease.[32] The heart was a nexus for debates over the emotions because it allowed writers to evade the necessity to ascribe emotion either purely to physical causes or to mental ones. The materiality (or otherwise) of all feeling and thought was a crucial area of debate, and the heart, because of its status as a physical organ with spiritual connotations, was central to this investigation. E. Warwick Slinn has recently argued that Victorian poetry functions as a critique of contemporary culture partly because it interrogates the division between material and spiritual: in this regard, the heart was a useful image to exploit.[33] In addition, arguments about the social construction of emotion in modern theory have implications for the nineteenth-century language of the heart, the 'system of commonplace' associated with it.[34] 'Heartsickness' as both term and condition, for example, was clearly socially constructed as a disorder affecting particular groups within society even while it might be experienced by individuals as personal and embodied. Statements such as Honoria's 'My heart is so compressed, and I am sure it is breaking' might function as what William Reddy has described as 'emotives'—performative statements which create the condition they describe. Emotives, in Reddy's discussion, are partially shaped by the prescriptions of society:

> Because emotions are closely associated with the dense networks of goals that give coherence to the self, the unity of a community—such as it may be—depends in part on its ability to provide a coherent set of prescriptions about emotions . . . Because intentional shaping of emotions is possible,

---

[32] For a general account of the Victorian discourse of the emotions, see Gesa Stedman, *Stemming the Torrent: Expression and Control in the Victorian Discourses on Emotions, 1830–1872* (Aldershot: Ashgate, 2002).

[33] E. Warwick Slinn, *Victorian Poetry as Cultural Critique: The Politics of Performative Language* (Charlottesville: University of Virginia Press, 2003).

[34] Max Black uses the term 'system of commonplace' to describe the cultural knowledge required to understand particular metaphors. See *Models and Metaphors* (Ithaca, NY: Cornell University Press, 1962), 40.

> . . . a community's emotional order must take the form of ideals
> to strive toward and strategies to guide individual effort.[35]

In the decades I consider, for instance, one prevalent ideal of healthy emotion rested upon the healthy, well-regulated heart, working smoothly and unobtrusively. Medical texts often promote this goal and suggest ways to achieve it. Although this might seem an individual ambition, it also had implications for the community in that the health of the state as a whole might be affected by the weak hearts of its citizens.

If the intense discussion of emotion and its containment in Victorian literature shows a sophisticated understanding of the emotions (whether physiological or mental) interacting with and influencing rational thought and behaviour, Victorian poets had an equally clear understanding of the transmission of affect from poet to poem and poem to reader. Contemporary critical comments on Tennyson, for example, included: 'Nature has taught him to throw his whole heart into his harmonies'; 'He has a deep knowledge of the human heart'; his poetry is 'timed to the beating pulses of the living present'; it 'belongs to those deepest forms of poetic expression which grow out of the heart'; 'he is among those *poets who enrich the blood of the world*' —this last a citation from Tennyson's own work *The Princess*.[36] According to these writers, as a poet he has a greater sensitivity to human emotion and an ability to pick up on the affects of the living present and respond to them. Furthermore, he responds to his emotional environment, enriching it. These critical comments are, however, considerably more optimistic about affective transmission than many of Tennyson's speakers would prove to be.

Besides the description of feelings in poetry, poets have at their disposal a vital agent in the transmission of affect: their use of rhythm. Brennan argues that:

---

[35] Reddy, 61.

[36] Edgar F. Shannon, *Tennyson and the Reviewers* (Cambridge, Mass.: Harvard University Press, 1952), 6, 86, 114, 143, 115.

> Rhythm is a tool in the expression of agency, just as words
> are. It can literally convey the tone of an utterance, and, in
> this sense, it does unite word and affect. Rhythm also has a
> unifying, regulating role in affective exchanges between two or
> more people.[37]

'Entrainment', the scientific term to describe two or more bodies
coming to share rhythmic processes (pendulums swinging together,
women in shared environments menstruating at the same time),
is a common trope in Victorian poems and is often described
in terms of hearts beating in time. But entrainment might also
happen on a physiological level between poem/poet and reader,
if the rhythm of a poem draws the reader into participation in a
bodily sense, affecting blood and breath. As I discuss in Chapter 2,
new theories of rhythm emerging in this period moved towards
perceiving it as an organic force, related to bodily movements
and hence able to influence the breath or heartbeat of both poet
and reader.

Expanding Brennan's argument on how people sharing a space or
with a strong emotional bond can influence one another to encompass
forms of affective reading might also extend its radical implications,
suggesting that the experience of being 'caught up' in reading, made
to experience another's emotions or the sensory surroundings of the
poem, might be enough to create those sensations or emotions in the
subject. The anxiety that we will see in nineteenth-century poetry,
however, is that such affect might be pathological, creating illness
or instability. In the light of this, it is again the interaction between
literature and medicine which becomes vital. The period between
1800 and 1860, which constitutes the main focus of this study,
has been characterized as the age of 'grand reform' in medicine, the
point at which it was poised on the verge of great discoveries. Yet
while medical culture was gradually modernizing and reaching ever
more accurate diagnoses of the processes within the body, British
physiological research prior to the 1860s, as Gerald Geison notes

---

[37] Brennan, 70.

in his excellent study of later Victorian physiology, was still mainly the province of amateurs, doctors taking time off from practice to investigate, and thus 'remained ... largely submerged in anatomy and in essentially religio-philosophical concerns'.[38] The immense physiological advances made in this period were still necessarily assimilated to a world-view in which Christian morality and older theories of the body based on the passions or humours were crucial factors. The popularity of heartsickness, discussed in the first chapter and throughout this book, in part stemmed from this fact; it could be used as a symbol of virtually any of society's ills, from the decline of manly patriotism, to the loss of religious faith, to the increased hardness of heart caused by a material and industrialized society. Chapter 1 therefore examines Victorian medical research into heart disease in some detail. It shows that during this period cardiac disease came to be regarded as a widespread and to some extent popular illness, particularly common in those possessing poetic talent. The question here is not simply how medicine influenced literature, or even vice versa. Rather, I hope to show that both poets and doctors were engaged in a mutual exchange of ideas about the heart which helped to shape a 'culture of the heart' specific to Victorian Britain.

The succeeding chapter turns to rhythm and the pulse, and argues that poetic theory in the nineteenth century gradually caught up with practice, as rhythm came to be envisaged as organic and variable. The use of the pulse to represent this idea of living rhythm raised questions about agency within the human body: who controls the heart and why does it beat? These questions had spiritual as well as immediate physical significance, given a tendency to link the heart-beat to cosmic processes and rhythms—what Tennyson famously

---

[38] Gerald Geison, *Michael Foster and the Cambridge School of Physiology: The Scientific Enterprise in Late Victorian Society* (Princeton: Princeton University Press, 1978), 1–78 (p. 4).

called 'the deep pulsations of the world'.[39] Far from alone in perceiving these pulsations, the speaker here uses an image repeated in
some of the most popular poetry of the 1840s and 1850s. The 'spasmodic school'—a loosely affiliated group of radical poets, mostly
from working-class backgrounds—were particularly vehement in
propagating the use of physical, heart-based imagery in poetry and
in suggesting that the pulsation of verse might have affective and
organic properties.

The final three chapters turn to specific poets: Elizabeth Barrett
Browning, Matthew Arnold, and Alfred Tennyson. What these
writers have in common (besides the fact that they all believed
themselves to suffer from heart disease) is that they published major
works in the 1850s, corresponding with important advances in
metrical theory and with a poetic craze for 'spasmodism'. The 1850s
have been read as the most confident decade of Victoria's reign: in the
title of one study by J. B. Priestley, her heyday.[40] In terms of poetry
they are also something of a golden age, a decade which opens with
the publication of *In Memoriam* and Wordsworth's *The Prelude* and
continues via Arnold's 'Empedocles on Etna', Clough's *Amours de
voyage*, Browning's *Men and Women*, Tennyson's *Maud*, and Barrett
Browning's *Aurora Leigh*, to mention only the obvious examples. Of
these poems, the various strands in the culture of the heart described
above seem to be best represented by Arnold's 'Empedocles on
Etna' and 'The Buried Life' (and of course by his later repudiation
of the themes contained within them), *In Memoriam, Maud*, and
Aurora Leigh. Chapter 3, on Barrett Browning, considers her work
in relation to gendered ideas about writing from the heart and
concerns with the heart as commodity. In both her private letters
and published poems, she is evidently very interested in the body

---

[39] Alfred Tennyson, *In Memoriam*, XCV. 40. *The Poems of Tennyson*, ed. Christopher
Ricks, 2nd edn., 3 vols. (Harlow: Longman, 1987), vol. ii. All further references are to
this edition and will be given in the text.

[40] J. B. Priestley, *Victoria's Heyday* (London: Heinemann, 1972).

and in the emotional impact of grief, love, and desire. As a woman writer well aware of the tradition to which she would inevitably be consigned, Barrett Browning knew that the heart was frequently gendered female and that there was a strongly perceived link between the suffering heart and the fragile woman's body. Her poems are interested in the heart in many different ways, but I suggest that in *Aurora Leigh* she is particularly concerned with ways of rewriting the cliché of the woman's heart and wrestling, through her heroine, with the concept of 'writing from the heart' and the related assumptions that poetry must be personal and emotional. Although this interest in reworking standard ideas about the heart was to some extent shared with Robert Browning, in his works the heart is only one cliché of many which he considers and disassembles. Relatively speaking, Browning writes of the heart less than most of his contemporaries. While an investigation of why this is lies outside the scope of this study, Browning could be described as a poet more interested in the movements of the mind than of the heart, eschewing simple emotional effects in favour of an appeal to the intellect. Unlike Barrett Browning's repeated and passionate invocations of the heart, he uses it but without apparently having much invested in it, personally or poetically.

Matthew Arnold was another poet who feared for his own heart, and his poetry is perhaps the most pessimistic about the heart's health and prospects written in this period. In Chapter 4, I read his poems in relation to religious discourse and suggest that some of their deeply felt ambiguity about feeling and emotion can be traced back to High Anglican anxieties about the use of feeling to determine religious faith. As the brief extract from Arnold discussed above demonstrates, a sense of heartsickness pervades his poems. He himself, of course, recognized their morbidity in his 1853 preface, allowing the possibility that their affect might be negative and even potentially dangerous. Like the poets cited in Chapter 2, he also uses rhythmic effects to represent this affect (or lack of affect). The final chapter of the book deals with Tennyson's *In Memoriam* and

Maud. Tennyson's work is cited throughout and to a significant extent his poetics underpin this study. While Tennyson invokes the heart throughout his early career, *In Memoriam* and *Maud* are the focus because they exemplify two different elements in his use of it. *In Memoriam* is a poem deeply interested in the curative possibilities of poetry, in which the speaker moves from an Arnoldian despair about the possibilities of sympathetic communication and heartfelt emotion, to a reintegration into world and community and an acceptance of the poem's power to convince with or without the poet's full assent. *Maud*, on the other hand, is perhaps the finest example in Victorian poetry of a speaker suffering from heart-related problems, including though not limited to cardiac disease. The speaker of *Maud* constantly pathologizes references to his heart and apparently cannot be saved by the healing influence of love or grief. Tennyson displays his medical knowledge both here and in *In Memoriam*, and shows that he can play with the established rhythms of the pulse and circulation, presenting affect as much in form as content.

This study concludes with the 1860s and a short discussion of poetic developments in this decade and beyond. The poets discussed in the conclusion—Whitman, Swinburne, Hopkins, and Christina Rossetti—could easily be the subject of separate chapters, not to mention the significant deployment of heart imagery in major poems of the same period, like Dante Gabriel Rossetti's *The House of Life* or George Meredith's *Modern Love*. The heart is such a common image in nineteenth-century poetry that no study could hope to be comprehensive. But what I hope to do here is to focus attention back onto the language and imagery of the heart and related formal effects, so that, rather than twenty-first-century readers glossing over references to the heart, pulses, and circulation in these poems, we recognize that there might have been a great deal at stake in what now might seem like a dead metaphor or a sentimental commonplace. To question what the heart did, or is doing, in Victorian poems is to examine some of the central cruxes of the period. Above all, it brings anxieties about the power of poetry itself, its affective communication, into sharp relief. Poetic representations of the heart's actions and discussion about the implications of these are fundamentally also arguments about the function and future of poetry itself.

1

Proved on the Pulses: Heart Disease in Victorian Literature and Culture

In 1824 Anne Lister, an English landowner staying in Paris, confided to her journal the details of a parlour game which involved taking the pulse of the other guests in her lodgings:

> Felt pulses, mistaking Mlle de Sans several times. Said I could not feel hers correctly. Said she reminded me of the following, which I gave her in pencil; 'When in my hand thy pulse is prest, I feel it alter mine, and draw another from my breast, in unison with thine.' 'Indeed', said she, 'if you were a man I know not what would be the end of all this.'[1]

The poem which Lister flirtatiously gives Mlle de Sans is a nice example of the transmission of affect: she cannot produce an accurate reading of de Sans's pulse because she is distracted by its effect on her own heart. De Sans's response to Lister's poetic communication clearly shows that she recognizes the possibilities of sexual desire created by this scene. Taking pulses was apparently a fashionable pursuit, but these Parisian women were slightly behind the times in that they were not playing with the new tool recently invented for this purpose, the stethoscope. As *The Times* reported in the same year, 'A wonderful instrument called the stethoscope . . . is

---

[1] 13 Oct. 1824, in *No Priest But Love: The Journals of Anne Lister 1824–1826*, ed. Helena Whitbread (Otley: Smith, Settle, 1992), 27. Lister's journals are famous for their explicit discussion of her lesbianism, and this incident is part of an ongoing flirtation with the women in her Parisian boarding house.

now in complete vogue in Paris … It is quite a fashion … to have recourse to the miraculous tube.'[2] René Laennec's invention of the stethoscope in 1819 was in fact fuelled by the need to prevent the hint of intimacy and potential indecency in pulse-taking (as in Lister's game) by removing the necessity for the doctor to touch his patient. It is a nice example of the feeling heart apparently becoming subject to technology, its beatings classified and reduced to medical symptoms as the possibility of affective communication between doctor and patient is denied.

In practice, however, the stethoscope also drew attention to the irregular and affective pulse. Along with the related technique of 'auscultation' (tapping the chest with a hammer and listening to the reverberations), it gave the Victorian heart a chance to be more eloquent than ever before and encouraged a growing fascination in medicine and in popular culture with the operations of the heart, pulses, and circulation. In order to analyse the newly audible sounds of the pulse, doctors and other investigators resorted to a 'poetic' language, using striking and inventive similes like the sound of bellows, a rasping file, the cooing of a dove, the purring of a cat.[3] As the eminent doctor Peter Mere Latham, known as 'Heart Latham' because of his fame as a cardiac researcher, wrote on the praecordial region in 1846:

> Within this space we cannot see. But at this space we can listen,
> and feel, and knock, and so put it to question, whether all be

---

[2] Cited in P. E. Baldry, *The Battle against Heart Disease* (Cambridge: Cambridge University Press, 1971), 63.

[3] James Hope discusses the 'bellows-murmur' and 'purring tremor' in his classic work *A Treatise on Diseases of the Heart and Great Vessels* (London: William Kidd, 1832), p. xv. He is clearly following Laennec's descriptions in *A Treatise on the Diseases of the Chest and on Mediate Auscultation*, trans. John Forbes, 3rd edn., revised (London: Thomas & George Underwood, 1829), 555, 573. Laennec also describes hearing sounds like a whip, and like a dog lapping water (p. 558). John Elliotson describes a sound like a file or saw and one 'exactly resembling the cooing of a dove' in *On the Recent Improvements in the Art of Distinguishing the Various Diseases of the Heart* (London: Longman, Rees, Orme, Brown and Green, 1830), 15, and J. J. Furnivall hears a 'creaking, or new leather sound' and 'the rumpling of silk or parchment' in *The Diagnosis, Prevention and Treatment of Diseases of the Heart* (London: John Churchill, 1845), 8, 36.

right beneath. And there is no spot of it which does not in its turn make answer to the ear, to the touch, or to the tapping of the finger, and tell something of the organ that lies herein.[4]

Latham envisages a highly responsive heart, although his phrasing suggests that it is not the heart answering the investigator, rather the echoes from the dark space in which it lies that allow a process of deduction as to the mysterious organ within. Asking 'whether all be *right* beneath', in his terms, raises the likelihood that in that obscure and dark region something might be wrong. He is addressing a readership of medical students, but his comments imply that anyone in possession of a stethoscope or guide to auscultation could attempt to diagnose the heart's problems; adding a medical gloss to the common trope of listening to another's heartbeat. In one poetic example of this, from 'A Death-Sound' by Ebenezer Jones (a minor working-class poet whose sole volume, *Studies of Sensation and Event*, caused some controversy in the 1840s and was rediscovered by the Pre-Raphaelites in the 1860s), a lover resting on his beloved's breast is suddenly struck by an anomaly in the sound of her heart:

> Then heard he through her frame the busy life-works ply,
> But the sound was not of life; and he knew that she must die.

As he 'urged his ear unto her bosom', what starts out as an erotic scene turns morbid, and the lover's delight in his beloved's heart changes to horror. He becomes vividly aware of his own pulse and circulation and their potential disturbance: 'The life within his veins did press at every pore.'[5] His privileged access to his lover's heart is terribly ironized, as he conceals his knowledge of her imminent death and goes through with their marriage. Jones shows how the physicality of the heart, and its susceptibility to disease, might intrude upon a scene of love, and how a little medical knowledge could be a dangerous

---

[4] Peter Mere Latham, *Lectures on Subjects Connected with Clinical Medicine, Comprising Diseases of the Heart*, 2nd edn., 2 vols. (London: Longman, 1846), i. 2.

[5] Ebenezer Jones, 'A Death-Sound', in *Studies of Sensation and Event*, ed. Richard Shepherd, with memorial notices by Sumner Jones and W. J. Linton (London: Pickering, 1879 (first published 1843)), 17.

thing. He is typical of many Victorian poets in that the heart in his works is sensationalized, subject to passion and emotion, throbbing and palpitating rather than doing its work unnoticed. In a kind of stethoscopic reading, if the stethoscope can be used as a symbol for the close attention paid to the heart's sounds and movements here and elsewhere, the pulse speaks at amplified volume of the sensations it experiences.

When poets listened to the heart and responded to it, they were often acting on personal grounds as well as deploying a standard poetic image. As this chapter and succeeding chapters demonstrate, poets were held to be particularly subject to heart disease and virtually every major and minor Victorian poet expresses anxiety about the state of his or her heart at some point. Summing up the general opinion, Elizabeth Barrett wrote to Robert Browning in 1845:

> I had a doctor once who thought he had done everything because he had carried the inkstand out of the room — 'Now', he said, 'you will not have such a pulse tomorrow.' He gravely thought poetry a sort of disease and held as a serious opinion, that nobody could be properly well who exercised it as an art — which was true, he maintained, even of men — he had studied the physiology of poets.[6]

Barrett's doctor assumes that such a thing as the 'physiology of poets' exists and is a legitimate object of study. He reads her ill health through her heart, the organ primarily affected by writing, and attempts a cure by regulating and normalizing her pulse. This is in line with standard medical practice. 'The action of writing raises the pulse considerably,' as an 1837 writer remarked, 'that of composition still more.'[7] Poetry, even more than her gender (note that 'even of men'), is the cause of Barrett's sickness. Although her tone in this letter is gently mocking, she herself fostered this

---

[6] EBB to RB, 11 Aug. 1845, in Kelley and Lewis, xi. 24.
[7] Dr Knox, 'Physiological Observations on the Pulsations of the Heart, and on its Diurnal Revolution and Excitability', *Edinburgh Medical and Surgical Journal*, 47 (1837), 358–77 (p. 372).

belief through her constant references to her poor health, and she takes pains to associate this illness with the heart and circulation. She expresses comic exasperation with her doctors' use of the stethoscope: 'Yes—and they could tell from the stethoscope, how very little was really wrong in me .. if it were not on a vital organ—and how I should certainly live .. if I didn't die sooner.' [8] But to some extent she seems proud that her body might resist analysis by these mechanical means: 'My whole illness has arisen from this excessive rapidity of the circulation,—medical watches being often put aside in despair of catching the uncountable time!' [9] Barrett boasts here of how her pulse and circulation defy calculation because she knows that possessing a rapid heartbeat could be a signifier of a poetic temperament. Moreover, the fact that such comments are frequent in her letters to Browning suggests that as in Lister's parlour games there is an element of flirtation and a hint of desire in these references to her disturbed pulse. During the serious illness of one of her brothers, for instance, she recorded his pulse every day in her letters to Browning, eventually asking archly, 'Are you learned in the pulse that I should talk as if you were? *I*, who have had my lessons?' In the context of a love letter, these 'lessons' imply those learnt from love as well as from illness. 'Pulses I know very little about,' Browning responded drily.[10]

By focusing on their hearts, nineteenth-century writers both sought to position themselves and were positioned as sufferers from cardiac disease, precisely because it was popularly believed to stem from acuteness of feeling, emotional sensitivity. As we can see in Lister's pulse-taking, in Jones's poem, and in Barrett's letters, the heart was always linked to affect and its actions had emotional as well as physical connotations and influences. Physical symptoms of heart disease, which came to be considered characteristic of the peculiar physiology of the Victorian poet, mark the bodies of poets and poetic

---

[8]   EBB to RB, [23 June 1845], Kelley and Lewis, x. 277.
[9]   16–17 June 1844, ibid. ix. 19.
[10] EBB to RB, [17 Oct. 1845], and RB to EBB, 20 Oct. 1845, ibid. xi. 129, 131.

characters and leave their traces in form, rhythm, and language. The significance of the emerging medical and physiological discourse of the heart in this context is twofold. First, poets such as Barrett were aware of medical developments and could read the discourse of the pathological heart onto (or into) their bodies, besides incorporating it into their poetic accounts. In addition, however, the medical texts discussed here and in the following chapter show that nineteenth-century physiologists found in the heart the qualities which poetry had already taught them to look for. The vast body of texts published on the heart in this period, in all discourses, show a much closer relation between the poetic and the physical heart than has previously been recognized. While the poets and other writers whom I discuss in this book were in many cases demonstrably familiar with the medical culture of early–mid-Victorian Britain, it is at least as likely that the authors of medical treatises were reading Tennyson as vice versa. Nineteenth-century physicians seldom if ever manage to discuss the heart without introducing a sense of its purpose, its agency, its role in the emotional and spiritual life of the patient. Medical writers borrowed from earlier metaphorical descriptions of the heart, and more specifically read and cited contemporary poetry in their works. Meanwhile, poets were engaging with the new vocabulary of the pathological heart and the new sense, indicated in comments such as Latham's, that the heart was an important subject for investigation and indeed for dialogue. The question as to 'whether all be right beneath' meshed with general cultural disquiet about illness and heartsickness, again partly fostered by poetry which concentrated on the abnormal actions of heart and circulation rather than their quiet continuation. The poetic heart in Victorian literature tends to be strongly physicalized and is frequently subject to disease, but the physical, physiological heart is always shaped by a priori perceptions based, in some degree, on poetry.

Medical perceptions of heart disease in Victorian Britain shaped the developing culture of the heart by focusing on its pathology and hence the dangers of affective transmission through heart or pulse. There is considerable evidence that heart disease was a 'popular'

nineteenth-century condition, not only at the forefront of physiological and medical research, but also ubiquitous in popular diagnosis
and social commentary on disease, discussed in the pages of news-
papers and periodicals, in private letters and published accounts,
in dinner table conversations as well as coroners' courts. As Gerard
Manley Hopkins noted wryly in a sermon describing the significance
of the Sacred Heart both as spiritual signifier and as Christ's real,
fleshly heart:

> Nay I have remarked it, so honourable, so interesting to us
> is the heart, that there are people who whatever in head or
> throat or back or breast or bowel ails them will always have you
> believe it is the heart that is affected, that their complaint is of
> the heart.[11]

Hopkins's comment suggests that heart disease was perceived as
in some sense a high-status disease, still tinged with romance. It
was not embarrassing, humiliating, or unacceptably rude to discuss
cardiac illnesses in company, as it might have been to discuss a bowel
complaint. Moreover, if heart disease were associated with a sensitive,
poetic nature then suffering from it might actually enhance a certain
type of self-image. Reading Barrett Browning's letters, it is notable
that she deliberately emphasizes her suffering from the heart rather
than from consumption. Similarly, on Christina Rossetti's painful
death from cancer, William Michael Rossetti's letters suggest that
cardiac disease was the major contributory factor: 'She is undoubtedly
dying, owing to a malady of the heart and, other grave matters.'
Cancer is hidden under 'other grave matters'. In a letter to Theodore
Watts-Dunton giving information for an obituary, he writes: 'Her
illness was functional malady of the heart, with dropsy in left arm
and hand: there was another matter, painful to dwell upon, which I
leave in the background.'[12] While Rossetti may technically have died

---

[11] Sermon on the Sacred Heart, 26 June 1881, in *Sermons*, 102.
[12] To Alice Boyd, 17 Sept. 1894, and Theodore Watts-Dunton, 29 Dec. 1894,
in *Selected Letters of William Michael Rossetti*, ed. Roger Peattie (University Park:
Pennsylvania State University Press, 1990), 574, 575.

of heart failure (since ultimately, any death results from the cessation of the heart), William Michael appears deliberately to construct her death as heart related. In nineteenth-century medical discourse, 'functional' is the opposite of 'organic' and usually indicates that the heart is suffering in sympathy with another organ rather than from an inherent disease. William Michael thus implies that Rossetti's death had a background source elsewhere in the body, but suggests that the malady of the heart this created was the actual cause of death. As an adolescent, Rossetti had been diagnosed as suffering from angina—again a diagnosis that seemed to rest upon her sensitivity, poetic interests, and attachment to a 'somewhat sensational brand of High Anglican religious belief' rather than on any recognizable physical symptoms.[13] This and William Michael's letters on her death would imply that Rossetti had died of an illness aptly suited to, if not caused by, her poetic career.

For the poets in this study, cardiac disease was 'honorable and interesting' because it confirmed their position as poets. But one of the points of this chapter is to show that heart disease was more widely of interest, that in early–mid-Victorian culture and society it served almost as cancer does today, in terms of being the most feared yet most readily assumed interpretation of any set of symptoms. Susan Sontag compares the metaphors associated with cancer and AIDS in the twentieth century with the important set of metaphors surrounding consumption in the nineteenth century.[14] Yet there is evidence that heart disease was almost as feared as consumption, and may have had a greater tendency to attract metaphorical implications. By tracing what doctors, patients, and medical researchers were saying about the heart in the decades between the invention of the stethoscope in 1819 and the emergence of a new psychology in the 1870s, we can see how

[13] *The Letters of Christina Rossetti*, i: *1843–1873*, ed. Antony H. Harrison (Charlottesville: University of Virginia Press, 1997), 5 n.

[14] Susan Sontag, *AIDS and its Metaphors* (New York: Farrar, Strauss and Giroux, 1989). Sontag briefly mentions heart disease but suggests that it has been 'little culpabilized' because it suggests purely mechanical failure (p. 25). As the material presented here suggests, I strongly disagree with this in relation to the 19th century.

the heart was still held to retain extensive influence over other organs within the body, how heart disease seemed to infiltrate diagnoses of other ailments, and how traditional connections between the heart and emotional disturbance retained medical power.

In an influential medical textbook on the heart, written in the 1870s, the eminent doctor J. Milner Fothergill confidently claims that cardiac disease has been a topic of widespread interest in the preceding decades:

> [C]uriously, both the public who furnish the patients and the medical men who give advice, have to a great extent neglected the normal working of the heart; both, however, feeling keenly the fascination which the diseases of this organ unquestionably possess for all.[15]

As a brief indication of this 'fascination' on the part of medical men, it should be noted that the decades preceding Fothergill's study saw an unprecedented rise of knowledge about and investigation into heart disease. The early nineteenth century was the era when most major heart diseases were first classified and named, including angina in 1802, endocarditis (inflammation of the lining membrane of the heart) in 1809, pericarditis (inflammation of the membranous sac enclosing the heart) in 1799, and 'fatty degeneration of the heart', first described in 1816. 'Hypertrophy'—distension and hardening of the heart—and 'syncope'—a sudden cessation of its action—were also fully classified in this period.[16] This was also the time when,

---

[15] J. Milner Fothergill, *The Heart and its Diseases, with their Treatment*, 2nd edn. (London: H. K. Lewis, 1879), 2.

[16] For an account of these discoveries, see Frederick A. Willius and Thomas Keys (eds.), *Cardiac Classics* (London: Henry Kipton, 1941). On medical research into the heart in this period, see also Frederick Willius and Thomas Dry, *A History of the Heart and the Circulation* (Philadelphia: W. B. Saunders, 1948); Terence East, *The Story of Heart Disease* (London: William Dawson, 1958); J. O. Leibowitz, *The History of Coronary Heart Disease* (London: Wellcome Institute, 1970); P. R. Fleming, *A Short History of Cardiology* (Amsterdam: Rodopi, 1997); R. K. French, *The History of the Heart: Thoracic Physiology from Ancient to Modern Times* (Aberdeen: Equipress, 1979); Robert G. Frank, 'The Telltale Heart: Physiological Instruments, Graphic Methods and Clinical Hopes, 1854–1914', in William Coleman and Frederick L. Holmes (eds.), *The*

according to Kenneth Keele, the sounds of the heart 'were to be sufficiently rationally elucidated as to satisfy most clinicians' demands ever since'.[17] All these discoveries were hotly debated in the numerous books published on cardiac disease and in the pages of pioneering medical journals such as the *Lancet*. With regard to the cause and actions of the pulse, for instance, there was a much-discussed ongoing dispute between Charles Williams and James Hope, two of the leading writers on the subject, and from 1832 to 1835 this had moved into a heated technical debate in the *Lancet*.[18] Probably in response to this, the British Association for the Advancement of Science appointed a committee in 1835 to enquire into 'the heart's sounds and movements'.[19] By 1860, George Britton Halford notes that at least thirty different explanations of the pulse had already been offered.[20]

During the first decades of the nineteenth century, as the practice of medicine became more professionalized with the introduction of teaching hospitals, reform-minded journals like the *Medico-Chirurgical Review* and the *Lancet*, and new independent professional organizations, cardiac disease was an up-and-coming topic for ambitious young researchers.[21] Many well-known medical researchers launched their careers by publishing on heart disease, while at the

---

Investigative Enterprise: Experimental Physiology in Nineteenth-Century Medicine (Berkeley and Los Angeles: University of California Press, 1988), 211–90 and Christopher Lawrence, 'Moderns and Ancients: The "New Cardiology" in Britain 1880–1930', in W. F. Bynum, C. Lawrence, and V. Nutton (eds.), *The Emergence of Modern Cardiology* (London: Wellcome Institute, 1985), 1–33.

[17] Kenneth D. Keele, 'The Application of the Physics of Sound to 19th-Century Cardiology: With Particular Reference to the Part Played by C. J. B. Williams and James Hope', *Clio Medica*, 8 (1973), 191–221 (p. 198).

[18] On this rivalry, see ibid. For an example of the *Lancet* debate, see Archibald Billing, 'On the Auscultation and Treatment of Affections of the Heart', *Lancet* (1831–2), ii. 198–201.

[19] E. L. Bryan, letter to editor on committee's report, *Lancet* (1835–6), i. 501–2.

[20] George Britton Halford, *The Actions and Sounds of the Heart: A Physiological Essay* (London: John Churchill, 1860), 20.

[21] On the increasing professionalization of Victorian medicine see M. Jeanne Peterson, *The Medical Profession in Mid-Victorian London* (Berkeley and Los Angeles: University of California Press, 1978) and A. J. Youngson, *The Scientific Revolution in Victorian Medicine* (London: Croom Helm, 1979).

newly established University College Hospital in London (one of the most influential teaching hospitals), at least four professors were researching the heart between 1830 and 1860.[22] When the Pathological Society was formed in 1846 to draw professionals together and provide a new forum for discussion, thirty-one heart cases were discussed in the opening season; perhaps not surprisingly given that the first president (Charles Williams) was an expert on the pulse.[23] The first hospital specifically for the treatment of heart disease also opened in London in this period, and in 1857 the National Hospital for Diseases of the Heart (generally known as the 'National Heart') was founded.[24]

This new research into cardiac disease, allied to older cultural perceptions of the centrality of the heart to health and well-being, undoubtedly fostered a sensitivity to heart disease as a common and widespread contemporary ailment. One medical writer observes that in 1845 a third of all deaths in London were recorded as caused by 'diseases of the chest'.[25] While tuberculosis would have accounted for many of these deaths, the distinction between consumption and heart disease, both 'diseases of the chest', was not always clear given that consumption was associated with heart problems, broken blood vessels, and palpitation. Similarly, many other symptoms were blamed on the underlying presence of heart disease, whether detected or not. The well-known doctor and researcher James Paget wrote to his fiancée in 1839, when he was in the early stages of his career:

---

[22] James Paget wrote an early article on pericarditis. James Hope, Richard Quain, P. M. Latham, and Allan Burns began their careers by publishing on heart disease. Their works are cited below. John Elliotson, author of at least one significant work on cardiac disease, helped to establish University College Hospital and worked there until 1838. Richard Quain was Professor of Anatomy there in 1830, W. H. Walshe was Professor of Morbid Anatomy in 1841, and John Marshall was Professor of Surgery in 1866. All three published on heart disease.

[23] Reported in A. D. Morgan, 'Some Forms of Undiagnosed Coronary Disease in Nineteenth-Century England', *Medical History*, 12 (1968), 344–58 (p. 346).

[24] Lawrence, 11.

[25] Herbert Davies, *Lectures on the Physical Diagnosis of the Diseases of the Lungs and Heart* (London: John Churchill, 1851), 1–2.

> I have found out something . . . by which I hope I shall gain a
> little more reputation: for I shall be able to prove that nearly
> half the adult population have had a disease of the heart at some
> time of their lives—not indeed an important, not perhaps an
> injurious one, but still one that is discernible.[26]

The breadth of his claim makes 'a little more' seem like understate-
ment. In an atmosphere where the sick heart was 'fascinating' Paget
might well think that his discovery could cause a sensation. One
year later, *The Times* reported this summing up of a case of sudden
death by the chief coroner, who was also the influential editor of the
Lancet:

> Mr Wakley said he had no doubt that deceased's death was
> occasioned by disease of the heart, which was now fearfully
> prevalent; and which an eminent physician had told him
> recently was the cause of 95 sudden deaths out of 100.[27]

By 1863, the inquest on Sir F. W. Slade (which concluded he had
died from heart disease) reported with gruesome irony that he said
shortly before his death 'that no-one knew who had a diseased heart,
and God only knew who would die from it next'.[28] Reports on
the frequency and unpredictability of heart disease clearly carried a
frisson of interest, and the statistics circulating in popular and medical
reports about the likelihood of contracting it were high enough to
be definitely alarming.

Many nineteenth-century writers and intellectuals would have
encountered medical opinions on heart disease through personal
acquaintance with doctors and scientists—George Eliot was a close
friend of James Paget, for instance, and he also knew Tennyson and
Browning; Latham was family doctor to the Arnolds and possibly

---

[26] Letter to Miss North, 20 July 1839, cited in Stephen Paget (ed.), *Memoirs and
Letters of Sir James Paget*, 3rd edn. (London: Longmans, Green, 1901), 107–8. His
argument was based on finding white spots on the surface of anatomized hearts, which
were taken to be a sign of undiagnosed pericarditis.

[27] Inquest on Sir W. H. Pringle, *The Times*, 29 Dec. 1840, p. 7.

[28] *The Times*, 15 Aug. 1863, p. 8.

treated Christina Rossetti; the mesmerist John Elliotson, whose early research was on the heart, later befriended Dickens and Thackeray; Richard Quain, famous for his work on fatty degeneration, was Coventry Patmore's doctor—and even for those without these connections, several periodicals, such as the *Quarterly Review*, regularly reported the latest advances in pathological research.[29] George Henry Lewes, for example, published striking essays on the heart and circulation in *Blackwood's* before reprinting them in *The Physiology of Common Life*. Popular medical encyclopedias, at various prices and levels of sophistication, included detailed analyses of diseases of the heart and blood.[30] And besides its inquests, in which diagnoses of heart disease crop up again and again, *The Times* occasionally contained descriptions of medical lectures about the heart.[31] Eliot, always interested in new scientific and medical research, provides a good example of a novelist engaging with medical investigations into the heart. Her evident familiarity with developments in heart disease and her interest in it as an illness reflecting the emotional life of a character is shown in *Middlemarch*, where the emotionally stunted Casaubon is diagnosed by Lydgate as suffering from fatty degeneration of the heart.[32] Since the novel is set barely more than a decade after the classification of this disease, this demonstrates Lydgate's up-to-date medical knowledge as well as Eliot's awareness that by the 1860s fatty degeneration was a 'fashionable complaint'.[33] Heart disease is also present in 'Mr Gilfil's Love-Story' from *Scenes*

[29] For details of Paget's literary friends and interests, see Stephen Paget. On Latham and Arnold, see below. On Latham and Rossetti, see Rossetti, ed. Harrison, p. lv. Elliotson's friendships are discussed in Alan Gauld, 'Elliotson, John (1791–1868)', *DNB*: www.oxforddnb.com/view/article/8671, accessed 7 June 2005. On Quain and Patmore, see Basil Champneys, *Memoirs and Correspondence of Coventry Patmore*, 2 vols. (London: George Bell, 1901), i. 77.

[30] For example, John Conolly, John Forbes, and Alexander Tweedie (eds.), *The Cyclopaedia of Practical Medicine*, 3 vols. (London: Sherwood, Gilbert & Piper, 1833).

[31] *The Times*, 22 May 1827, describes Abernethy's lectures on 'Sympathy of the Heart' (p. 3).

[32] George Eliot, *Middlemarch* (1872), ed. W. H. Harvey (Harmondsworth: Penguin, 1965), 460–1.

[33] Archibald Billing, *Practical Observations on Diseases of the Lungs and Heart* (London: S. Highley, 1852), 73. See also Morgan, 349.

of Clerical Life, where the untrustworthy seducer Captain Wybrow suffers from 'terrible palpitations' and dies from syncope (a disease where the heart stutters and stops, thus indicating his lack of consistency in love); and in 'The Lifted Veil', where the sensitive, nervous narrator, Latimer, suffers equally appropriately from angina, an illness linked to excessive sensibility.[34] Latimer sees himself as possessing a poetic temperament, and it seems as if this, besides his inappropriate passion for Bertha, might be one cause of his fatal weakness at the heart.

Eliot's knowledge was clearly exceptional. Yet while it is unlikely that the lay public had access to the kind of specialized medical treatises she and Lewes knew, she still expects her readers to appreciate the irony inherent in the particular type of disease she attributes to each sufferer. Such interconnections between medicine and literature suggest that information about heart disease and its symptoms was infiltrating popular culture. John Ruskin, for example, wrote to his father in 1861 after attending a party, 'Miss Cooke thought I must be threatened with disease of the heart, and spoke almost with tears in her eyes to me about minding what I was about in time—she is herself a sufferer from heart disease.' In the same letter he adds, 'It's very tiresome the way people notice my face now. A lady. . .was dining here to-day, and I had no sooner gone out of the room than she asked Miss Bell if I had heart disease.'[35] If we assume Ruskin's report is accurate, here we have two women who independently read his appearance as symptomatic of heart disease (which does suggest informed knowledge, as at least one popular medical writer warns that a 'violet or red tint to the face' can be a sign of hypertrophy) and two potential sufferers from that disease.[36] Although this letter undoubtedly

[34] George Eliot, *Scenes of Clerical Life*, ed. Graham Handley (London: J. M. Dent, 1994), 140, 176 and 'The Lifted Veil', in *The Lifted Veil and Brother Jacob*, ed. Helen Small (Oxford: Oxford University Press, 1999), 3.

[35] Ruskin to his father, Mar. 1861, in Cook and Wedderburn, xxxvi. 360.

[36] Thomas J. Graham, *On the Diseases of Females: A Treatise. . .Containing also an Account of the Symptoms and Treatment of Diseases of the Heart*, 7th edn. (London: Simpkin, Marshall, 1861), appendix, 10.

reflects Ruskin's hypochondria, it does suggest that heart disease was an illness in common discussion. In another instance, Mark Pattison writes in his *Memoirs* that when he and his fellow dons began discussions about revising the Oxford syllabus in 1845, 'The great discoveries of the last half-century in chemistry, physiology, etc, were not even known by report to any of us.' Two years later, however, when he was suffering from 'palpitation of the heart' due in his analysis to overwork, fasting, and an intense emotional investment in Tractarianism, Pattison tells the reader that he went to London 'to take the advice of Dr Williams, or Dr Latham, I forget which'.[37] Williams (probably either John Williams, known for his work on sympathetic palpitation, or Charles Williams, the leading researcher on the pulse) and Latham were experts on nervous diseases of the heart. Not only did Pattison evidently know of them at the time, his casual reference also implies that he assumes readers in 1885 will recognize the names and perhaps be impressed by his connection to such eminent doctors.

Knowledge and anxiety about heart disease was apparently disseminated among those who might be most expected to fear it. Roughly speaking, this applied to anyone engaged in pursuits associated with emotional excitement. The philosophical and medical writer Benjamin Richardson lists four types of people more liable to contract heart problems: those engaged in politics; those involved with commerce and speculation; those pursuing a career in science, art, or literature; and scholars and students.[38] As this indicates, heart disease (like nervousness) was frequently troped as a disease of the professional middle classes, and was particularly associated with intellectual pursuits—the following chapter examines in more detail how both reading and writing were thought to affect the pulse. Gender, as I discuss in Chapter 3, was also a crucial factor, since women were believed to be much more liable to develop heart-related problems. Barrett and her contemporaries, including Ruskin and Pattison, would have perceived cause to worry.

---

[37] Mark Pattison, *Memoirs* (London: Macmillan, 1885), 237, 229.
[38] Benjamin Richardson, *Diseases of Modern Life* (London: Macmillan, 1876), 120.

If many Victorian writers were fascinated by the possibility of cardiac disease, was this fascination caused by medical interest in the heart or did it contribute to it? Medical engagement with cardiac problems emerged at the same time as anxieties about sensibility called the feeling heart into question—but again, the question of which came first is impossible to answer. What is clear, however, is that medical writers were participating in a wider culture of the heart in early–mid-Victorian Britain and that much beyond physiological advance was at stake in descriptions of the pathological heart, pulse, or circulation. The reason why cardiac disease specifically became a focus for many researchers may be because it permitted them to combine detailed physiological research with philosophical speculations, to participate in developments in medical understanding without entirely abandoning traditional beliefs. The heart was also, as noted in the Introduction, a crucial site of negotiation between materialist and spiritualist concepts of body and mind. James Garth Wilkinson, doctor, philosopher, and later a leading Swedenborgian, notes the resulting clash in his 1851 work:

> Every man is still valued by his heart. Every feeling comes from it and goes to it ... The most touching thing in the world, it is the most tangible too; it feels before the fingers, and pulls the words from the speaker's tongue by an anticipated hearing. We should rather say, that all this is attributed to it since the beginning of time ... But we cannot overlook the fact, that another heart has come upon the carpet. The scientific heart ... has not been slow to suggest, that the ancient heart is a figure of speech, and only exists metaphorically ... Hence arises imperfection and struggle.[39]

In Wilkinson's language the heart seems to feel, hear and speak independently; even the 'scientific' heart 'suggests'. 'Touching' and 'tangible' play on this lack of distinction between science and the feeling heart by being almost exact equivalents divided by the Latinate diction of 'tangible' and the range of emotional, affective associations

---

[39] Wilkinson, 216.

carried by 'touching'. Wilkinson's writing does not maintain any distinction between metaphorical and actual actions performed by the heart. If the heart could be explained purely as a scientific mechanism, one cog in a smoothly working machine, and heart disease as the result of identifiable organic factors, then medical science would have set perceptions of the body on a new rational and materialist ground, rejecting tradition. On the other hand, if it could be demonstrated that the heart did respond to emotions (the emotions of others, as well as the emotions of its host), that it operated independently of other organs and often in unpredictable or inexplicable ways, and that disease was frequently the result of external factors, then a rigorously materialist standpoint would be disavowed. Most medical writers on the heart are, like Wilkinson, reluctant to abandon the 'ancient', feeling heart, implying it by their language even if their argument disavows it.

In this effort, medical writers found an ally in literature. Gillian Beer and other critics have noted how the existence of 'one culture' in Victorian Britain meant that 'not only *ideas* but metaphors, myths, and narrative patterns could move rapidly and freely to and fro between scientists and non-scientists'.[40] In relation to the heart, medical writers exploited the consonance between physiology and literature in two ways. First, as noted of Wilkinson, medical textbooks describe the heart in ways which implicitly give it agency. Latham, whose books were widely read and who was described by Matthew Arnold as 'the usual man to consult in heart cases',[41] observes that:

---

[40] Gillian Beer, *Darwin's Plots: Evolutionary Narrative in Darwin, George Eliot and Nineteenth-Century Fiction* (London: Routledge, 1983), 7. On the connections between medical and literary language, see also G. S. Rousseau's classic essay 'Medicine and Literature: The State of the Field', *Isis*, 72 (1981), 406–24. Many writers have made similar points with regard to Victorian science in general. See especially George Levine (ed.), *One Culture: Essays in Science and Literature* (Madison: University of Wisconsin Press, 1987); Gillian Beer, *Open Fields: Science in Cultural Encounter* (Oxford: Oxford University Press, 1996); Tess Cosslett, *The 'Scientific Movement' and Victorian Literature* (Brighton: Harvester, 1982); Susan Gliserman, 'Early Victorian Science Writers and Tennyson's *In Memoriam*: A Study in Cultural Exchange', *Victorian Studies*, 18 (1974–5), 277–308, 437–60.

[41] Letter to Mary Arnold, 2 Nov. [1856], in Lang, i. 346.

'Often the Heart is a more delicate test of something wrong within the man than his own consciousness. His Heart is beforehand with him.'[42] Strictly speaking, Latham's comments are accurate, in that the heart might have developed disease which the individual cannot feel. But metaphors lurk behind his phrasing, which works with a number of assumptions about the heart and its behaviour. If the first sentence suggests that the heart is being passively tested by the pathologist, the copula in the second makes it an active agent, which (or who?) knows more about the individual than he does himself. Latham does not always capitalize the word 'heart' in his writings, so it is possible that he does so deliberately here to emphasize its importance. 'By its all-pervading sympathy, [the heart] feels all that is hurtful throughout the body;' he writes elsewhere in this essay, 'and by its own peculiar mode of action it tells all that it feels, and telegraphs intelligence of it through every artery that can be felt.'[43] Again, he describes a physical action of the heart in language which extends into the figurative, introducing a productive uncertainty as to how far concepts like 'sympathy' can be taken. 'Intelligence' conveys a sense that the heart is the thinking operator of this system. In a metaphor borrowed from contemporary technology, it is simultaneously the telegraph operator and the mechanism itself, as the pulse beats out the messages. Such suggestions that the heart is implicitly conscious, knowing and controlling, run throughout Latham's writings: and in terms of Victorian textbooks on cardiac disease, his work is the rule rather than the exception.

Secondly, medical writers explicitly used literary allusion to suggest the role of the physical heart in metaphysical concerns. By citing poetry and other forms of literature, they perhaps hoped to demonstrate that physiological explanations did not entirely destroy the mystery of the heart or detract from its long-standing associations. Poetic allusions position these doctors or scientific researchers as

---

[42] Latham, 'The Heart and its Affections, Not Organic' (1861), in *The Collected Works of P. M. Latham*, ed. Robert Martin, 2 vols. (London: New Sydenham Society, 1878), ii. 516–54, 528.

[43] Ibid. ii. 521.

men in touch with a wider culture, speaking to an audience outside specialists in the field, and they additionally serve to provide imaginative insight into complex physiological events. In *The Physiology of Common Life*, for example, G. H. Lewes cites the awakening of the Sleeping Beauty in Tennyson's 'The Day-Dream' as an instance of the resumption of suspended circulation.[44] After quoting Shakespeare's *Henry VI* in the second edition of his authoritative treatise on the heart, James Wardrop (one of the most frequently cited researchers into heart disease of the time) informs his readers that 'The condition of the cutaneous circulation in congestion of the heart, is admirably delineated by our immortal poet.'[45] Shakespeare's lines are valued for the quality and accuracy of their medical description, and the way in which Shakespeare seems to anticipate nineteenth-century medicine lends credibility both to his work and to Wardrop's. Further literary quotations are scattered throughout Wardrop's books. His contemporary Thomas Burgess cites Byron in a treatise on the blush:

> Is it not pleasing, that we are enabled to look back and trace *ab origine*, that beautiful train of action by which 'the heart, and soul, and sense in concert move' . . . What other parts of our organic structure are more capable of exciting our wonder, or of filling us with gratitude for the plenitude and richness of the gifts of our Creator, than the heart and its blood vessels.[46]

These rhetorical questions have a ring of self-justification, both because they enable Burgess to restore religion to a place above scientific analysis, and because they excuse the actual vagueness and uncertainty of his account of the workings of the heart and blood vessels by attributing their complex actions to God's will. He cites

[44] G. H. Lewes, *The Physiology of Common Life*, 2 vols. (London: William Blackwood, 1859), i. 342–3.

[45] James Wardrop, *On the Nature and Treatment of Diseases of the Heart*, 2nd edn., revised (Edinburgh: Thomas Constable, 1859), 471. See also pp. 146, 149, 273, 480.

[46] Thomas Burgess, *The Physiology or Mechanism of Blushing* (London: John Churchill, 1839), 93. Christopher Ricks makes interesting use of this text in *Keats and Embarrassment* (Oxford: Clarendon Press, 1974).

the moment of heart/earth-shaking passion when Byron's Don Juan and Haidee experience:

> Such kisses as belong to early days,
> Where heart, and soul, and sense, in concert move,
>   And the blood's lava, and the pulse a blaze,
> Each kiss a heart-quake.[47]

Soul and sense are less evident than the heart in these lines, suggesting that it is the organ which displays the symptoms of passion most acutely. The leisurely, drawn-out iambic rhythm in the second line here speeds up with the interspersed anapaests on 'aňd thĕ blóod', 'anď thĕ púlse', while the double emphasis on 'blóod's lávă' and 'heárt-quáke' further stresses the variations in the heartbeat in a moment of passion. Burgess is deeply concerned with the drama of the effects of emotion on bodily processes, and by alluding to this famous passage he can hint that his discussion has dealt with sexual desire without making this explicit. The allusion to *Don Juan* is also appropriate given the later career of Haidee, who, distraught at the loss of her lover, collapses and dies from a broken blood vessel—suffering from the excessive emotion which Burgess warns against elsewhere in his text. In one of his footnotes, Byron carefully assured the reader of the medical basis for her death:

> This is no very uncommon effect of the violence of conflicting and different passions . . . I was witness to a melancholy instance of the same effect of mixed passions upon a young person; who, however, did not die in consequence at that time, but fell a victim some years afterwards to a seizure of the same kind, arising from causes intimately connected with agitation of the mind.[48]

Haidee's passion for Juan becomes physically dangerous, as she is transformed from a poetic heroine to a medical case study. Her

---

[47] *Don Juan*, II. 1484–8. *Lord Byron: The Complete Poetical Works*, ed. Jerome McGann, 7 vols. (Oxford: Clarendon Press, 1986), v.
[48] Ibid., v. 704 n.

death is more than symbolic: the volcanic feelings stirred up by love, desire, and grief have a medically apt outlet in her burst blood vessel. Byron's poem and Burgess's allusion to that poem thus enter into a mutually dependent relationship.

The fact that the heart, blood, pulse, and circulation could be linked to 'mixed passions' and to older humoral theories provided another reason why medical writers continued to assert their dominance. The heart had authority, based on its long history and also on its apparently controlling position within the body. Yet doctors who chose to focus on heart disease were also entering into a debate over this authority, as it was challenged by new medical discoveries about the action of the nerves and the working of the brain. Unlike the lungs (the source of consumption), which were generally perceived as reliant on the heart and circulation and were not seen as vitally linked to emotion, nerves and brain did seem to offer an alternative source of power and influence within the body and were much discussed in Victorian medicine. Many literary critics working on the Victorian period have for this reason concentrated on psychology, mental illness, or the nervous system in their studies of literature and medicine.[49] But irrespective of the heart's strong literary presence, a study of the medical works published on the heart in the early–mid-Victorian period demonstrates that the supremacy of nerves and brain was not readily assumed. Heart, nerves, and brain were perceived as possessing an intertwined, almost symbiotic relationship, and various arguments for the dominance of one of these three tended to rest on the commentator's personal investment in

---

[49] On Victorian psychology, see Ekbert Faas, *Retreat into the Mind: Victorian Poetry and the Rise of Psychiatry* (Princeton: Princeton University Press, 1988); Sally Shuttleworth, *Charlotte Brontë and Victorian Psychology* (Cambridge: Cambridge University Press, 1996); Rick Rylance, *Victorian Psychology and British Culture 1850–1880* (Oxford: Oxford University Press, 2001). On nerves, see Janet Oppenheim, *'Shattered Nerves': Doctors, Patients and Depression in Victorian England* (Oxford: Oxford University Press, 1991); Athena Vrettos, *Somatic Fictions: Imagining Illness in Victorian Culture* (Stanford, Calif.: Stanford University Press, 1995); Peter Logan, *Nerves and Narratives: A Cultural History of Hysteria in Nineteenth-Century British Prose* (Berkeley and Los Angeles: University of California Press, 1997); Jane Wood, *Passion and Pathology in Victorian Fiction* (Oxford: Oxford University Press, 2001).

a particular area of research. Nervous disease, mental illnesses (such as insanity), and cardiac disease were frequently linked together, in poetic imagery as well as physiological studies.

To determine the mixed messages which such imagery sends, it is important to consider where the heart stood in terms of bodily hierarchy. Was it still perceived as dominant, or had it been superseded? This question has obvious implications for the poetry of the time in terms of whether the literary heart retained its force as an image. Tennyson can speak of the 'unquiet heart and brain' in the same phrase in *In Memoriam* V, and writes of heartsickness, a sluggish circulation, and nervous distress as effectively synonymous:

> When the blood creeps, and the nerves prick
> And tingle; and the heart is sick,
> And all the wheels of Being slow. (L. 2–4)

The double stress on 'blood creeps', slowing the movement of the line, suggests the halted circulation, while the comma after 'tingle', coming before the natural caesura and preceding two unstressed beats, further introduces a sense of stops and starts, a lack of smooth flow. Heartsickness here is of a piece with disturbed nervous and sanguinary movements. Nonetheless, elsewhere in *In Memoriam*, for reasons more fully explored in Chapter 5, it is clear that the sick heart carries a metaphorical resonance for Tennyson which establishes it as central to the poem. The same, I would argue, holds true for medical commentators. Despite the mutual dependence of heart, nerves, and brain, the heart was frequently depicted as one of few organs in the body that was *not* entirely subject to the vacillations of the nervous system, and for that reason it assumed further importance.

The case for the heart's independence of the rest of the body, first put forward in the mid-eighteenth century and restated by Claude-Xavier Bichat in 1800, rested on evidence that the heart continued to move after the brain and nervous system had been destroyed, and on the belief that the heart was directly influenced by the passions, a belief stemming from long-standing attribution.[50] If this were demonstrably true, it would seem that the heart was an independent organ which enjoyed unmediated physical responses, and communicated them to the rest of the body. Such views had potential political significance. L. S. Jacyna has studied how medical research was politicized in early nineteenth-century Edinburgh, as Whig doctors sought to shape and intervene in debates over the nerves in order to promote a 'view of the body as decentralized' which fitted with a social conception that 'refuses to acknowledge the predominance of any central power'.[51] The heart provided an even more obvious controlling force than the nerves, and discussions of its predominance create a reassuring sense of central agency, further underpinned by Christian associations. Although some writers might seek to use the heart for more radical political aims (Barrett Browning's repeated use of heart imagery in *Casa Guidi Windows* provides one example), asserting its significance tends to be a conservative move.

Debates over the relative importance of heart or nerves therefore have wider implications than the merely medical, and opinion could be fiercely polarized. In an 1815 article, A. P. Wilson Philip comments that 'there seems never to have been any difference of opinion respecting the direct dependence of the nervous on the sanguiferous system', before going on to argue that this common opinion is misguided, because the nerves do generally control the heart.[52] His book two years later attempts to satisfy both camps by claiming that although the heart is definitely 'independent' of the nerves it is nonetheless influenced by them, and even here he

[50] Bichat's work is summarized by almost every British writer on this subject. See, for example, A. P. Wilson Philip, *An Experimental Inquiry into the Laws of the Vital Functions, with Some Observations on the Nature and Treatment of Internal Diseases* (London: Thomas and George Underwood, 1817), 1–20.

[51] L. S. Jacyna, *Philosophic Whigs: Medicine, Science and Citizenship in Edinburgh, 1789–1848* (London: Routledge, 1994), 67.

[52] Philip, 'Experiments Made with a View to Ascertain the Principle on which the Action of the Heart Depends, and the Relation which Subsists between that Organ and the Nervous System', *Philosophical Transactions of the Royal Society*, 105 (1815), 65–90 (p. 65).

rescinds part of this claim by reassuring his reader that the influence is mutual.[53] In 1829, Joseph Swan's book on the relation between heart and nervous system claimed that the former controlled the latter, but in the same year George Calvert Holland disagreed with his and Philip's conclusions, arguing that the heart was a dependent organ.[54] Yet he too found difficulties in explaining the heart's apparent emotional responsivity:

> Although I am fully persuaded that the contractions of the heart are to be ascribed to the nervous power . . . yet I do not consider that this . . . explains the frequent and violent disturbance in the function of circulation observed in the exciting or depressing effects of passion.[55]

It is the heart and circulation's passionate responses which these writers cannot reconcile with their dependence. Despite the reduction of the heart's influence in his argument, Holland still ascribes extensive powers to the blood: '*every . . . function, whether intellectual or organic, operates in extent and correctness, according to the nature and quantity of this fluid.*'[56] The title of his 1844 book— *The Philosophy of the Moving Powers of the Blood*—itself suggests more than a physiological interest in circulatory 'powers'. 'Moving' acts as a pun, in that blood not only moves around the body but also emotionally 'moves' the mind.

Similarly, James Wilson, author of a medical treatise on spasm in the 1840s, noted that 'between the blood and the nerve there are at present great and competing claims', but concluded that the circulation, unlike the nervous system, 'is not merely passive and

---

[53] Philip (1817), 119, 259.

[54] Joseph Swan, *An Essay on the Connection between the Action of the Heart and Arteries and the Functions of the Nervous System* (London: Longman, Rees, Orme, Brown and Green, 1829).

[55] G. Calvert Holland, *An Experimental Inquiry into the Laws which Regulate the Phenomena of Organic and Animal Life* (Edinburgh: MacLachlan and Stewart, 1829), 261–2.

[56] Ibid. 343. Holland argues again for the importance of the circulatory system in disease in *The Philosophy of the Moving Powers of the Blood* (London: John Churchill, 1844).

subordinate; it originates its own actions'.[57] This is interesting in that Wilson bypasses the heart in his language in favour of the decentralized circulation, although the heart's motive power must lie behind the movements of the blood. Most forcibly, Henry Ancell upheld the primary role of the blood in a series of lectures published in the *Lancet*: '[T]here is no nervous structure without blood,—no nervous function without blood ... nerve, nervous action, and nervous power are wholly and at all times dependent on the BLOOD.'[58] As another polemical book states, 'Thirty years of professional observation have sufficed to convince me that the Mosaic doctrine—"The blood is the life"—is too often fatally overlooked,' a comment which neatly implies that the cultural and religious significance of the blood is as much at play here as medical fact.[59]

Arguments over whether and to what extent derangements of the heart and circulation could affect the brain, and vice versa, are almost as frequent in medical textbooks around the 1830s and 1840s as discussions about the relation between the nervous and circulatory systems. The relation between heart, blood, and brain had equally important cultural implications: if the heart was predominant, this might suggest that feeling could prevail over reason; whereas if the brain transmitted sensations to the heart via the blood, mind and consciousness could be seen triumphing over purely physical responses. The sensitive nature of this debate, in terms of queries about the possible material basis of feeling and thought, meant that doctors were reluctant to deny that the brain had a role in producing (rather than responding to) sensations. The general medical theory was that overexcitement, caused by excess thought or intense mental emotion, could force the blood to rush from the heart to the head, damaging the blood vessels in the brain and disturbing the cerebral

[57] James Wilson, *On Spasm and Other Disorders, Termed Nervous, of the Muscular System* (London: John W. Parker, 1843), 2–3, 37.

[58] Henry Ancell, *Course of Lectures on the Physiology and Pathology of the Blood*, Lecture XVIII, *Lancet* (1839–40), ii. 548–56 (p. 554).

[59] Robert Hull, *Essays on Determination of Blood to the Head* (London: John Churchill, 1842), p. xi.

circulation. All kinds of cerebral ailments, from headaches to insanity, were thus believed to be caused by the heart and circulation even if these were technically responding to a mental impulse. The medical terms for this were 'determination' of blood or the more general 'congestion'.[60] In the earliest commentary on these diseases which I have found, from 1829, George Warren argues that 'manifest and painful determinations to the head, so frequent in hysterical, nervous and debilitated constitutions', cannot lead to death, although he gives the circulation destructive intent and malign agency: 'it would appear as if every effort were strained by the circulatory powers, to effect some lesion in the brain.'[61] Again, this associates a deranged circulation with nervousness. Later writers gave still more power to the heart and circulation. Robert Law, for instance, writes that: 'serious cerebral mischief will result, and has been proved in many instances to have resulted, from an hypertrophied left ventricle impelling the blood with undue force to the brain.'[62] The heart is perceived as the stronger and more threatening organ. 'It is marvellous how the tender vessels of the brain ever resist the strokes of the heart,' writes Robert Hull in his *Essays on Determination of Blood to the Head* (1842).[63]

In an important treatise on the relation between disease in heart and brain, George Man Burrows concludes: 'I believe it will be found that diseases of the heart play their part as an excentric cause of irritation, exciting or increasing disorders of the intellect to an extent which is not at present suspected.'[64] Burrows argues that the brain does in fact find it difficult to resist the strokes of the heart, and hence that insanity itself should be read as the outcome of

[60] In Conolly et al., E. Barlow notes in his entries for 'determination' and 'congestion' that these two phrases are commonly (but in his view erroneously) used to denote the same state (i. 455–6, 528–9).

[61] George Warren, *A Commentary, with Practical Observations, on Disorders of the Head* (London: Longman et al., 1829), 22.

[62] Robert Law, 'Disease of the Brain Dependent on Disease of the Heart', *Dublin Journal of Medical Science*, 17 (1840), 181–210 (p. 204).

[63] Hull, 25.

[64] George Man Burrows, *On Disorders of the Cerebral Circulation; and on the Connection between Affections of the Brain and Diseases of the Heart* (Philadelphia: Lea and Blanchard, 1848), 176.

cardiac illness. In 1859 Wardrop writes that he is similarly convinced that heart disease is the root cause of insanity, 'especially in those examples of mental aberration where the heart has been "broken" ': another example of the broken heart as a life-threatening illness.[65] Wilkie Collins has an example of a sufferer from simultaneous mental and cardiac disease in Anne Catherick, the eponymous Woman in White. He probably chose heart disease for its unpredictability, in that the plot requires Anne to die suddenly and surprisingly, but it is interesting to speculate whether Collins—generally well informed about science and medicine—expected his readers to note the link between insanity and the sick heart, which raises the possibility that Anne's mental instability might all along have resulted from organic illness.[66] The name of his hero, Hartright, also becomes particularly meaningful in this context.

'Determination' appeared to be pervasive in mid-Victorian society, at least among the middle and upper classes. 'Scarcely can an individual complain of pain and occasional throbbing in the head', writes Henry Searle in 1843, 'without being pronounced to have a determination of blood to the head.'[67] Literary men and women were particularly anxious about symptoms deriving from the relation between blood and brain, given that intellectual thought and writing were supposed to divert the normal circulation from the heart, threatening rupture. R. R. Madden warned in *The Infirmities of Genius* (1833) that an over-strong circulation in the brain could have extreme consequences:

> [I]f by constant application, the blood is continually determ-
> ined to the brain, and the calibre of the vessels enlarged to the

---

[65] Wardrop, 181–2. See also John Webster, 'On Insanity', *Medico-Chirurgical Transactions*, 26 (1843), 374–416. Webster describes finding evidence of heart disease after the death of many of the patients in his asylum. While he does not make the connection between insanity and heart disease explicit, several writers, including Burrows and Wardrop, cite his results as proof.

[66] Wilkie Collins, *The Woman in White* (1860), ed. John Sutherland (Oxford: Oxford University Press, 1996), 409, 469, 471.

[67] Henry Searle, *A Treatise on the Tonic System of Treating Affections of the Stomach and Brain* (London: Richard and John E. Taylor, 1843), 75.

extent of causing pressure or effusion in that vital organ . . . giving rise to a long train of nervous miseries—to hypochondria
in its gloomiest form, or mania in its wildest mood . . . who
can deny that the sufferer has . . . drawn the evil on himself?[68]

The circulation here *causes* nervousness and 'mania'. Throughout
his book Madden claims that writers are almost inevitably sufferers
from this illness. He reports, for example, that Byron, on seeing
his daughter suffering from 'determination', told the doctor 'that it
was a complaint to which he himself was subject', and that William
Cowper's religious mania led to a 'sudden determination to the
brain'.[69] Two decades later, Herbert Spencer, exhausted after too
much intellectual work, writes: 'The fact is, I have been making
blood faster than the weakened blood vessels of my brain will bear,
and I see that I must live low for a while.'[70] Robert Browning's friend
Alfred Domett urged him to give up writing and thinking for the
state of his health and to plunge his head regularly into cold water,
which 'will lower the circulation of the blood within and with it the
necessity for thinking'.[71] This phrasing seems to suggest that thought
is a physiological function, an irresistible impulse caused directly by
the rapid circulation of the blood.

In 1864, Frederick Tennyson told his brother Alfred that Edward
FitzGerald 'has been ill with his old complaint, blood to the head'.[72]
Alfred Tennyson had reason to sympathize. Besides his famed fear of
inheriting the 'black blood' of the Tennysons, his father had suffered
from 'spasms of the chest', and he himself wrote in 1829, 'For the last
quarter of a year I have been most distressed by a determination of
blood to the Head.'[73] Given the emphasis on hereditary transmission

[68]   R. R. Madden, *The Infirmities of Genius*, 2 vols. (London: Saunders and Otley,
1833), i. 18–19.
[69]   Ibid. ii. 136, 94.
[70]   Letter to his father, 29 Sept. 1855, in *The Life and Letters of Herbert Spencer*, ed.
David Duncan (London: Routledge/Thoemmes, 1996 (first published 1908)), 79.
[71]   Alfred Domett to RB, 30 Jan. 1846, Kelley and Lewis, xii. 31.
[72]   *Memoir*, i. 494.
[73]   Charles Tennyson to George Tennyson, 23 Sept. [1828], and Alfred Tennyson to
George Tennyson, 12 July 1829, in Lang and Shannon, i. 23, 41. On the 'black blood'

of heart disease in the early part of the century, he might well have believed he had significant grounds for anxiety. He certainly had an incentive to dwell on the implications of 'determination'. For, most notably, Arthur Hallam allegedly died of this disease. His father ascribed his death to 'a sudden rush of blood to the head' (in fact cerebral haemorrhage) and 'the symptoms of deranged circulation'.[74] Throughout his Cambridge years, Hallam reportedly suffered from bouts of 'blood in the head', or 'a too rapid determination of blood towards the brain', serious enough to cause him to miss nearly the whole of one term.[75] John Brown, doctor, popular author, and friend of Ruskin, Thackeray, and other writers, wrote that Hallam's sufferings from his heart, 'that organ out of which are the issues of life' (a quotation from Psalm 4), made him 'easily moved for others—more alive to pain—more filled with fellow-feeling'.[76] Hallam's allegedly diseased heart supposedly made him sympathetic in the wider sense of that word. Yet this contradicts his own poetic emphasis on his heartsickness. In letters and poems written as an undergraduate, Hallam repeatedly bewails his inability to achieve a healthy state of feeling. Borrowing a phrase from Coleridge's *Aids to Reflection* where he laments 'a dark cold speck on the heart', he wrote gloomily: 'The damnable part of me now is that I cannot be happy without forecasting unhappiness: there is a cold speck on the heart, even when it glows with enjoyment.'[77] Despite the fact that he is referring to his own feelings, Hallam keeps Coleridge's definite article (rather than writing 'my heart'), which serves to make his

of the Tennysons and family anxieties about insanity see Ann C. Colley, *Tennyson and Madness* (Athens: University of Georgia Press, 1993), 16–17, 34–50.

[74] Henry Hallam (ed.), *Remains, in Verse and Prose, of Arthur Henry Hallam* (London: W. Nichol, 1834), p. xxxiv.

[75] R. M. Milnes to his parents, 12 June 1829, cited in *The Letters of Arthur Henry Hallam*, ed. Jack Kolb (Columbus: Ohio State University Press, 1981), 295 n. Henry Hallam, p. xvii.

[76] Cited in Hallam Tennyson (ed.) *Tennyson and his Friends* (London: Macmillan, 1911), 455.

[77] Hallam to Joseph Blakesby, [13 Apr. 1830], in Hallam, Kolb, ed. 361. For Coleridge's quotation in full see above, p. 8.

own condition the index of a more general malaise. The 'cold speck' recurs in the early poem 'Wordsworth at Glenarbach', where the poet's heart is described as 'burning with immedicable thirst | As though a plague-spot seared it'.[78] This state, the poem argues, could be eased if not cured by reading Wordsworth's poetry.

Hallam's claims of heartsickness, and indeed his constant stress on the heart in his poems, are evidently a deliberate attempt to position himself as an intelligent, slightly morbid young man possessed of acute poetic sensibility and hence suffering from an illness that was particularly apt for writers. But when we know that the post-mortem report on his body described 'a weakness of the cerebral vessels, and a want of sufficient energy in the heart', should we therefore read Hallam's self-conscious literary references to heartsickness as also an actual indication of his bodily state?[79] The line between the poetic heart and the real heart within the body becomes blurred. Perhaps the demands of Hallam's intellect did indeed prove too much for his heart. On the other hand, the pathologist might well have found symptoms of a weak heart because he was looking for them. In 1833, a sensitive and clever young man, already a writer of promise, who died suddenly and unexpectedly, could safely be assumed to have had something wrong with his heart. If Hallam's poetry did not cause his death, it may at least have contributed to the way in which that death was read and interpreted.

The relations between heart, nerves, and brain, and the kinds of heart disease associated with these, were conceived in terms of sympathy. Illnesses such as Hallam's would be described as 'sympathetic' because the heart affected the brain through the network of the circulation, the brain sympathizing with the heart's disturbances. As John Williams, author of an 1852 book entitled *Practical Observations on Nervous and Sympathetic Palpitation of the Heart*, suggests:

---

[78] ['Wordsworth at Glenarbach: An Episode'], 130–1, in *The Writings of Arthur Henry Hallam*, ed. T. H. Vail Motter (London: Oxford University Press, 1943).

[79] Henry Hallam, p. xxxv.

> From the intimate connection that exists through the medium
> of the nervous system, between the heart and other organs
> ... symptoms may arise 'par sympathie', so similar, in every
> respect, to those which proceed from absolute disease of the
> heart itself, as to baffle the closest inquiry.[80]

This concept of sympathetic disease and its mimicry of organic disease was immensely influential, not least because it meant that any mysterious ailment could ultimately be ascribed to the heart's influence. 'Sympathy' as a term also encapsulated notions of the transmission of affect, because it could occur between the sufferer and another as well as within the suffering body, and because it was associated with the physical effects of emotion. Sympathetic disorders of the heart were assumed to be more common among those who were unduly sensitive or over-emotional; particularly young men, women, and artists. Robert Semple writes in his medical textbook on the heart that sympathetic heart disease is associated with 'mental emotion and excitement, a very common cause, especially in this active and enterprising age; the influence of the passions, especially that of love; the pursuit of study to an excessive degree'.[81] Note that the pursuit of study here, rather than being seen as dry and intellectual, is linked to passion and feeling. Several medical writers also specifically cite sexual excess (including masturbation) as a direct cause, because moments where the heart is unduly excited, if prolonged, could lead to permanent collapse.[82] Elizabeth Gaskell's *Wives and Daughters* (1865) provides a good example of a typical candidate for sympathetic heart disease. Osborne Hamley, a sensitive young man with an interest in poetry who marries unwisely for love, dies from 'Something wrong about the heart'. His illness is technically defined as 'aneurism of the aorta' but

---

[80] John Williams, *Practical Observations on Nervous and Sympathetic Palpitation of the Heart*, 2nd edn. (London: John Churchill, 1852), 3.

[81] Robert Hunter Semple, *A Manual of the Diseases of the Heart: Their Pathology, Diagnosis, Prognosis and Treatment* (London: John Churchill, 1875), 265.

[82] Horace Dobell, *On Affections of the Heart and in its Neighbourhood: Cases, Aphorisms and Commentaries* (London: H. K. Lewis, 1872), 127–8.

implicitly linked to his emotional susceptibility and the pain he suffered in concealing his marriage from his father: 'care killed him. They may call it heart disease—.'[83] The question in this case (as with Eliot's Casaubon or Latimer) is whether this is simply dramatic irony in assigning the appropriate disease to a character, or whether the reader should assume that the disease would be a logical result of the feelings or actions of that character. The difficulty, in the imagined case of Osborne Hamley and in many medical case studies, in distinguishing between the organic and the 'functional' or sympathetic, emotional and physical causes, was highly significant in giving heart disease wider implications because it created a strong belief that 'real' heart disease could be directly caused by emotion and passion.

Nineteenth-century medical writers frequently observe that while those actually suffering from cardiac disease are relatively unlikely even to realize that their heart is unhealthy, those undergoing sympathetic or nervous heart disorders experience symptoms so alarming that they will insist they have organic disease. James Hope remarks on palpitation:

> There are few affections which excite more alarm and anxiety in the mind of the patient than this. He fancies himself doomed to become a martyr to organic disease of the heart, of the horrors of which he has an exaggerated idea; and it is the more difficult to divest him of this impression, because the nervous state which gives rise to his complaint, imparts a fanciful, gloomy and desponding tone to his imagination.[84]

By imitating the symptoms of 'real' disorders, palpitation could induce such apprehension in the sufferer that organic disease would eventually be produced. Hope's language—'fancies', 'idea', 'impression', and 'imagination'—emphasizes that heart disease acts upon the mind as much as the body. The patient is trapped, because the

---

[83] Elizabeth Gaskell, *Wives and Daughters*, ed. Pam Morris (Harmondsworth: Penguin, 1996), 554, 381, 567.
[84] Hope, 488.

nervous state associated with inorganic, sympathetic disease, in itself, by manifesting the symptoms of heart disease (a disordered pulse, an unbalanced circulation) is likely to cause these symptoms to become permanent and thus lead to organic disease. As Elliotson observes: 'when the heart has been labouring under morbid irritability for a length of time, it is very possible for one part to give way, and to have organic disease set up.'[85] Belief in the sick heart was itself enough to make the heart sick. Such theories of a causal link between sympathetic and 'real' heart disease were very tempting, not least because they indicated the need for mental and moral regulation and control over impulsive emotions.

Sympathetic heart disease, as the title of Williams's book suggests, was characterized by 'palpitation', one of the most frequent and alarming symptoms of cardiac disease. This appears to have been another term in common parlance. Charles West Cope, an artist known for his story paintings, produced a painting titled 'Palpitation' in the 1850s which shows a woman apparently on the verge of fainting as a man arrives at the door.[86] The spectator, alerted by the title, could read a story of either disappointed love or painful expectation into her pose. The title invites imagination and sympathetic identification with her physical symptoms even though these are minimally visible in the painting. Other fictional sufferers would include the speaker of Tennyson's early poem 'Eleanore':

> From thy rose-red lips MY name
>   Floweth; and then, as in a swoon,
>   With dinning sound my ears are rife,
>   My tremulous tongue faltereth,
>   I lose my colour, I lose my breath,
>   I drink the cup of a costly death,
> Brimmed with delirious draughts of warmest life. (128–39)

---

[85] Elliotson, 'Clinical Lecture on Disease of the Heart', *Lancet* (1830–1), i. 487–95 (p. 494).

[86] Charles West Cope, *Palpitation*, Victoria and Albert Museum, London. I am grateful to Sonia Solicari for drawing my attention to this image.

Tennyson deliberately recalls Sappho here, in a move which might feminize his speaker.[87] Burgess writes, on sympathetic palpitation under the influence of love:

> There is a thrill or throbbing of the heart, which is oftentimes visible externally—we feel a momentary oppression ... the breathing becomes affected in the general sympathy ... and a stifling follows as in grief—all self-possession is lost for the moment—*the voice becomes changed.*[88]

These signals are all present in Tennyson's poem. The 'cost' of this orgasmic death relates it both to Victorian conceptions of sex as 'spending' the vital forces of the body, and to the potential price paid by the heart for this dangerous palpitation. 'Delirious draughts' might be related to warm blood rushing through the circulation, and the heart's presence and sudden vehement action are embodied in the rhythm. 'My tremulous tongue faltereth' is extremely awkward to say in regular metre, and with 'Ĭ losé mў cólŏur, Ĭ losé mў bréath' an extra hurried beat is added, an anapaest disturbing the underlying iambics, as in Byron's *Don Juan*. Passionate moments of intense feeling, such as those experienced in 'Eleanore' or in Cope's painting, are tinged with pathology.

The fear that sympathetic heart disease could be created by emotional disturbances and that it might prove infectious is evident in medical works which trace the supposed increase in heart disease to societal factors. If the heart could sympathize with external events, cardiac disease could be seen as a national ailment, almost an epidemic, caused by wider social ills in addition to individual weaknesses. John Williams remarks:

> For nearly fifty years Europe has been continually under the influence of political commotion of the most exciting kind. In the more civilised parts, states have been changing and unsteady

---

[87] See Margaret Reynolds, *Fragments of an Elegy: Tennyson Reading Sappho* (Lincoln: Tennyson Society, 2001).

[88] Burgess, 134.

in their foreign and domestic policy; commerce has been of the most fluctuating and speculative character; individual feelings have been powerfully called into exercise, and the passions, which fan into flame the morbid energies of the nervous system, have revelled in the luxuries of gratification ... When we reflect, therefore, on the powerful influence that mental emotions exercise over the action of the heart ... when we know that functional derangement is daily and hourly produced by the activity of these feelings; then we are bound to believe, that disorders of the circulation and the heart have increased of late years.[89]

Williams's move into the first person plural, 'we reflect', 'we know', assumes that the link between disease and emotion is unproblematic for his audience, and his constant use of adjectives and repetition of clauses and words builds up rhetorical force, so that this passage itself seems to revel in the chaos it describes. He does not state that the heart is directly affected by the outside world, but rather by the 'mental emotions' created by it, which in turn act upon the heart. Heart, brain, and nervous system are again linked in terms of the 'morbidity' caused by modern life. Williams's view that national traumas or upsets could seriously damage the hearts of the population was relatively common. Jean-Nicholas Corvisart, one of the pioneers in the study of cardiac pathology, claimed at the start of the century, in an oft-quoted passage, that heart disease rose as a direct consequence of the French Revolution.[90] William Newnham, for one, refers to his work in arguing that:

[D]isease of the heart has been of much more common occurrence of late years, especially after any season of commercial distress, or political excitement. This was very remarkably exemplified after the revolution in France, and in our own country after seasons of great and unfortunate speculation.[91]

[89] John Williams, 8.

[90] J. N. Corvisart, *A Treatise on the Diseases and Organic Lesions of the Heart and Great Vessels*, trans. C. H. Hebb (London: Underwood and Blacks, 1813), 323.

[91] William Newnham, *The Reciprocal Influence of Body and Mind Considered* (London: J. Hatchard, 1842), 258.

Associating heart disease with the aftermath of the French Revolution literalizes the pervasive sense that the revolution had been an affair of passion and emotion, which then soured and decayed, and that the overexcitement of political revolution could be physically dangerous. Like Williams, Newnham also hints at the importance of economic factors. Halts or disturbances in the smooth circulation of capital—common in this period of booms, speculative mania, panics, and sudden slumps—might alter the circulation of those affected.[92] Newnham in fact published his book at the lowest point of a period of pronounced economic depression, in 1842.[93] He does suggest that the apparent spread of heart disease might simply reflect the attention paid to it by medical writers, but he emphasizes that this does not entirely explain the sudden rise in cases. Forbes Winslow, in a popular book on avoiding insanity from the same year, notes on the heart:

> Diseases of this organ are, I regret to say, alarmingly on the increase, and I much question whether the circumstance is not to be attributed to the unnatural political excitement in which the people of this country have been kept for the last few years.[94]

Winslow also stresses economic anxiety as well as apprehension about the possibility of revolutionary disturbances. He neatly lays the blame for heart disease on the politicians, not on the weak hearts of the people.

While an explosion of theory about the difference between sympathetic and organic disease, the question of emotional response, and the heart's status in relation to the rest of the body made heart disease more visible in the nineteenth century, it was not therefore

---

[92] David Trotter's excellent study of circulation in the novel makes similar points and expands upon the economic implications of this metaphor. *Circulation: Defoe, Dickens and the Economies of the Novel* (London: Macmillan, 1988).

[93] Asa Briggs claims that 'there was no gloomier year in the whole nineteenth century' in *The Age of Improvement, 1783–1867*, 2nd edn. (Harlow: Longman, 2000), 255.

[94] Forbes Winslow, *On the Preservation of the Health of Body and Mind* (London: Henry Renshaw, 1842), 92.

more curable or more explicable. The fears associated with heart failure still rested on the idea that the heart's actions could not be fully predicted or analysed, and that the subject might at any point be suffering from an unrecognized, incurable illness which could result in sudden death. The author of one of the most important early treatises on the subject, Allan Burns, writes:

> The heart, from the intricacy of its structure, and from its incessant action, is liable to many diseases, and these from the importance of the function of this organ, are at all times highly alarming. Some of them are extremely insidious in their commencement, are attended with obscure and perplexing symptoms, and in their result are almost uniformly and speedily fatal.[95]

Burns presents the heart as a delicate organism subjected to deliberate attack by disease. His repeated use of intensifying adverbs ('highly', 'extremely', 'uniformly', 'speedily') heightens the rhetorical urgency of his warning. Rather than reassuring his readers (whether they are a doctor hoping to diagnose heart disease or a patient), Burns plays on their fears, painting an exaggerated and foreboding picture. 'Observation has traced back, with fearful fidelity,' writes Latham, 'a long line of formidable and fatal diseases to their pathological parentage in the heart.'[96] The heart becomes a parent, or a womb, generating diseases as its offspring, an image which taps into contemporary fears about heart disease and heredity. The relish in Latham's alliteration deliberately adds a dramatic flourish, portraying the physiologist as an intrepid investigator, fearing what he will encounter—the sensational hidden source of all disease, the sick heart.

The Victorian heart was an organ that, despite endless discussions of its behaviour, remained mysterious, unquantifiable, and

---

[95] Allan Burns, *Observations on Some of the Most Frequent and Important Diseases of the Heart* (Edinburgh: James Muirhead, 1809), 1.

[96] Latham (1846), i, p. x.

rife with significance. Nineteenth-century physiologists made crucial advances in the description of the circulation, the blood vessels, and the heart's movements, but vexing questions of why the heart beat or the blood circulated, and what precisely caused derangement in heart and circulation, were unanswerable, often still simply referred to as acts of God. As in Tennyson's *The Princess* (1848), the heart is beyond (or above) comprehension:

> [S]omething wild within her breast,
> A greater than all knowledge, beat her down. (VII. 222–3)

Princess Ida gives way at this moment to her nascent love for the Prince. The ambiguity of 'something' and '*A* greater' position the heart as a separate, inhuman and potentially uncontrollable entity, capable of overcoming the will and intellect. Tennyson's pun on 'beat'—common in his poems—suggests that the heart's emotional beats can 'beat' the combined forces of the self. The heart possesses its own 'knowledge', sometimes more powerful than any conscious or intellectual force.

In *The Physiology of Common Life*, Lewes describes a heart completely removed from the body and still beating. He stresses the 'thrill' and 'tremulous awe' felt by the anatomist, in language itself associated with unusual activity in the heart. But the main feeling produced is that of alienation:

> The beating of the heart, which from his childhood he has learned to associate in some mysterious manner with life and emotion, he here sees occurring under circumstances removed from all possible suggestions of emotion or life. What mean these throbbings?[97]

This is a question that resonates throughout nineteenth-century literature as well as nineteenth-century science. The observer here has 'learned' to associate heart and emotion. In other words, when

---

[97] Lewes, i. 332.

seen in purely physiological terms, the heart is not intrinsically and naturally an emotional apparatus. It does not need human feelings, but if the observer cannot read emotional significance into its actions he is at a loss. This fear fuels anxiety about the heart throughout this period. As threatening as the worry that the heart will feel and suffer too much, and become diseased is the misgiving that it is unresponsive, in some sense even inhuman—that there is nothing to connect the body with the external world, no spiritual part or connection with God, nothing even to unite the different organs within the body. Hence the need for both poets and doctors to offer reassurance that the heart still meant something. Tennyson's Ida refuses to teach her students anatomy because:

> We shudder but to dream our maids should ape
> Those monstrous males that carve the living hound,
> .   .   .   .
> Or in the dark dissolving human heart,
> And holy secrets of this microcosm,
> Dabbling a shameless hand with shameful jest,
> Encarnalize their spirits.
>
> (*The Princess*, III. 292–8)

She sees anatomy as resolutely physical, involving a demeaning and dangerous separation of the physical aspects of the body from their spiritual significance. Anatomists and physiologists are carnal beings, 'monstrous' and demeaned by the verbal association with apes. This gendered critique of the new culture of physiology (one not necessarily supported by Tennyson) acts as a defence of the 'ancient' heart against the scientifically analysable heart. 'Dark, dissolving human heart' seems to imply either that the heart acts as a solvent or that it is itself 'dissolving', coming apart, decaying within the body. There is a sense of the heart receding from the probings of the anatomist, hiding its secrets. 'Dark' suggests that these secrets might be disturbing. But in this mystery, despite the threat that the heart is falling apart, there is the possibility of something 'greater'; even 'holy'. It is a possibility, as the next chapters show, that is simultaneously highlighted and questioned by the investments and investigations of nineteenth-century poets.

2

Shocks and Spasms: Rhythm and the Pulse of Verse

Poetic rhythm, in its emphasis on the beat, the regular but flexible pattern of stresses and stops, has long been read in relation to the pulse, so much so that discussion of the 'poem's heartbeat' might seem clichéd.[1] As Adam Piette argues in connection with Tennyson's *Maud*:

> *All* poetic clichés and conventions may be said to derive their force from the myth of origins in blood and heartbeat, but the fact that the heart is thought to be anything more than just a pump is itself a function of poetic cliché and convention. The heart's regular beat is the dubious source of all repetition: mechanical pump methodically keeping a body regular and alive, and emotional source of the rhythm of all passion.[2]

Piette identifies a key paradox with regard to rhythm and the heart: the separation between the mechanical and the organic. The pulse serves as a model for rhythm in that it always involves the possibility of variation from the steady beat, the deviation from a set metrical pattern on which poetic rhythm depends. Yet at the same time, in nineteenth-century literature, there is an evident anxiety that the heartbeat might be purely mechanical, equivalent to the ticking of a clock or other repetitive, 'methodical' action, that it might not be

---

[1] A study of metre by Alfred Corns, for example, is titled *The Poem's Heartbeat: A Manual of Prosody* (Ashland, Ore.: Story Line Press, 1997).

[2] Adam Piette, 'Sound-Repetitions and Sense, or How to Hear Tennyson', *Swiss Papers in English Language and Literature*, 7 (1994), 157–70 (p. 166).

responsive to emotion. The Victorian period, I want to suggest, was both the point at which the link between poetry, poetics, and the heartbeat seemed more than mere convention and was imagined as a physical, felt connection, and the point at which fear was greatest that this link might simply be conventional, that ideas of affect were hollow and poetic form was a fossilized, inert structure, not a living force. The poets discussed in the following chapters—and perhaps Tennyson in particular—were deeply concerned with the heart and pulse as poetic cliché. Tennyson himself, as Piette implies, was dubious about taking the heart as the source of feeling, yet his poetry nonetheless continually engages with this idea and repeatedly plays on the notion of pulse as rhythm. While the link between poetry and the pulse was already becoming hackneyed by the Victorian period, then, it was still a charged association. This was partly because of the physiological studies described in the previous chapter and partly, as we shall see, because new investigations into English prosody suggested that rhythm might be somatic, the means by which emotion could be transferred between poem, poet, and reader. It was hence a primary medium for conveying affect. Although poets had played on the idea of a link between rhythm and the body for centuries, the mid-Victorian period was the point at which it was first fully theorized in relation to metre.

Recent considerations of the affective role of rhythm, notably Amittai Aviram's *Telling Rhythm: Body and Meaning in Poetry*, have discussed the affective pleasures created by rhythmic utterance in terms of freedom, excitement, self-surrender. Aviram argues that rhythm is above social and historical constraints; it possesses a sublime, non-cognitive power which speaks directly to the body: '*Poetic meaning is to the rhythm of poetic form as social constructions of the body are to the body itself.*'[3] His argument, filtered through psychoanalytic accounts of our natural attraction to rhythm by Nicolas Abraham, Julia Kristeva, and others, is significant for Victorian poetics because

---

[3] Amittai Aviram, *Telling Rhythm: Body and Meaning in Poetry* (Ann Arbor: University of Michigan Press, 1994), 21.

writers at the time moved increasingly towards just such a concept of rhythm as innate, physical, and, at least in part, representative of motions within the body. But my argument differs from Aviram's in suggesting that the Victorian conception of rhythm as pulse was less a recognition of a transhistorical truth than a historically constructed perception. Questions of affect and rhythmic embodiment are deeply informed by the wider culture of the heart in Victorian society. Rhythms which self-consciously reference or represent the pulse were meaningful (as opposed to Aviram's suggestion that rhythm is deliberately 'outside of meaning') in that they were interpreted in the light of popular beliefs (and anxieties) about the heart's behaviour.[4] Furthermore, Aviram's celebration of surrender to rhythm does not quite fit in a Victorian context. In a very suggestive account of how to read Victorian rhythms, Matthew Campbell has examined how prosody at this time is engaged in a sounding of the rhythms of will, the attempt to create and sustain agency.[5] In my addition to this, the rhythm of the heart stands in opposition to the will because it represents an alternative source of control. If rhythm is dictated by the heart, giving in to it would mimic the kind of bodily surrender Aviram celebrates. It would also, however, involve a loss of will and might imply that the body rather than the mind was in control. Such surrender was feared as well as welcomed by Victorian writers. At the start of the century, in *Natural Theology* (1802), one of the standard textbooks of the period, William Paley writes:

> We cannot consider but with gratitude, how happy it is that our vital motions are *involuntary*. We should have enough to do, if we had to keep our hearts beating ... We must have been continually upon the watch, and continually in fear: nor would this condition have allowed of sleep.[6]

Paley seeks to reassure, but there is something frightening in this account. He makes it clear that the motions of the heart have nothing

---

[4] Ibid. 5.
[5] Matthew Campbell, *Rhythm and Will in Victorian Poetry* (Cambridge: Cambridge University Press, 1999), *passim*.
[6] William Paley, *Natural Theology*, 3rd edn. (London: R. Faulder, 1803), 175.

to do with human agency, that we cannot hope to keep our own hearts beating. An anatomist, Paley notes, would expect that the heart 'should always be liable to derangement, or that it would soon work itself out. Yet shall this wonderful machine go, night and day, for eighty years together.'[7] This blithe assurance, counteracting the threatening possibilities of derangement introduced immediately beforehand, rests on Paley's belief that if human will is redundant when it comes to the heart, God's will still predominates. Since He is the creator of this 'wonderful machine', we effectively have a guarantee of its operation. Perceval Barton Lord, writing in *Popular Physiology* in 1834, agreed that:

> It is an equally wise and prudent provision, that parts the constant and uninterrupted action of which is necessary to life, should have been withdrawn from the immediate direction of the will; else would a slight inattention or forgetfulness be attended by death.[8]

Again, Lord implies that the heart is controlled by an external force equivalent to God's will, which is considerably safer than the fragile human control he describes here. Later writers were less convinced. As the century progressed and Paley and Lord's confident faith became questionable, the surrender of will in relation to the material body was an anxious topic of debate. When Victorian rhythm is read in terms of the heartbeat, or the breath, as in Eric Griffiths's influential account, it introduces a suggestion that the poet may not quite be in control of his or her physical actions as they impinge upon the creation of a poem, nor of the affect they might create and transmit.[9]

This chapter examines both the specific links between poetic rhythm and the pulse, fostered by physiological investigations and potentially intensified by new scientific studies of motion, force, and time, and the general implications of a new theory of prosody.

---

[7] Paley, 170.

[8] Perceval Barton Lord, *Popular Physiology* (London: John W. Parker, 1834), 234.

[9] Eric Griffiths, *The Printed Voice of Victorian Poetry* (Oxford: Clarendon Press, 1989).

The negotiation between an older view of metre, based on classical prosody and involving the strict measurement of accent and quantity, and a more flexible stance, is evident, I argue, in the increased use of cardiac imagery in poetry and poetic theory.[10] The pulse seems to represent this negotiation because, as Piette observes, it is both mechanical and variable, throbbing, spasming, and palpitating. The emphasis on pathology in the literature of the heart complicates this further. As we saw in the last chapter, heart disease was conceptualized as a disorder strongly related to an individual's habits, career, and emotional susceptibility, yet also bound up with social conditions and burdened with extensive metaphorical implications. The rhythms of the human heart, similarly, are on one hand perceived as private, internal, affected by personal feeling; yet on the other, they are linked to universal movements and processes. Depending on the point of view of the commentator, these wider rhythmic processes—frequently described in terms of pulsation—might either show the harmony of all living things or indicate that all human motions stemmed from God. Rhythm, that is, could be seen as part of a scientific, natural unity in which such forces as electricity, sound, and light waves are in tune with the same pulse, or as a religious tool, dictated by the will of God. Poetry of this period oscillates between representing the pulse of and in the poem as part of these wider unities and concentrating on its individual movements and variations.

Literary and medical discourse argued that poetry could act directly upon the heart, creating and hence embodying the effects it describes—a rapid, sluggish, or intermittent pulse, which in turn acts upon the circulation. Reading as well as writing is represented as a somatic experience. This has been well discussed by literary criticism but the focus has largely been on the novel (and sensation

---

[10] For a brief analysis of classical prosody, see Karl Shapiro and Robert Beum, *A Prosody Handbook* (New York: Harper and Row, 1975). On its significance in the 19th century, see A. A. Markley, *Stateliest Measures: Tennyson and the Literature of Greece and Rome* (Toronto: University of Toronto Press, 2004), 87–9.

fiction in particular) rather than on poetry, despite the potential for affective transmission contained in poetic rhythm.[11] 'We confess our blood circles rapidly again as we hold these volumes in our hands,' wrote one reviewer of Barrett Browning.[12] The anticipation, the excitement aroused by opening and reading Barrett Browning's poetry, is akin to that created by passion or desire. Thomas Carlyle wrote approvingly (and reassuringly) to Tennyson, after reading his 1842 volume, 'Truly it is long since in any English Book, Poetry or Prose, I have felt the pulse of a real man's heart as I do in this same.'[13] He echoes a comment by William Hazlitt on Robert Burns's poetry: 'He had a real heart of flesh and blood beating in his bosom—you can almost hear it throb.'[14] Tennyson's and Burns's 'manly' hearts and Barrett Browning's rapid circulation implicitly infuse their verse and touch the reader. Gauging the health of the poem (and determining the gendered characteristics of the writer) depends on an ability to 'take its pulse'.

Direct links between disturbed rhythms and the health of the poet's and reader's hearts meant that poetic affect had the potential to be either curative or dangerous. A number of theorists of rhythm in the period argue that it can materially assist the calmative efforts of poetry, and that a steady rhythm will act to soothe the heart, quieting the emotions. The well-known doctor James Wardrop, in his work on heart disease, cites the case of a woman suffering from palpitations and an irregular pulse who was cured by participating

[11]　See, for example, Kate Flint, *The Woman Reader* (Oxford: Clarendon Press, 1993), 53–70 and Helen Small, 'A Pulse of 124: Charles Dickens and a Pathology of the Mid-Victorian Reading Public', in James Raven, Helen Small, and Naomi Tadmor (eds.), *The Practice and Representation of Reading in England* (Cambridge: Cambridge University Press, 1996), 263–90.

[12]　Anon., Review of Barrett Browning's *Poems* (1844), *The Prospective Review* (1845), reprinted in Kelley and Lewis, xi. 337. This may have been an especially common critical response to female authors. Edward Dowden wrote on Eliot, 'When we read what she has written the blood circulates through every part of our system,' 'George Eliot', *Studies in Literature 1789–1877* (London: Kegan Paul, 1878), 243.

[13]　*Memoir*, i. 213.

[14]　'On Burns, and the Old English Ballads', from *Lectures on the English Poets* in *Collected Works of William Hazlitt*, ed. A. R. Waller and Arnold Glover, 12 vols. (London: J. M. Dent, 1902), v. 123–43 (pp. 127–8).

in church worship: the reassuring rhythms of the psalms and hymns eased her pulse.[15] In contrast, stops, starts, halts, and momentary disruptions to rhythm threaten the stability of the pulse and the smooth continuation of the poem itself. In poems written by poets who believed themselves to be acute sufferers from heart disease, these rhythmic signals can suggest the failure of the poet's heart to maintain a steady and healthful rhythm, and given the widespread belief in sympathetic heart disease, inducing similar symptoms in the reader's heart might spread functional disturbances rather than healthful empathy.

The minor Scottish poet Robert Leighton wrote in 'Art' (1855):

> Art is medicinal. If I am long
>   Without the exercise of poesie,
> My spirit ails, my body's somewhat wrong,
>   My heart beats 'Woe is me!'
>
> And if the rhythmic measure is my choice,
>   'Tis also my necessity. I weave
> The threaded thought: it makes no laurell'd noise;
>   But all my ailments leave.[16]

'Necessity' suggests that 'choice' may be deceptive; rhythmic measure is less a function of the poet's will than of a physical need. The fact that the stress falls on 'if' at the start of the second stanza also supports this by calling the idea of choice into question. Note that poetry has the potential to cure both the 'spirit' and the heart and body. Leighton's troubled heart beats quite neatly in tune, in terms of rhyme and rhythm: 'poesie' and 'Woe is me', for example, are exact rhyming equivalents. 'And so, I doubt not, his creation makes | A healthier current in the painter's veins', he continues. Despite the slight troubling of the metre in 'healthier', which could take either two or three syllables, Leighton is complacent about the relation

---

[15] James Wardrop, *On the Nature and Treatment of Diseases of the Heart, with Some New Views on the Physiology of the Circulation* (London: John Churchill, 1837), 44–5.

[16] Robert Leighton, 'Art', from *Records and Other Poems* (London: Kegan Paul, 1880), 169.

between artistic creation and a healthy circulation. Others would have disagreed. Ruskin, for example, cites a report in the *Pall Mall Gazette* of a young painter who died while frantically trying to complete his masterpiece. The cause of his death was recorded as fatty degeneration of the heart, 'the latter having probably ceased its action due to the mental excitement of the deceased'.[17] 'Art' might also stand as a jaunty relation of Tennyson's anguish in *In Memoriam*, a poem which interrogates the relations between rhythm, affect, and health. Leighton's argument is perhaps even (given the 'laurell'd') a reproachful response to Tennyson's doubts about the value of poetry, the 'sad mechanic exercise' of metre (V. 7).

A contrasting view to Leighton's assurance is represented by Elizabeth Barrett Browning's 'The Student', from her 1838 collection. The poem consists of a description of a scene of reading—or potentially writing, if we assume that the student is a poet—in which a young overambitious student is found dead at his desk with his 'breast and brow' pressed to those

> Words which had often caused that heart to throb,
> That cheek to burn; though silent lay they now,
> Without a single beating in the pulse,
> And all the fever gone![18]

The last line here contrasts ironically with Leighton's 'And all my ailments leave': the student too is 'cured' by art but in the sense that it has removed him from earthly cares. The implication is that these words led to the student's death by creating a fevered pulse. Barrett Browning uses regular metre to produce the opposite effect to that of Leighton's poem. While the trochaic reversal in the first line creates a brief effect of speed, like the heightened throb of the heart, the steady iambic pulse in the second and third lines, and particularly in the latter, unbroken by punctuation, does not indicate a return

---

[17] Cook and Wedderburn, xix. 133.
[18] Lines 41–4. *The Complete Works of Elizabeth Barrett Browning*, ed. Charlotte Porter and Helen A. Clarke, 6 vols. (New York: AMS Press, 1973 (reprint of 1900 edn.)). All further references are to this edition, unless otherwise stated, and will be given in the text.

to health but rather ironically signifies the absence of that which it represents. The beat of rhythm continues, but the student's pulse has stopped. Rhythm here does not simply enhance the meaning of the lines, it adds an extra dimension by presenting a counterpoint to them. These lines also shift so that the heartbeat and blush of the student, caused by the excitement of reading (or writing, if these words are his) are strangely transferred to the written page. The pulse belongs to the words themselves, and came alive in the act of reading, when the student animated it with his own fever and desire. With his death the affective power of these words dies also, until they find a new reader. Barrett Browning does not need to state explicitly the cause of the student's death, when the symptoms clearly allude to an excess or 'determination' of blood to the head.

The division between 'Art' and 'The Student' is apparent in wider debates over the dangers of reading and specific questions about the function of rhythm. From the late eighteenth century onwards, writers argued over whether metrical language heightened or contained the passions it expressed, whether it excited emotions or soothed them. Could the metres associated with particular affective results be identified, and was a steady, regular beat more desirable than one which incorporated shocks and starts? As this chapter makes clear, no definitive answer was found, but by the 1860s there was nonetheless a perceptible shift towards viewing rhythm as an agent to express emotion rather than as a regulated check upon it. This 'new prosody', as identified by Dennis Taylor and recently by Yopie Prins, may have been influenced by physiological and scientific research, and perhaps particularly by poetry which engaged with this research.[19] After a consideration of these interchanges, the second part of this chapter focuses on the loosely defined 'spasmodic' poetry written between 1840 and 1860—a genre which was much discussed at the time, and both influenced and was influenced

---

[19] Dennis Taylor, *Hardy's Metres and Victorian Prosody* (Oxford: Clarendon Press, 1988). Yopie Prins, 'Victorian Meters', in Joseph Bristow (ed.), *The Cambridge Companion to Victorian Poetry* (Cambridge: Cambridge University Press, 2000), 89–113 (p. 89).

by Tennyson and the Brownings. Spasmodism is the only poetic movement of this period which implies in the name it came to bear that its chief characteristics might be formal. There is, moreover, something about the idea of 'spasmodic' verse which immediately implies that poetry is *felt*. Although in practice the spasmodic poets whom I discuss—Alexander Smith, Sydney Dobell, J. Stanyan Bigg, and others—often lacked the formal skills needed to back up their poetic theories, they nonetheless mimicked and anticipated metrical theories produced in these decades by attempting to introduce radical discussions of affect and embodiment into poetry. In their writing, the heart and pulses are defining metaphors which suggest emotional disturbance and heartsickness within the individual, but also relate individual shocks and spasms to larger principles of time and measure and use them to reflect upon the process of poetry itself.

In 1847, when he was acutely ill, Edgar Allan Poe wrote a poem, 'The Beloved Physician', to the nurse who took his pulse, in which he attempted to represent what he saw as a pathologically dangerous heartbeat in terms of metre.[20] The nurse, Marie-Louise Shew, later destroyed most of the poem (perhaps because taking the pulse could be a gesture of dubious intimacy) but recalled:

> *[A]t best*, when he was well Mr Poe's pulse beat only ten regular beats, after which it suspended or *intermitted* ... The Poem was written in a singular strain, a verse describing the Doctor watching the pulse, etc. There was in every verse a line 'The Pulse beats ten and intermits'.[21]

Interestingly, in the fragment that was preserved, Poe chose to represent his heartbeat not in a disturbed rhythm but in short regular lines, and not in ten beats but in eight:

---

[20] There is a good discussion of Poe's investment in the heart by Claude Richard, 'The Heart of Poe and the Rhythmics of the Poems', in Eric Carlson (ed.), *Critical Essays on Edgar Allan Poe* (Boston: G. K. Hall, 1987), 195–206. Richard argues that Poe despises the poet's abandon to his heart and seeks to keep the pulse in check, although his poetic speakers often fail to do so.

[21] Marie-Louise Shew, letter to Poe's biographer in 1875, cited in Mabbott, i. 401–2.

> The pulse beats ten and intermits.
> God nerve the soul that ne'er forgets
> In calm or storm, by night or day,
> Its steady toil, its loyalty.[22]

Although this extract is outwardly reassuring, the full stop after 'intermits' introduces a potentially life-threatening pause, enhanced by the suggestion that we might be waiting for the missing two beats out of the ten, before the pulse takes up its accustomed rhythm. The half-rhymes of the couplets also lack a confident chime. In order to maintain a strong iambic pulse, the final syllable of the last word in each line (i.e. 'forgets', 'loyalty') would have to be decisively stressed in a way which seems unnatural: this is particularly evident in 'loyalty', which trails off anticlimactically. Alternatively, reading the lines so that they ended firmly on a rising note would subject natural pronunciation to the dictates of metre and suggest that the pulse was beating mechanically, insensitive and untuneful. 'God nerve' (rather than 'God nerves') seems to imply that the soul, perhaps morbidly aware of the pulse's continual toil, needs to be 'nerved' to face this knowledge. The fragments left of the second and third stanzas make this even more explicit by substituting 'God shield' and 'God guide'. Why should the soul need God's guidance and shelter from the knowledge of the heart's workings, unless the pulse itself was frighteningly beyond individual control?

Engagement with the pulse in nineteenth-century physiology and pathology, and the perceived connections between writing poetry and particular forms of disordered pulse and circulation, meant that the analogy of pulse and rhythm was taken very seriously by doctors and investigators into the heartbeat as well as by poets. Early nineteenth-century writers on the heartbeat often used metrical analogies, so that physiological terminology was frequently similar to that used of poetic rhythm. James Hope, for example, divided the sound of the pulse into four beats and assigned a relative time value to each, as did

---

[22] 'The Beloved Physician', ibid. i. 403.

Herbert Davies, and many writers after him.[23] This measurement of the pulse in terms of quantity and particularly an interest in whether its beats were perfectly isochronous mirrored the focus on these issues in classical prosody. George Balfour, in an 1873 article from the *Edinburgh Medical Journal*, uses metrical notation and terminology to describe—effectively to scan—particular rhythms of the heart, concluding that at the apex of the heart the pulse resembles a trochee, and at the base an iambus.[24] By the 1870s the general assumption was that the heart's beat had four parts: the first sound, followed by a short silence, then the second, and a longer silence. Each beat could be compared to the movement within an iambic or trochaic foot, equally consisting of two 'beats' or sounds, with a short pause between them and a longer pause before the next unit. Many medical writers turned towards a musical analogy. Charles Williams, for instance, cites Laennec, who divided the pulse into time periods and separated the beat into four parts using musical notation.[25] A comparison to music was significant because it meant that pauses, silences, had to be taken into account (as rests are in musical notation) as integral parts of the heartbeat. While the invention of the metronome had brought mechanization, to some extent, into musical time, it remained necessarily variable, with early nineteenth-century composers like Beethoven, who wrote several pieces in the time of his pulse, working in counterpoint to the steady beat as much as with it.[26] Musical comparisons might therefore demonstrate that investigators into the heartbeat were moving away from the norm of mechanical regularity. In Williams's analysis, although the diseased

---

[23] James Hope, *A Treatise on Diseases of the Heart and Great Vessels* (London: William Kidd, 1832), 28–30. Herbert Davies, *Lectures on the Physical Diagnosis of the Diseases of the Lungs and Heart* (London: John Churchill, 1851), 226.

[24] George W. Balfour, 'Clinical Lectures on Diseases of the Heart', *Edinburgh Medical Journal*, 19 (1873–4), 1057–87 (p. 1074).

[25] Charles Williams, *The Pathology and Diagnosis of Diseases of the Chest*, 4th edn. (London: John Churchill, 1840), 203.

[26] See Curt Sachs, *Rhythm and Tempo* (London: J. M. Dent, 1953). Berndt Lüderitz briefly discusses Beethoven in *History of the Disorders of Cardiac Rhythm* (New York: Futura, 1995), p. vii.

heart always produces 'all varieties of measures, very unequal both in time and strength', similar variations can also occur in the relatively healthy heart: 'The two rates of pulsation seem to be variously mixed; three or four beats of the quick movement being followed by a strong one of the slow, or a pause, or some other such combination.'[27] Although the irregular pulse as described here was still generally seen as a symptom of disease, the concept of responsive, organic measure in the heartbeat was nonetheless gaining ground in comparison to an ideal of perfectly timed repetition.

As physiologists considered the pulse in relation to measure, so both poets and poetic theorists in this period can be seen moving towards a 'physiological' view of poetic metre, as opposed to the classical scansion which earlier writers had attempted to impose upon English. T. S. Omond, writing in 1921, suggests that until the 1750s English prosodic criticism was obsessed by quantity, despite the fact that classical standards were highly difficult to apply to English verse.[28] It was not until the later eighteenth century that a more abstract and fluid sense of 'rhythmus', influenced, like the physiological accounts above, by new musical theories, started to develop in literary criticism and philosophy. For my argument, what is notable about these accounts of rhythm is the way in which they deploy imagery of the pulse to signal their dissent from classical norms. In Joshua Steele's 1779 *Prosodia Rationalis* (one of the sources later used by Coventry Patmore in formulating his metrical theory), he writes:

> Our animal existence being regulated by our pulse, we seem to have an instinctive sense of *rhythmus*, as connected with, and governing, all sounds and all motions; whence it follows, that we find all people feel the effects of *rhythmus* . . . so that, without searching for the reason, it has generally been passed over as a first principle, or self-evident truth.[29]

---

[27] Charles Williams, 228–9.
[28] T. S. Omond, *English Metrists* (Oxford: Clarendon Press, 1921), 42.
[29] Joshua Steele, *Prosodia Rationalis*, 2nd edn. (London: J. Nichols, 1779), 67.

Steele was the first writer to apply musical methods to metre and he perceives poetic rhythm as innate and in some degree embodied. Writers influenced by him included Richard Roe, who saw 'pulsation' as a more accurate term than 'accent' and uses it throughout his discussion of metre, and J. Odell, whose 1806 treatise argued that metre was governed by 'the pulsation of alternate emphasis and remission'.[30] Odell also comments:

> Man alone is sensible of a rhythmus in his motions ... it is transfused through every sentence that we utter. It is felt in silence and repose, as well as actual speech and motion. It regulates the pauses both of motion and of speech, and measures even the current of our thoughts.[31]

Odell's imagery throughout the volume makes it clear that he too is thinking of the pulse as one location of this felt 'rhythmus' and that he sees this bodily rhythm as all-encompassing, influencing all thought, speech, and action. These theories were given form by contemporary poets. In Shelley's 'Alastor', for example, the poet-hero encounters a mysterious woman in whose body music, pulse, and rhythm are blended to powerful effect:

> Her fair hands
> Were bare alone, sweeping from some strange harp
> Strange symphony, and in their branching veins
> The eloquent blood told an ineffable tale.
> The beating of her heart was heard to fill
> The pauses of her music, and her breath
> Tumultuously accorded with those fits
> Of intermitted song.[32]

The 'eloquent blood' appears to speak inside this woman's veins, not, as would be more usual, in an externalized blush, as though

---

[30] Richard Roe, *The Principles of Rhythm* (Dublin: R. Graisbury, 1823), 33–5. J. Odell, *An Essay on the Elements, Accents and Prosody of the English Language* (London: Lackington, Allen, 1806), 129.

[31] Odell, 146, 127–8.

[32] *Alastor, or the Spirit of Solitude* (1815), 165–72. *The Complete Poetical Works of Percy Bysshe Shelley*, ed. Neville Rogers, 4 vols. (Oxford: Clarendon Press, 1972), vol. ii.

the hero is reading the interior of her body rather than the surface. Her breath 'accords' with the heart in a near-pun, since the root of 'accord' is the heart itself, 'cor'. 'Tumultuous', 'fits', and especially the 'intermittency' of song (and implicitly of breath and heartbeat) are terms suggestive of a disrupted heart and excessive sensibility, and might therefore be prophetic of disease.

For nineteenth-century poets and metrical theorists, the best-known theories of rhythm were probably those of Wordsworth and Coleridge, as laid out in their poetics and in the Preface to *Lyrical Ballads* and *Biographia Literaria*. In the former, Wordsworth writes on the function of metre:

> [T]he co-presence of something regular, something to which the mind has been accustomed when in an unexcited or a less excited state, cannot but have great efficacy in tempering and restraining the passion by an intertexture of ordinary feeling.[33]

His sense of the customary and 'ordinary' nature of metre suggests that some form of rhythm is always consciously or subconsciously present, though in mind rather than body. Metre, he continues, ensures that even while hearing or reading the most tragic verse we experience 'small, but continual and regular impulses of pleasurable surprise'.[34] There is some equivocation here, because Wordsworth wants to suggest that metre is affective in that it produces feelings of pleasure in the reader, but also that it prevents pleasure from becoming passion, an overmastering and hence dangerous sensation. It is simultaneously a channel for conveying feeling and for containing it. Coleridge expands upon this in *Biographia Literaria* (1817), famously tracing the origin of rhythm to 'the balance in the mind effected by that spontaneous effort which strives to hold in check the workings of passion'.[35] When commenting further on the Preface

---

[33] William Wordsworth and S. T. Coleridge, *Lyrical Ballads*, ed. R. L. Brett and A. R. Jones, 2nd edn. (London: Routledge, 1991), 264.

[34] Ibid. 265.

[35] *Collected Works*, vii: *Biographia Literaria*, ed. James Engell and W. Jackson Bate, 2 vols., ii. 64.

to *Lyrical Ballads*, Coleridge does not use the words 'metre' or 'rhythm', but, intriguingly, he writes instead that, 'as every passion has its proper pulse, so will it likewise have its characteristic modes of expression'. 'Pulse' seems to become analogous to rhythm, and poetry and the body are again linked through the physical sense of the word 'passion'.[36] 'Passion' in both Wordsworth and Coleridge is significant because it suggests both passive suffering and active excitement: an ambiguity which Wordsworth later picked up on in his 'Essay, Supplementary to the Preface' (1815).[37] In a well-known 1802 letter, Coleridge wrote, 'But *metre itself* implies a *passion*, i.e. a state of excitement, both in the Poet's mind, & is expected in that of the Reader—and tho' I stated this to Wordsworth ... yet he has [not] done justice to it.'[38] J. R. Watson notes that 'implies' can be read in an older sense of the word: metre 'folds in the passion, enwraps and entangles it' as well as generating it.[39] Wordsworth's original Preface, while accepting the origin of metre in impassioned speech, had shied away from a too close link between poetry and passion. For Coleridge, however, metre also implies passion in the sense that the presence of one immediately indicates the presence of the other, and because the particular kind of passion (anger, grief, love) expressed in the poem could be identified from the metre chosen by the poet.

In 1825, Bryan Waller Procter (who also wrote as the popular poet 'Barry Cornwall') confidently asserted that 'Verse is the *limit*, or shape by which poetry is bounded: it is the adjunct of poetry, but not its living principle.'[40] Yet this was a view which was gradually becoming unfashionable as the influence of earlier theorists filtered through and, crucially, as Romantic poetic experimentation reinvented forms

---

[36] *Biographia Literaria*, II, 71. Coleridge is citing Kenelm Digby's *Treatise on Bodies* (1645): 'Physicians do tell us, that every passion has a distinct pulse' (p. 71 n.).

[37] *Selected Prose*, ed. John O. Hayden (Harmondsworth: Penguin, 1988), 410.

[38] To William Sotheby, 13 July 1802, *Collected Letters of S. T. Coleridge*, ed. Earl Leslie Griggs, 6 vols. (Oxford: Clarendon Press, 1956), ii. 812.

[39] J. R. Watson, *The English Hymn: A Critical and Historical Study* (Oxford: Clarendon Press, 1997), 40.

[40] [Bryan Procter], 'On English Poetry', *Edinburgh Review*, 42 (1825), 31–64 (p. 34).

and genres and introduced a more flexible sense of metrical patterning within a poem. Hints that rhythm could have an affective function, often described in terms of regulating the heartbeat, were increasingly taken up by writers from the 1830s onward, and the focus gradually shifts from discussing metre primarily as an agent of control to considering rhythm as expressive in itself. R. H. Horne, for example, suggested in the introduction to *Poems of Chaucer Modernized* (1841) (a volume including a translation by Barrett Browning): 'It would be far nearer the truth were we to call our scanning gear by such terms as systole and diastole,—metre being understood as muscle, and pulsation as rhythm—varying with every emotion.'[41] The distinction between metre and rhythm here suggests that the former is the form—the flesh, the solid structure—and the latter the more flexible 'life' infusing it. In this analogy the poem is a living body, and rhythm is a matter of contraction and dilation, an opening outward in the long syllables or stressed beats, and a closing in on the shorter ones. Horne evidently sees this association with the heart as freeing rhythm from the constraints of traditional scanning and allowing it a sensitivity of response. Again, regarding rhythm as variable meant that analysing poetry was less a question of scanning for a fixed metre than of identifying the emotions conveyed by aspects of the form; in Coleridgean terms, its 'proper pulse'. Consider, for example, an instance from Tennyson's early poem 'The Lover's Tale', written in the 1820s and 1830s but not completed and published until the 1870s. The hero, Julian, describes his sufferings after the shock of discovering that his beloved is marrying another man:

> [M]y blood
> Crept like marsh drains through all my languid limbs;
> The motions of my heart seemed far within me,
> Unfrequent, low, as though it told its pulses: (ii. 51–4)

These lines provide a brilliant demonstration of the way in which rhythm could embody the disordered pulse. Metre implies passion

---

[41] R. H. Horne, *The Poems of Geoffrey Chaucer, Modernized* (London: Whittaker, 1841), p. lxxxiv.

in that the motions of the lines correspond to Julian's heartbeat. The plosive nature of the end-stopped word 'blood', and its position at the end of the line, leaves an uneasy pause here, a halt in the circulation. The reversed foot at the start of the next line, and the double emphasis on 'marsh drains', weigh down the line. Regular metre reasserts itself in line 53, but the long vowel sounds, assonance, and internal rhyme ('marsh', 'heart, 'far') mean that these iambic beats might themselves seem slow, muffled. 'Unfrequent' then introduces a disturbance as the sharpness of the 't' introduces another jerky stop, followed by further halts in the commas. Moreover, these lines deviate from iambic pentameter by introducing an extra syllable in each line, meaning that the lines trail off on a feminine ending, perhaps reflecting Julian's loss of will and manhood here.

Such imagery, carefully embodied in these metrical effects, recalls Lord's *Popular Physiology* (potentially significant because Tennyson was given a copy for Christmas in 1838) where two pages are devoted to the comparison of the circulatory system with the drainage system of a city. The blood circulating through Julian's veins is not purified blood, 'bright and lively' through exposure to the air in the lungs, but 'black and impure' blood, compared to sewage, that has been moving sluggishly around the body.[42] The pun on 'told/tolled' remembers the wedding bells for Camilla's marriage, which are also the funeral bells of Julian's nightmares, and also suggests that the heart is telling over its pulses, like rosary beads, perhaps. The 'sunken' heart, another common image, shows his isolation from human feeling—the heart has withdrawn into the depths of the body so that its movements are scarcely perceptible. In medical terms, a shock such as the one Julian has suffered could leave the heart permanently weakened: 'In *grief,* or long protracted and severe affliction, such is the influence of the mind on the heart, that the circulation of the blood becomes extremely languid, and sometimes to such a degree as to produce syncope.'[43] Tennyson thus combines the literary trope of broken-heartedness at the loss of a lover with medical conceptions of sympathetic heart

[42] Lord, 206–10.   [43] Wardrop (1837), 67.

disease, and deploys metre to express the affective qualities of this heartsickness. As the literary critic George Brimley argued in 1855:

> [A]s regards the reader, [form and rhythm are] an index to the singer's intensity of poetic temperature—a kind of metronome—and the medium through which the same heat of emotion is kindled in the reader, and he is infused with the passion as well as the imaginative perception of the subject.[44]

Reading of Julian's sufferings, according to this account, might induce the same helpless languor. Formal qualities express emotion more strongly than the meaning of the words used. They act on the reader's sensible body, his or her passions; he or she will be made to share what Brimley describes as 'that rhythmical condition of emotion'.[45] Imagery of heat and passion in his account makes a virtue of the poet's intensity; it is welcomed rather than being regarded with suspicion. But when the intensity conveyed is one of grief, as in 'The Lover's Tale', then such affect becomes less welcome.

Brimley's comparison of form and rhythm to a metronome, presumably intended to suggest that the speed of the beat has some correlation to the effects created, implies a link between poetic rhythm and mechanical time which to some extent counteracts his physical imagery. The intimation that metre might be regular and mechanical is a common poetic conceit and one which becomes prominent in much nineteenth-century poetry. It is most often seen in the comparisons between clock time and the heartbeat. As the standardization of time in the period heightened the focus on clock or watch time, this was set in contrast to notions of a human, physical time, in tune with the processes of nature.[46] The heart negotiates

---

[44] George Brimley, 'Poetry and Criticism', *Fraser's Magazine* (1855), reprinted in *Essays*, ed. William George Clark (Cambridge: Macmillan, 1858), 188–208 (p. 207).

[45] Ibid. 206.

[46] In his classic account of Victorian attitudes to time, Jerome Buckley argues that the period saw the conception of 'private time' as 'arbitrary, relative in quantity to the passing personal emotion, continuous, yet variable in tempo'. *The Triumph of Time* (Cambridge, Mass.: Harvard University Press, 1966), 7. The heartbeat stands in an uneasy relation to this, however, because it also participated in public (or national) time or rhythm.

between these extremes. It is comparable to a mechanism—John Abercrombie, in an early medical article, described a case where a man suffering from 'painful feeling' at the heart heard a sound 'exactly resembling the loud tick of a watch', a sound also audible to those around him.[47] But it is also flesh, variable and fallible. Tennyson uses the heart/watch comparison in *In Memoriam*, in the image of the clock which 'Beats out the little lives of men' (II. 8), contrasted to the various human beats and pulses associated with the poet's and Hallam's hearts. In 'Two in the Campagna', Browning turns to a clock, or perhaps even a metronome, to express the cliché of two lovers' hearts beating in time:

> I would I could adopt your will,
>   See with your eyes, and set my heart
> Beating by yours (41–3)

The speaker wants to regulate his pulse by his lover's, synchronized heartbeats, in a form of sympathetic communication. 'Set' makes the heart seem mechanical. Matthew Reynolds suggests that there is an edge of 'tyranny' in such imagery, a suggestion that one will (or heart) will predominate over the other.[48] The image here is recalled in *Aurora Leigh*, where Barrett Browning plays with the conceit that Romney and Aurora are like two clocks striking out of time with each other, but gradually working towards a mutual rhythm.[49] This is an image of mechanical entrainment which speaks to the physiological and emotional entrainment, occurring slowly over the course of the poem, of their hearts. Aurora also uses the heart/clock analogy to express her feelings of exposure and intrusion as her aunt's household tries to identify her feelings for Romney:

> I lived on and on,
>   As if my heart were kept beneath a glass,

[47] John Abercrombie, 'Contributions to the Pathology of the Heart', *Transactions of the Medico-Chirurgical Society of Edinburgh* (1823), 48.

[48] Matthew Reynolds, *The Realms of Verse: English Poetry in a Time of Nation-Building* (Oxford: Oxford University Press, 2001), 59.

[49] *Aurora Leigh*, ed. Margaret Reynolds (Athens: Ohio University Press, 1992), book 4, line 421. All further references given in the text.

> And everybody stood, all eyes and ears,
> To see and hear it tick. (II. 856–9)

Aurora's heart is expected to behave mechanically, perhaps conventionally, leaving no room for emotional variation. The image of it as a clock in a glass case suggests alienation. Such bitterness in *Aurora Leigh* comes from Aurora's sense that her heart—representing her most private and inmost feelings—is being examined and commodified, its workings detachedly assessed.

Gerard Manley Hopkins provides an outstanding instance of this trope in the unpublished poem 'To his Watch', written in the 1880s:

> Mortal my mate, bearing my rock-a-heart
> Warm beat with cold beat company, shall I
> Earlier or you fail at our force and lie
> The ruins of, rifled, once a world of art?
> The telling time our task is; time's some part,
> Not all, but we were framed to fail and die—[50]

In this meditation on the relation between heart and mechanism, Hopkins may well be thinking of the famous opening of Paley's *Natural Theology*, in which he posits that the consideration of a watch immediately leads us to assume that 'there must have existed at some time and at some place or other an artificer or artificers who formed it for the purpose which we find it actually to answer'.[51] By analogy, Paley argues, we should ask the same questions of beautifully designed natural creations, and will inevitably find God as the answer. Hopkins's poem, I think, takes issue with the idea that the human heart, like Paley's watch, might be a perfectly designed artefact produced to perform a specific task. If God has created the heart purely as a mechanism, a 'world of art', whose task is simply to keep time until it runs down, this strongly suggests a lack of human will and agency—although 'not all' does hint at the possibility of

---

[50] Lines 1–6. *The Poems of Gerard Manley Hopkins*, ed. W. H. Gardner and N. H. MacKenzie, 4th edn. (Oxford: Oxford University Press, 1970). All further references are to this edition and will be given in the text.

[51] Paley, 4.

another role. In this short poem it is not even clear whether the heart
or watch is more alive and responsive. The description of the watch
as mortal in Hopkins's opening address to it and a sentence structure
which potentially allows 'warm beat' to apply to either heart or
watch confounds distinctions between human and mechanism. The
poem also hints, disturbingly, that the watch might be stronger and
longer-lasting than the heart.

Despite the focus on mechanical time in Hopkins's poem, however,
these lines are not steady in their beat but rocking. The first line
alternates iambic and trochaic measures ('Mórtăl mў máte, béariñg
mў róck-ă-héart') to create a sense of expansion (on the repeated
long beats) and contraction, slowing down and speeding up. The
repeated four-syllable phrase ('Wárm beăt wĭth cóld' | 'Fail at
our force'), with the first and last syllables stressed, 'rocks' because
it descends from an initial emphasis to two unstressed syllables
and then rises to another emphasis. As if to highlight the absence of
conventional metre, Hopkins's rhythm fails to stress 'beat'. Awkward
enjambements (I/Earlier) and the difficulty of reading the first four
lines in one breath further enhance the sense of ungainliness in the
verse. Mechanical rhythm starts to take over in the iambic beats
and alliteration on 't' and 'f' in lines 5–6—but is this a positive
move, if the heart's steadiness is achieved at the cost of becoming
a mechanism? The implications of this extract might be that this
poet's heart is already failing in force because it cannot maintain
steady measure; it is uncertain and unpredictable. On the other
hand, the very unpredictability of the rhythm hints that the heart
is more than a timekeeper, introducing possibilities of variation and
change.

This debate plays itself out in poetic theory as well as in poetry. E.
S. Dallas, in *Poetics* (1852), had already considered the vital question
of time in poetic rhythm, and its implications for a theory which saw
form as organic:

> The measure of time . . . which the imagination will provide, is
> not a uniform beat, like that of the clock, but one like the pulse,

varying according to circumstances. Even this, however—this throbbing—gives but a faint semblance of the manner in which ideas of time are conveyed by the modulations of verse.[52]

In this volume Dallas uses Kant's theories to argue that poetic rhythm is inherently linked to a subjective perception of time-processes. Kant argues that Time and Space are the only forms of inner sense, governing all our perceptions. Therefore, Dallas suggests, the poetic imagination (stemming from inner sense) must be shaped by these forms. Kant claims that Time is 'a subjective condition of our (human) intuition'. Everything is perceived to exist in it, but time itself has no 'absolute reality'. We order the world according to an abstract principle of perception, not an identifiable external order.[53] Dallas's borrowing of this idea is crucial for poetic metre in that metre can then be seen as a subjective way of creating and ordering, not of reflecting, the perception of time. The poet's subjective experience of time, which Dallas envisages as related to physical experience, shapes the verse. Likewise, the reader's similarly subjective experience means that they read a sense of time into poetry. In other words, poetic time is not *in* the verse but in the perception of the writer or reader. Dallas's use of the pulse as his measure implies that, for him, this perception is connected to body as well as mind.

Five years after Dallas's book was published, Sydney Dobell, well known in the 1850s as a spasmodic poet, delivered a talk in Edinburgh in which he argued that poetry, besides its connection to the Divine, is 'actually in tune with our material flesh and blood'.[54] The more 'perfect' a poem, the more it will be exactly in harmony with the vital rhythms of the body—and Dobell takes this vital rhythm to be the motion of a healthy heart:

---

[52] E. S. Dallas, *Poetics: An Essay on Poetry* (London: Smith, Elder, 1852), 160–1, 172.

[53] Immanuel Kant, *Critique of Pure Reason*, trans. and ed. Paul Guyer and Alan W. Wood (Cambridge: Cambridge University Press, 1997), 163, 164.

[54] Sydney Dobell, 'The Nature of Poetry' (1857), in *Thoughts on Art, Philosophy and Religion*, introd. John Nichol (London: Smith, Elder, 1876), 3–65 (p. 22).

Physiology has already shown that other recognisable organic motions of the body—for instance, the action of the lungs—bear definite relations to this motion of the heart: and in all modesty I would suggest to the great Physiologists here present whether there be not reason to infer that every portion of the incessant vital action of the system is keeping measured dance to that great *beater of time*? . . . Perfect utterance, therefore . . . must occur in a succession bearing proportional relations to a time marked by a series of equal intervals, that is, to the time beaten by a healthy heart.[55]

Note that Dobell is speaking to an audience containing physiologists, and is evidently knowledgeable about their research. The heart as 'beater of time' is both that which keeps regular time and that which 'beats', wins over, time, establishing an organic rhythm that is not necessarily that of clock time. Dobell emphasizes the need for 'equal' time intervals, an ideal of isochronic regularity. His association of this with the 'healthy' heart, moreover, implies that the unhealthy heart might lead to imperfectly timed utterance.

Both Dallas and Brimley were influences on Coventry Patmore's *Essay on English Metrical Law*, one of the most significant discussions of rhythm in the period, and Patmore may also have known Dobell's lecture or at least his theories, given that the two poets met on at least one occasion.[56] Hopkins also knew Patmore's work well, offering detailed comments and criticism on the *Essay* when Patmore was revising it in the 1880s.[57] Taylor argues that this essay, first published in 1857, and Patmore's earlier reviews of *In Memoriam* and *Maud*, inaugurated the 'new prosody'; which involves an abstract concept of metre as 'mental beat' and a dialectical understanding of harmony

---

[55] Dobell, 24–5.

[56] Patmore describes an evening spent with Ruskin, Tennyson, Browning, and Dobell (at which Dobell clearly felt out of place) in Basil Champneys, *Memoirs and Correspondence of Coventry Patmore*, 2 vols. (London: George Bell, 1901), i. 130.

[57] See Hopkins to Patmore, 7 Nov. 1883, in *Further Letters of Gerard Manley Hopkins, Including his Correspondence with Coventry Patmore*, 2nd edn., ed. Claude Colleer Abbott (London: Oxford University Press, 1956), 326–33.

as the result of control interacting with liberty.[58] Patmore takes ideas tentatively formulated by earlier writers, and gives them their most forceful articulation. His essay supports an identification of rhythm with a physiological impulse:

> Art, indeed, must have a body as well as a soul; and the higher and purer the spiritual, the more powerful and unmistakable should be the corporeal element;—in other words, the more vigorous and various the life, the more stringent and elaborate must be the law by obedience to which life expresses itself.[59]

Patmore's 'in other words' does not help to clarify his intention here in terms of identifying the referents of 'law' and 'corporeal element'. His attitude is hard to identify because he seems on the one hand to advocate powerful physicality as an essential attribute of poetry while on the other suggesting that this vigour needs stringent control. Although it would seem natural (particularly in the light of earlier writings on metre) to identify form with the body, the corporeal element, Patmore appears to link metre instead to an implicitly spiritual law. This law controls the 'life' within the verse, which suggests the inference that its physical impulses are subdued by principles of order imposed by a higher power. Again, the identification of this principle of order with metre can be inferred from Patmore's immediately succeeding discussion, in which he states that metre should 'continually make its existence recognised', and that 'The language should always seem to *feel*, though not to *suffer from* the bonds of verse' (8). In a Wordsworthian sense, metre is the agent that balances and rules thought and feeling. Rather than being measurable, it does the measuring. But despite this association of metre with law Patmore also describes metrical expression as 'sensible' (a term still strongly associated in the mid-century with bodily sensibility) and consisting of 'an instinct, and not an artifice (9). This seems to imply that it is organic

---

[58] Taylor (1988), 18–48.
[59] *Coventry Patmore's 'Essay on English Metrical Law': A Critical Edition with a Commentary*, ed. Mary Augustine Roth (Washington: Catholic University of America Press, 1961), 7. All references are to this edition and will be given in the text.

rather than mechanical. Patmore then argues that metre has '*no material and external existence at all*' (15) by pointing to the human tendency to read rhythm into purely monotonous sounds, such as the ticking of a clock (16). Finally, he emphasizes that alterations in rhythm have an emotional effect: '*Such change is as real a mode of expressing emotions as words themselves are of expressing thought*' (48).

For both Dallas and Patmore, the subjectivity or otherwise of rhythm is a crucial issue. Do we impose rhythm upon our surroundings, or is it already inherent in them as a natural principle? Are thoughts, emotions, and physical motions shaped by rhythmic processes or do we simply perceive them to be so? In relation to the heart, which seems to have been the most cited example, a kind of test case, does it possess its own rhythm or do we read rhythm into its beats, in the same way as we do into the monotonous beat of a watch hand? Patmore's treatise to some extent supports a reading of rhythmic perception as subjective while maintaining that this tendency to perceive rhythm is both a natural instinct and imposed from without. The rules of prosody come to seem universally applicable because they relate to the general way in which 'life expresses itself' (7). This fits with a discourse of 'universal rhythm', that is, not only the idea, as expressed by Steele and later writers, that all humans have an innate sense of rhythm, but the concept that this natural rhythm relates to a wider force evident in all living things. 'If life is not always poetical, it is at least metrical,' Alice Meynell wrote in the 1890s, summing up this concept in terms of the laws of periodicity discovered by nineteenth-century scientists.[60] If poetic rhythm could be related to some collective metrical force, the same force that dictated the movements of particles and waves and the flow of sound, light, and electricity, then poems would be literally in tune with the universe, or even with God. As Dallas put it, 'Poets have come from God ... to attune the times to the time of their verse.'[61] Tennyson, as Chapter 5 explores in more detail, is one of many Victorian poets

---

[60] Alice Meynell, 'The Rhythm of Life', in *The Rhythm of Life and Other Essays* (London: Mathews and Lane, 1893), 1–6 (p. 1).

[61] Dallas, 172.

fascinated by such concepts. In 'Perdidi Diem', a fragment from one of his early, unpublished poems, the speaker describes the 'last beat of the thunder of God's heart' (81) thrilling through the universe in 'intense pulsation' (44); while at the climactic moment of the Cambridge prize poem 'Armageddon':

> There was a beating in the atmosphere,
> An indefinable pulsation
> Inaudible to outward sense, but felt
> Through the deep heart of every living thing,
> As if the great soul of the Universe
> Heaved with tumultuous throbbings (IV. 28–33)

Tennyson is creatively vague about the source of the heartbeat here, making it 'indefinable' and associating it with the Universe rather than directly with God. 'There was a beating in the atmosphere' has an iambic, measured beat, but 'indefinable pulsation', where the last syllable of 'indefinable' is a weak stress, and the line is truncated, suggestively embodies a degree of uncertainty about the source (and perhaps the reliability) of this pulsation. While these lines are reminiscent of Wordsworth's apprehension of 'something far more deeply interfused', the 'motion and the spirit' Wordsworth identifies in 'Tintern Abbey' acts on all '*thinking* things': rather than being 'felt' in the body it is apprehended in thought and imagination ('Tintern Abbey', 97, 101–2). 'Armageddon' replaces this intellectual apprehension with a confused physical recognition.

Such ambiguous imagery again united physiology and poetry, as scientists and doctors as well as poets considered whether the heartbeat was related to this general principle of natural rhythm. In the Croonian Lecture at the Royal Society in 1857, James Paget argued:

> [T]he peculiarity we have to study is not one of force ... but one of *time* as an element in the organic processes. No explanation of the rhythmic action of the heart, therefore, would be sufficient, which did not involve or appear consistent with some general law to which we may refer all other rhythmic

organic processes, that is, all such as are accomplished with
time-regulated alternations, whether of motion or any other
change.[62]

He spoke again in 1859 on his theory that 'each species has a
certain time-rate for the processes of its life', examples of a law of
'chronometry'.[63] Paget seeks to link the heartbeat to all organic life,
envisioning it as part of a natural law. In this he is perhaps influenced
by scientific developments in other fields, such as physics, in which
inorganic processes—the movements of particles and waves—had
been described in terms of repetitive movements. By adding time, he
stresses that organic processes mimic this except that they are moving
towards an end-point, their death. Applying this theory to poetry, if
the heartbeat is related to a general law of nature and is also the motor
for poetic rhythm, then rhythm itself is part of this general law.

Scientists writing in the 1860s and 1870s commonly used the pulse
as an analogy for the connections between various kinds of rhythmic
motion. In his essay on 'The Constitution of Nature' (1865), John
Tyndall discusses the 'rhythmic play of nature', the constant variation
in attraction and repulsion, and concludes: 'Thus beats the heart
of the universe, but without increase or diminution of its total
stock of force.'[64] The 'heart of the universe' is a vague rhetorical
phrase (reminiscent of similar lines in Tennyson), but Tyndall's
reference does allow the reader anxious about the implications of his
materialist theory to associate this unlocated heart with traditional
representations of the heart of God. He may be borrowing here
from the work of Herbert Spencer, who wrote in a footnote to *First
Principles* two years earlier, 'After having for some years supposed
myself alone in the belief that all motion is rhythmical, I discovered

---

[62] James Paget, 'On the Cause of the Rhythmic Motion of the Heart', *Proceedings of
the Royal Society of London*, 8 (1856–7), 473–88 (pp. 480–1).

[63] Id., 'On the Chronometry of Life', *Proceedings of the Royal Institution*, 3 (1858–62),
117–24 (p. 124).

[64] John Tyndall, 'The Constitution of Nature' (1865), reprinted in *Fragments of
Science*, 5th edn. (London: Longmans, Green, 1865), 20. Cosslett has pointed out the
possible influence of this essay on Tennyson.

that my friend Professor Tyndall also held this doctrine.'[65] Spencer, however, expanded his 'doctrine' beyond physical science to argue that the movements of thoughts and feelings were also rhythmical. He also suggested that rhythmical motion could be 'sympathetically' conveyed between objects:

> Little as we habitually observe it, it is yet certain that the impulses our actions impress from moment to moment on surrounding objects, are propagated through them in vibrations. It needs but to look through a telescope of high power, to be convinced that each pulsation of the heart gives a jar to the whole room. If we pass to motions of another order—those namely which take place in the etherial medium—we still find the same thing.[66]

Spencer moves from discussing 'impulses' to a literal 'pulse', thus implying the association between the two. Our body imposes on its surroundings through its unwilled motions, transmitting affect to both inanimate and animate objects. Spencer's oddly disembodied and magnified heartbeat has a sinister correlation in the threatening pulse of Edgar Allan Poe's 'The Tell-Tale Heart', which appears to the obsessed narrator to shake the room and drown out all other perceptions.[67]

Spencer's argument that impulses, in this case stemming from the human ('our actions'), can be transferred to other objects was attested to by other scientists working on sound and light waves. Charles Wheatstone, for instance, who acquired fame as the developer of the electric telegraph, demonstrated in the *Quarterly Journal of Science* in 1828 that vibrating bodies could put in motion 'all bodies whose pulses are coincident with their own'.[68] Again, while 'pulse' here is not used with reference to the heart itself but simply in the sense

---

[65] Herbert Spencer, *First Principles* (London: Williams and Norgate, 1863), 315–35 (p. 316). [66] Ibid. 315.

[67] 'The Tell-Tale Heart', from *Tales* (1843–4), Mabbott, ii. 789–98.

[68] Charles Wheatstone, 'On the Resonances and Reciprocated Vibrations of Columns of Air', *The Scientific Papers of Charles Wheatstone* (London: Taylor and Francis, 1879), 36–46 (p. 36).

of a regular beat, the connotations that it carries implicitly suggest a human dimension to these inorganic vibrations. The atmosphere, as scientific research advanced, came to seem increasingly filled with such pulsations, and an imperceptible but nonetheless apparent rhythm, it seemed, kept the body in time with them. Nineteenth-century poetry was not the first to discuss and incorporate these ideas of an innate sense of rhythm in tune with universal process, but it was the first poetry written in a period when science had quantified them and given them a firm basis in the physical world.

In the 1850 'Prelude', Wordsworth associated his perception of a 'vital pulse' with the connection to Nature he felt as a destined poet:

> That bursting forth
> Of sympathy inspiring and inspired,
> When everywhere a vital pulse was felt,
> And all the several frames of things, like stars,
> Through every magnitude distinguishable,
> Shone mutually indebted.[69]

The passive tense ('was felt') can suggest that it is not just Wordsworth himself who experiences this. It is more than a subjective perception. 'A vital pulse' is ambiguous; as in Tennyson's early verse, it is not clearly located in either God or Nature. Wordsworth altered this line from the 1805 version, 'The pulse of being everywhere was felt', a line which suggests more strongly that the pulse might stem from a singular entity. This passage is celebratory, congratulatory, as the sense of all things working harmoniously together confirms Wordsworth's status as a poet, his possession of insight and a sense of sympathetic connection. But by the time these lines were published in mid-century, Victorian poets were considerably less convinced about the mutual sympathy or shared pulse between poet and universe. Also in 1850, for instance, Charles Mackay, a scientific writer and minor poet later associated with the spasmodic school, described

---

[69] William Wordsworth, *The Prelude 1799, 1805, 1850*, ed. Jonathan Wu, M. H. Abrams, and Stephen Gill (New York: Norton, 1979), VIII. 479–84 (1850).

a vision of harmonious nature as presented to his morbid young hero, Julian:

> 'Oh misery!—Oh utter misery!'
> Said Julian, shuddering through all his frame.
> 'Are great Orion and the Pleiades,
> Arcturus, and the heavenly galaxy—
> Is all this boundless universe of stars,
> This dread infinitude of worlds and suns,
> One great pulsation of incessant pain?'[70]

Mackay, in this volume, avowedly seeks to unite science and poetry, and his descriptions of natural motion and rhythm deploy the new scientific imagery: the northern lights are 'electric threads of throbbing light', for example.[71] Unlike Wordsworth's inclusive vision, it is made clear that this is Julian's individual outlook. Inasmuch as he perceives 'sympathy' here, it is pathological and threatening. His shudders might indicate the affective relation his body has to this painful pulsation.

Mackay's *Egeria, or The Spirit of Nature* was published by the same firm who took on Alexander Smith's *A Life-Drama and Other Poems* three years later, the volume which chiefly contributed to the perception that a new poetic school was emerging. Julian, in Mackay's lengthy title-poem, fulfils all the characteristics of a 'spasmodic' hero. He is interested in artistic pursuits but deeply anxious about his inability to fulfil them, he is characteristically gloomy about the state of society, he feels intensely and acutely, but has no outlet for these feelings, and he is concerned about his lack of connection to the natural and human world, yet senses that sympathy will only bring suffering. This is the new breed of anguished, impotent poet-hero of the 1850s, represented by Smith's Walter in 'A Life-Drama', Sydney Dobell's eponymous Balder, J. Stanyan Bigg's Alexis in 'Night and the Soul' (1854), and in poems by Arnold, Clough, and Tennyson.

---

[70] Charles Mackay, 'Egeria', in *Egeria, or The Spirit of Nature* (London: David Bogue, 1850), 18.
[71] Ibid. 48.

In relation to form, affect, and the heart, these spasmodic heroes are significant because the problems of sympathy they experience, in terms of either feeling too much or failing to feel anything, are imaged through the heart and pulses and perceived in relation to wider natural and religious rhythms.

'Spasmodism' was known for introducing 'bursts of hectic excitement' and moments of intense feeling into poetry and was characterized by an uneasy mixture of different styles and forms within long poems, creating awkward hybrids.[72] Patrick Alexander, the editor of Smith's last works, commented:

> What, as exactly defined, really *is* 'Spasmodic Poetry'?—the Poetry of unrest and despair; of irregular struggle; of baffled effort, wild, bewildered and mistaken ... not cool in the intellect ... but raging, like mutiny of passion in the blood, with the whole perverted might of the heart and the moral emotions.[73]

'Irregular' and 'perverted' combined with the idea of the impassioned heart and blood committing mutiny suggest sexual and political depravity. The perverted heart indicates a turn towards dangerous passion and sensuality, besides suggesting that the roots of spasmodic poetry lie not in the mind but in the body, the heart and blood. In 'irregular' and 'unrest' Alexander's analysis also points towards the characteristic formal irregularities of these poems, in which rhythmic unevenness becomes a virtue and the looseness of a poem's structure might signify an adherence to poetry as organic and unpredictable. Yet although those spasmodic poets who theorized their practice suggested that form, and especially rhythm, served to represent spasms, this actually occurs relatively seldom in these poems. In the most straightforward sense, this is because the leading spasmodic

---

[72] Robert Buchanan, 'Sydney Dobell and the "Spasmodic School": A Souvenir', in *A Look around Literature* (London: Ward & Downey, 1887), 185–203 (p. 186). Buchanan is actually referring to Dobell's own behaviour here, but in terms which overtly link him to the themes and actions of *Balder*.

[73] Alexander Smith, *Last Leaves: Sketches and Criticisms*, ed. Patrick Alexander (Edinburgh: Nimmo, 1868), p. lxvi.

poets lacked the skill to play with form and rhythm in the way that other writers could. But it does also reflect how the radical statements of the poems ultimately turn to relatively conservative ends. If spasmodic poems are less unsettling and less novel than they proclaim (and than their poets may have hoped) it is partly because they are seldom truly innovative in form. Through their outspoken depiction of shocks, throbs, palpitations, and spasms taking place both within and without the body, however, and in their association of these motions with the practice of poetry itself, spasmodic writers set an agenda for other poets in this decade and beyond and advanced the increasing interest in poetry and prosody as organic, affective powers.

The term 'spasmodic' is itself drawn from medical discourse, meaning a sudden jerk or involuntary muscular motion. As I have explored in detail elsewhere, its pathological associations were strongly in play in these poems.[74] Spasmodic diseases were perceived as sympathetic in origin, and although they were often linked to nervous complaints, at least one medical writer at the time suggested that spasms ultimately originated in the circulatory system and were thus traceable to the disturbed heart or, as Alexander puts it, the 'raging' blood.[75] Both poetic heroes and spasmodic poets themselves were described in terms of heartsickness. As Dobell's biographer reports: 'The rheumatic fever was supposed to have left some weakness of action, or other affection, of the heart, which accounted for strange attacks of sudden illness to which he was from this time subject.' In 1848, for example, 'days spent in business, in study, or in composition' allegedly caused him to suffer a 'seizure' from 'spasmodic action of the heart'.[76] The fact that this spasmodic attack was immediately linked to the heart shows again the assumption that it is the source of poetic sufferings

---

[74] Kirstie Blair, 'Spasmodic Affections: Poetry, Pathology and the Spasmodic Hero', *Victorian Poetry*, 42 (2004), 473–90.

[75] See James Wilson, *On Spasm and Other Disorders, Termed Nervous, of the Muscular System* (London: John W. Parker, 1843), 37–8.

[76] Emily Jolly (ed.), *Life and Letters of Sydney Dobell*, 2 vols. (London: Smith, Elder, 1878), i. 96.

in action and indicates how the problems of poetic characters could be read into their creators. Dobell's tortured poet-hero Balder relates his sense of heartsickness and alienation to his inability to become a chosen poet, a Wordsworthian child of Nature. Once his heart 'Beat in the very breast and vital seat | Of all things' but now, exiled from this integration, it 'Resents the unblest deformity, and hath | No function of a heart'.[77] This seems to imply that when Balder's heart is reduced to the level of the individual human body it is deformed and malfunctioning. While imagery of the heart is used repeatedly throughout 'Balder', the hero seems to resent its actions and feelings. Balder tries to deny his heart in this poem, to sacrifice humanity in order to become a great poet, but his efforts are unsuccessful. When he attempts to write poetry, his body defeats him in a moment of spasm:

> That the head should write,
> And with a gush of living blood the heart
> Should blot it! (25)

The heart veers out of control—perhaps due to the act of writing itself—and impinges on the body of the poem, leaving its bloody traces in the work. Jason Rudy has noted that moments of spasm in *Balder* and other spasmodic poems are effectively feared as much as sought, as Balder laments 'the dangers of sensory overload, the intense impress of sensation on his physical and psychological being'.[78] The irony is that the physicality and surrender to sensation for which spasmodic verse was celebrated and critiqued is often represented in the poems themselves as dangerously pathological.

Spasmodic poems set such depictions of individual pathology in the context of a natural world filled with pulsations, echoing disturbances within the human body. They are notable for a deep insecurity about the relation between the body and the world.

---

[77] Sydney Dobell, *Balder* (London: Smith, Elder, 1854), 233. All further references are given in the text.

[78] Jason Rudy, 'Rhythmic Intimacy, Spasmodic Epistemology', *Victorian Poetry*, 42 (2004), 451–72 (p. 460).

Speakers within spasmodic poems frequently describe Nature and
God in terms of universal palpitation, motions and pulses which rule
all living things, but there is always, as in the extract from *Balder*
above, a concurrent emphasis on the disturbed beat of the human
heart, profoundly alienated from such cosmic rhythms. In J. Stanyan
Bigg's 'Night and the Soul' (1854), for instance, the hero, Alexis, tells
his companion that their 'very heart's pulsations' are 'out of tune'
with the night because 'they have something human in them'.[79] The
implicit disgust at humanity here indicates Alexis's Faustian desire
to become godlike, communing with Nature as an equal. Addressing
Nature, Balder comments: 'That ye have a heart | I know; but can it
beat for such as I?' (4), again suggesting the hero's separation from
the desired unity. As above, Balder repeatedly debates whether his
heart is in tune with nature (and God) or not:

> Whether my will
> Hath power on nature, or this heart of mine
> Is so compacted in the frame and work
> Of all things that in various kind they keep
> Attuned performance, I know not. (64)

Balder contrasts heart and will: the latter attempts to seek dominance
and assert itself over nature while the former inevitably defeats this
end by its own involvement in greater processes. In this passage, he
notes that he cannot even tell what his heart is doing.

Moments where a spasmodic hero can feel that 'The life of all
things beat and throbb'd in me' are rare and frantically sought.[80]
Dobell, Bigg, and Smith, however, also represent cosmic pulsation
as disturbed and spasmodic in its actions, thus perhaps suggesting
that these fragile, unpredictable human hearts are less isolated than
they might seem. In 'Night and the Soul' Earth possesses 'throbbing
veins, and surcharged heart', while in 'A Life-Drama' Smith's hero,
Walter, declares,

---

[79] J. Stanyan Bigg, *Night and the Soul* (London: Groombridge, 1854), 2.
[80] Ibid. 146.

Half-blind, I looked up to the host of palpitating stars,
'Gainst my sides my heart was leaping, like a lion 'gainst his
bars.[81]

'My heart was leaping' is a typical spasmodic formulation. Nodding
towards Wordsworth's 'My heart leaps up' from 'Intimations of
Immortality', it uses a common figure of speech suggesting a moment
of joyous excitement and takes it to implausible and potentially
ridiculous extremes. Philip Bailey's Festus similarly declares on an
emotional parting from his dying lover that his heart was 'like
a live engine booming up and down'.[82] These are attempts to
describe a physical sensation, the heart actually moving within the
breast, but while such similes emphasize the heart's aggressiveness
and the difficulty of containing it, they also blur the physicality of
this imagery into the metaphorical. Cosmic pulsation in Walter's
comment causes or responds to vehement physical reactions. In
Balder the hero similarly perceives the sun as a 'pulsing wave of
hyaline' (28) (an image which combines light waves and pulses),
the stars moving in 'systole and diastole' (223), and imagines 'the
beating heart o' the world | In palpitation mad and moribund' (40).
'Palpitation mad and moribund' is a nice example of how the metre
in spasmodic poems might contrast with the sense in a way that
effectively contradicts it. There is nothing 'mad' about this iambic
beat, unless its steadiness is itself suspicious.

If, as these comments suggest, the natural world is pathological,
does this indicate that it is in fact in harmony with the beat of the
disturbed individual heart, or does it simply show that these speakers
have a distorted view of nature? The would-be literary hero of Bigg's
later novel *Alfred Staunton* is told by a critic that he sees natural
objects 'distorted, as they would appear to one already labouring
under some strong excitement'.[83] If this pathetic fallacy is true of

---

[81] Ibid. 130. Alexander Smith, 'A Life-Drama', in *Poems* (London: David Bogue,
1853), 31.
[82] Philip Bailey, *Festus*, 3rd edn. (London: William Pickering, 1848), 6.
[83] Bigg, *Alfred Staunton* (London: Blackwood, 1861), 222.

Bigg and Dobell's spasmodic heroes, it might seem that spasmodism is less a characteristic of an intrinsically pathological world than a disorder evident in the speaker's heart and body. In other words, Balder, Alexis, and Walter are not reading their pulse in relation to universal pulsation, but projecting a vision of universal pulsation based on their individual pathology onto the external world. Again, this is a question of whether rhythmic experience is subjective or stems from some external force, and these poems also cannot provide a definitive answer.

If rhythmic turbulence is relatively rare in spasmodic poems, they nonetheless attempt both to describe and to represent the uncontrollable, unpredictable, and inexplicable nature of spasms through the very awkwardness of their verse, its startling metaphors, irregular punctuation (particularly the repeated use of exclamation marks), and constant shifts in form. Alexander commented on Smith's poetry that: 'If a Poem be boldly Spasmodic in its main motives, it will scarcely be much worth as a Poem if it does not, in the technic of detail, afford some significant reflex of *spasm*.'[84] 'Reflex' suggests involuntary muscular action. This belief that spasm should be revealed in the technical aspects of the poem was echoed by critical commentary, as in Gerald Massey's remark that Byron's punctuation 'was composed of the marks made by spasm', as though it was dashed onto the page, like Balder's poetry in the image of his heart seizing control.[85] Spasmodic poetry in itself did not appreciably advance theories of prosody, but by celebrating or at least drawing attention to the spasms and irregularities of verse, in terms both of subject matter and of form, it opened the way for a general theory of the place of 'spasmodism' in poetics. While Tennyson and the Brownings were themselves major influences on these young writers of the 1850s, the marked difference between the steady beat of *In Memoriam* and the shocks and starts of *Maud*, or the interest

---

[84] Smith (1868), p. lxix.
[85] Gerald Massey, 'Poetry: The Spasmodists', *North British Review*, 28 (1858), 231–50 (p. 240).

in pulsation in *Aurora Leigh*, may be in part attributable to the intervention of a culture of spasmodic poetics.

'In these funeral marches which our hearts are beating', wrote Oliver Wendell Holmes, poet and physician, in the late nineteenth century, 'we may often keep step to the cardiac systole more nearly than our poet suspected.'[86] It seems likely that this is an allusion to one of the most popular poems of the period, Henry Wadsworth Longfellow's 'The Psalm of Life':

> Art is long, and Time is fleeting,
>> And our hearts, though stout and brave,
> Still, like muffled drums, are beating
>> Funeral marches to the grave.[87]

Longfellow's lines use the four-beat rhythm associated most strongly with the heartbeat, but they are trochaic rather than iambic. This, and the feminine endings of lines 2 and 4, gives the lines a sense of declension, trailing off. The stress on 'brave' and 'grave' rings hollow because the reader allows a pause for the missing final beat, an uncertain silence. Ruskin, who particularly admired this stanza, described 'The Psalm of Life' as the modern poem which 'has had most practical influence on men's minds' and as 'a kind of trumpet note to the present generation'.[88] If this specific stanza is read as having a positive effect, however, it can only be in raising awareness of mortality in order to spur men to action, reminding them that the bravest heartbeat is still wearing down towards death. Poe, who used this verse as the headnote for 'The Tell-Tale Heart', a tale of murder, insanity, and a horrifying pulse that continues beyond the grave, showed his consciousness of the macabre elements of Longfellow's lines, and the way in which his moral 'carpe diem' message could be

---

[86] Oliver Wendell Holmes, 'The Physiology of Versification', in *The Writings of Oliver Wendell Holmes*, 13 vols. (London: Sampson Low, 1891), viii. 315–21 (p. 320).

[87] *Poetical Works of Henry Wadsworth Longfellow* (London: Oxford University Press, 1973 (first published 1904)), 3.

[88] Letter to father, 7 Dec. 1851, Cook and Wedderburn, xxxvi. 122–3.

perverted. In these lines, as in many other poems of the period, the heartbeat is inexorable. The pulse is not simply a positive assertion of life's continuity but rather a negative reminder of the frail hold of the body on life, and the speaker's lack of control over the heart's beat. Even Latham, debatably the best-known medical expert on the heart in this period, admits the impossibility of regulating or understanding it: 'What can be said of palpitations of the heart, and intermissions, and irregularities of its beats, which come and go during a man's whole existence ... They must come from something, but we know not what.'[89] The heart and the pulses, as we have seen, participate in processes outside as well as inside the body, but the origin of these processes is itself unfathomable. Poetic rhythm is endlessly renewable, preserving the pulse and recreating it in each act of reading, but the individual human heartbeat is not sustainable, threatening to break down or wear out.

Alba Warren, considering the significance of poetic theorists in the early nineteenth century, argues that, 'Of the relation of verse to meaning ... only hints are to be found here and there in Early Victorian criticism.'[90] Yet with regard to the question of poetic affect and the heart, theory, by the mid-nineteenth century, was catching up with poetry. As in the poetry itself, it appropriated elements from medical and scientific theories of bodily motion in order to formulate the relation between verse and meaning in physical, embodied terms. The contrast between, as the quasi-spasmodic poet Henry Ellison put it, 'A Heart, that watchlike, beats | Sixty Pulsations in a Moment's Space' and 'A Pulse harmonious in Nature's vast | And allembracing Bosom', feeds into debates over rhythm as well as questions of authority and affect in the body of poet and reader.[91] The difficulty of reconciling these mechanical and organic visions of the heart is

---

[89] *The Collected Works of P. M. Latham*, ed. Robert Martin, 2 vols. (London: New Sydenham Society, 1878), 519.

[90] Alba H. Warren, *English Poetic Theory, 1825–1865* (Princeton: Princeton University Press, 1950), 32.

[91] Henry Ellison, 'On the True Sources of Being', *Madmoments, or First Verseattempts of a Bornnatural* [*sic*], 2 vols. (London: Painter, 1839), ii. 28, 29.

evident in a wide variety of mid-century poems. Spasmodic poets sum up the mingled excitement and anxiety with which both poets and theorists—as well as medical and scientific writers—considered these questions. The chief subjects of the next chapters, Barrett Browning, Arnold, and Tennyson, extend the ideas raised by these writers, and in their repeated use of heart and pulse imagery and its embodiment in rhythm further the sense that the heart was becoming the most vital cliché of nineteenth-century poetics.

3

'Ill-lodged in a woman's breast': Elizabeth Barrett Browning and the Woman's Heart

The heart in the nineteenth century was often troped as feminine simply because of its associations with intense personal emotion and feeling rather than will or reason. Coleridge nicely demonstrates some of the complications of this in his short comic poem 'The Exchange':

> We pledg'd our hearts, my Love and I,—
> > Me in her arms the Maiden clasping;
> I could not guess the reason why,
> > But, oh! I trembled like an aspen!
>
> Her father's love she bade me gain,
> > I went, but shook like any reed!
> I strove to act the man—in vain!
> > We had exchang'd our hearts indeed.[1]

'The Exchange' was written for a journal in 1804, and republished at least four times in the 1820s in annuals. Coleridge would have known that his readership would be familiar with the kind of sentimental poetry often published in such collections, and its tendency to feature fainting, trembling heroines overcome with emotion. His own use of extravagant exclamation marks and a melodramatic 'oh!', plus the

---

[1] 'The Exchange of Hearts' (1804), *Poetical Works II: Poems (Variorum Text)*, part 2, ed. J. C. C. Mays (Princeton: Princeton University Press, 2001). *Collected Works*, vol. xvi.

deliberately bathetic rhyme on 'clasping/aspen', hint at parody. 'Me in her arms' implies that the woman is the instigator here and that the man may be reluctant to submit: Coleridge changed this line to 'I in my arms' in later versions, creating a more subtle interplay of 'masculine' and 'feminine' actions and feelings.[2] The male lover, unmanned by love, blames his condition on the female heart acting within his body. Despite his willed effort ('I strove') and without his mind's consent ('I could not guess the reason why'), the heart reveals his emotion through its own physical display.

Coleridge's poem is light and playful, but elsewhere the idea that properties of the 'woman's heart' could be transferred into a male body (or vice versa) created difficulties if also opportunities for both male and female poets. The heart's cultural status as the source of poetry meant that 'writing from the heart' was a trope continually deployed by male poets, and this in turn could serve to complicate imagery of the heart by introducing more masculine heart-behaviour. Poetic accounts of the heart's actions in a male speaker suffering from desire, like Byron's Don Juan or Tennyson's speaker in 'Eleanore', for instance, meant that its relation to sexuality was strengthened. By exploring, first, the reasons why male poets might have sought to appropriate the heart for their writing and the questions which surrounded this; and secondly, how Barrett Browning and her predecessors used the heart in the discourses of love, desire, politics, and poetics, this chapter shows how the gendered heart became a site of contest in relation to physical as well as emotional desires and forms of behaviour. To study what Barrett Browning in particular asked of the heart in her writing, and how she worked with and around it, is to see that, as Adela Pinch has argued in relation to eighteenth-century literature, 'the gendering of feelings may make feelings harder to place, rather than giving them a clearer meaning'.[3] The position of the feeling heart in literature, and the

---

[2] See Mays, 785.

[3] Adela Pinch, *Strange Fits of Passion: Epistemologies of Emotion, Hume to Austen* (Stanford, Calif.: Stanford University Press, 1996), 71.

question of poetic affect itself, becomes more, not less, contentious because of its traditional associations with femininity.

The cultural assumption that women are associated with the body and men with the mind is long-standing, and as numerous critics have established it was especially evident in the nineteenth century, as medical and scientific discourses constructed a 'natural' view of women which rested on their perceived closeness to emotion and the physical responses of the body.[4] In relation to heart disease, it is therefore not surprising that women were believed to be more liable to contract both organic and sympathetic or functional diseases, due to the perception that they were less able to control dangerous emotions and because of the circulatory system's apparent involvement in the menstrual cycle. Heart and womb were seen as inextricably linked (recalling an older discourse of the heart *as* a womb) by nineteenth-century medical writers, with the assumption that any failing in the one would result in disease in the other. W. O. Markham argues, for instance, that in young men, palpitation and other symptoms are the result of indulgence in 'vice' and 'over-exertion in study', while in women they are usually due to 'derangements of the uterine system', hence biological rather than cultural.[5] Hysteria, that crucial female sickness of the period, was perceived by several experts as a heart-related disease besides being coupled with the womb.[6] John Williams and other doctors discussed how 'irregular action of the

---

[4] See for example Susan Bordo, *Unbearable Weight: Feminism, Western Culture and the Body* (Berkeley and Los Angeles: University of California Press, 1993) and, on the 19th century, Cynthia Eagle Russett, *Sexual Science: The Victorian Construction of Womanhood* (Cambridge, Mass.: Harvard University Press, 1989).

[5] W. O. Markham, *Diseases of the Heart: Their Pathology, Diagnosis and Treatment*, 2nd edn. (London: John Churchill, 1860), 220–1. On 'uterine palpitation' see also Thomas J. Graham, *On the Diseases of Females: A Treatise ... Containing also an Account of the Symptoms and Treatments of Diseases of the Heart*, 7th edn. (London: Simpkin, Marshall, 1861), appendix, 26.

[6] James Wardrop, *On the Nature and Treatment of Diseases of the Heart*, 2nd edn., revised (Edinburgh: Thomas Constable, 1859), 200. John Williams, *Practical Observations on Nervous and Sympathetic Palpitation of the Heart*, 2nd edn. (London: John Churchill, 1852), 112–18. Other writers argued that hysteria caused heart disease, rather than vice versa, for example C. M. Durrant, 'Functional Affections of the Heart', *British Medical Journal* (1859), 3–4.

heart' was especially frequent in female puberty, at the onset of the menses.[7] Problems with the menstrual cycle were presumed to be the cause of diverse heart-related symptoms, including the ubiquitous 'determination of blood'. In her excellent article on 'female circulation', Sally Shuttleworth notes that 'If the menstrual flow were obstructed . . . it would, doctors warned, be forced to flood the brain and thus lead to irreparable psychological breakdown.'[8] The phenomenon of the 'flooding woman' (a phrase again suggesting a lack of control) is commonly discussed in medical texts. Rather than stemming from too much thought, too much mental action, as in the 'determination of blood' associated with literary young men, this 'determination' is caused by the uncontrollable forces of the body.

The pathological woman's heart had wider consequences than the suffering of the individual patient, as discussions of hereditary heart disease and its apparent spread in nineteenth-century culture demonstrate. Corvisart, one of the most influential European writers on the heart, stated that 'the intimate and immediate influence of the imagination of the mother on the foetus' was demonstrably the greatest cause of organic heart disease.[9] When a woman became pregnant, according to another writer: 'If any external agitation or passion make the heart beat unduly fast, or intermit, or for a brief period stop, the change of vibration passes to the child, which, unconscious though it be, is mechanically affected.'[10] This suggests the need for pregnant women to regulate their feelings and carefully

---

[7] John Williams, 112–18.

[8] Sally Shuttleworth, 'Female Circulation: Medical Discourse and Popular Advertising in the Mid-Victorian Era', in Mary Jacobus, Evelyn Fox Keller, and Sally Shuttleworth (eds.), *Body/Politics: Women and the Discourses of Science* (London: Routledge, 1990), 47–68 (p. 48). I disagree with Shuttleworth's argument that 'unlike women, men were not prey to the forces of the body' (p. 55). The male circulation was also liable to disorder, although often for different reasons. On the 'flooding woman', see also George Warren, *A Commentary, with Practical Observations, on Disorders of the Head* (London: Longman et al., 1829), 8–12.

[9] J. N. Corvisart, *A Treatise on the Diseases and Organic Lesions of the Heart and Great Vessels*, trans. C. H. Hebb (London: Underwood and Blacks, 1813), 316.

[10] Benjamin Richardson, *Diseases of Modern Life* (London: Macmillan, 1876), 36.

monitor their pulse, lest they produce a new generation of sufferers from heart disease. Tennyson seems to echo such popular medical theory in a passage from 'The Lover's Tale', in which the hero muses about the formation of his beloved's character in the womb. He describes how her mother carried:

> Camilla close beneath her beating heart,
> Which to the imprison'd spirit of the child,
> With its true-touchèd pulses in the flow
> And hourly visitation of the blood,
> Sent notes of preparation manifold,
> And mellowed echoes of the outer world— (I. 197–202)

This speaks directly to medical textbooks of the day. Heart and womb are perceived as close together, almost touching. The circulation, 'hourly visitation of the blood', gently inducts the child into the outer world. 'True-touchèd' perhaps indicates that the mother's heart responds 'truly', healthily, to external stimuli—her blood is pure and her heart untroubled. The passage also suggests that Camilla's emotional sensitivity, her closeness to love and to the body throughout the poem, was formed by the transmission of affect from her mother's heart.

Whereas heart disease seems to have been an occupational hazard and a badge of poetic identity for a Victorian male poet, a woman poet could be sick at heart either due to her writing or simply due to her femininity. This dual possibility that women would suffer from a deranged heart and circulation meant that intellectual work, and writing poetry in particular, was thought to be still more risky for them than for male writers. As we have already seen, Barrett Browning's doctor assured her that writing poetry was 'even' dangerous for men—pointing how much more dangerous it was for women—and Christina Rossetti was believed to be suffering from angina or a heart-related illness for many years, even though her primary illness had little to do with the heart.[11] Comments

---

[11] See above, pp. 29–30.

on women who allegedly contracted heart problems due to their writing career were often more judgemental than those on men. Letitia Landon, famous as the sentimental poetess L.E.L., apparently suffered from 'spasmodic affections' (a disease related to palpitation) due to her enthusiasm for writing poetry: 'She wrote with wonderful facility, but the mental excitement was unceasing, and much of her now constant ill-health was ascribed to that incessant wear and tear of every faculty.'[12] Her contemporary Felicia Hemans was reportedly a full-blown sufferer from heart disease. Citing a letter from her from Ireland, her biographer writes:

> 'I think that on the whole the soft climate agrees with me; my greatest foe is "the over-beating of the heart"' ... Of this beating of the heart Mrs Hemans had had very serious admonitions from her medical attendant, who told her that 'nothing but great care and perfect quiet would prevent its assuming a dangerous character'.[13]

Hemans also wrote that writing could be 'positively painful' and that she believed this to be caused 'entirely by irregular action of the heart, which affects my head with oppressive fulness': determination again.[14] As another biographer continues: 'sometimes the irregular pulsation of the heart, and the flush of blood to the head, from which she suffered, disabled her for many weeks together from using a pen.'[15] Both she and her nineteenth-century biographers were apparently keen to stress that her illness was potentially caused and enhanced by writing and involved symptoms of both palpitation and determination. This highlights Hemans's status as a poet of the

---

[12] Grace and Philip Wharton, *The Queens of Society* (London: James Hogg, 1861), 205.

[13] Letter from Felicia Hemans, 1831, cited in Sarah Elwood, *Memoirs of the Literary Ladies of England*, 2 vols. (London: Henry Colburn, 1843), ii. 251.

[14] Letter cited by Harriet Hughes in 'Memoir of Mrs Hemans', *The Works of Mrs Hemans, with a Memoir of her Life, by her Sister*, 7 vols. (Edinburgh: William Blackwood, 1839), i. 259. All further references to Hemans are to this edition and will be given in the text.

[15] Jane Williams, *The Literary Women of England* (London: Saunders, Otley, 1861), 463.

emotions, sensitive and feminine, but is also threatening to her poetic career: the 'perfect quiet' she is prescribed suggests that her female body cannot withstand the dangerous passions raised by writing. After her death, she was portrayed as a female singer whose heart was too weak to withstand the acute sensations it had been subjected to. As the epigraph to one of her poems reads, in a phrase she said 'could be her epitaph', 'Fermossi al fin il cor che balzò tanto.'[16]

When Matthew Arnold writes, in 'A Farewell',

> I too have felt the load I bore
> In a too strong emotion's sway;
> I too have wished, no woman more,
> This starting, feverish heart away. (29–32)

he emphasizes, in 'no woman more', the association between excessive emotion, the palpitating, irregular heart, and femininity. His apparent self-contempt and embarrassment at his heart's behaviour echoes Charles Kingsley's comments on Shelley's 'utterly womanish' poetics in the same year. These 'Words thrown off in the heat of passion; shameful self-revelings which [Shelley] has written with his very heart's blood' are not a sign of sincerity, rather they are unmanly and disturbingly sensual.[17] Writing from the heart is to be avoided, Kingsley suggests, as it encourages effeminacy and hence leads readers to mistake 'chronic disease for a new kind of health'.[18] While the speaker of 'A Farewell' appears to agree, note that he also stresses his connection to the feminine heart even as 'wishing' (a rather feeble word) it away. There is more pride in this stanza than is apparent, because Arnold's weakness, like that of other poets, can also be read as proof positive of his poetic destiny and hence as a mark of distinction. He makes a typical move here in that he

---

[16] Epigraph to 'Arabella Stuart', by the Italian poet Pindemonte (1753–1828). Cited in M. A. Stodart, *Female Writers: Thoughts on their Proper Sphere, and on their Powers of Usefulness* (London: Seeley and Burnside, 1842), 92.

[17] Charles Kingsley, 'Thoughts on Shelley and Byron', in *Literary and General Lectures and Essays* (London: Macmillan, 1890), 35–58 (pp. 47, 52).

[18] Ibid. 53.

deliberately appropriates a discourse of the sick heart which might seem to brand him as 'womanish', and turns it to advantage in emphasizing his poetic nature. As the literary critic George Gilfillan wrote, reviewing Barrett Browning's 1844 volume:

> We stay not to prove that the *sex* of genius is *feminine*, and that those poets who are most profoundly impressing our young British minds, are those who, in tenderness and sensibility—in peculiar power, and in peculiar weakness, are all but females.[19]

'Peculiar', an adjective often used of women's writing at this time, suggests something simultaneously highly individualized and not quite appropriate. Since Barrett Browning *is* female, she is removed from the group of poets who are 'profoundly impressing' the youth of England—indeed, women poets are neatly excluded by men wielding female powers. 'Sex' here seems less to do with the actual composition of the body, and more to do with the abstract qualities assigned to male or female. This enables genius to be viewed as something disembodied that can possess or inhabit the male poet and make him, not into a woman, but into a man with strongly feminine aspects. Femininity is then something which male poets might actively wish to possess.[20] Diane Hoelever and Anne Mellor claim that the process of appropriating feminine qualities for poetic ends began with late Romanticism, notably Keats, Shelley, and Byron, who incorporated 'the essence or idea of the feminine' into their work and implicitly into their bodies.[21]

---

[19] George Gilfillan, *Galleries of Literary Portraits*, 2 vols. (Edinburgh: James Hogg, 1856), i. 191.

[20] Claudia Nelson argues that a distrust of 'feminine' men did not begin until the 1850s and after, in 'Sex and the Single Boy: Ideals of Manliness and Sexuality in Victorian Literature for Boys', *Victorian Studies*, 32 (1989), 525–50. See also Karen Lystra, *Searching the Heart: Women, Men and Romantic Love in Nineteenth-Century America* (Oxford: Oxford University Press, 1989). Lystra argues that the central cultural position of romantic love meant that men developed a range of expression 'just as emotional and intense' as women in this period (p. 20).

[21] Diane Hoelever, *Romantic Androgyny: The Women Within* (University Park: Pennsylvania State University Press, 1990), 15. Anne K. Mellor, *Romanticism and Gender* (London: Routledge, 1993).

Continuing this line of thought, Joseph Bristow and others have persuasively argued that male Victorian poets deliberately sought to use the feminine to create a more affective model of poetry.[22] Bristow locates this shift in the gendered qualities of poetry at mid-century, which suggests that the argument over poetry and manliness, fostered in work such as Kingsley's essay on Shelley and Byron, was a direct response to contemporary poetic trends and heroes.

What these male poets incorporated into their poetry and their self-descriptions was something that could readily be described as the 'woman's heart'. J. C. Shairp comments, on John Keble's poetry:

> True, the woman's heart everywhere shows itself. But as it has been said that in the countenance of most men of genius there is something of a womanly expression not seen in the faces of other men, so it is distinctive of true poetic temper that it ever carries the woman's heart within the man's.[23]

Shairp is on the defensive here, alert to possible accusations of weakness and excess emotionalism. The suggestion that the poet has a woman's heart within his own neatly contains it, subsuming it as lesser to the male heart (Barrett Browning's Aurora Leigh strongly rejects as degrading Romney Leigh's proposal, 'Place your fecund heart in mine' (II. 375)). Possessing a woman's heart allows male poets to write affectingly without losing the mind and will of a man. It thus permits a certain liaison with femininity without hampering the poet's masculinity in all other areas of life. Owning a heart imaginatively gendered feminine, however, might also increase a sense of alienation or even of heartsickness. Arthur Hugh Clough,

[22] Joseph Bristow, 'Coventry Patmore and the Womanly Mission of the Mid-Victorian Poet', in Andrew Miller and James Eli Adams (eds.), *Sexualities in Victorian Britain* (Bloomington: Indiana University Press, 1996), 118–40. See also Carol T. Christ, 'The Feminine Subject in Victorian Poetry', *ELH* 54 (1987), 385–403.

[23] J. C. Shairp, *John Keble: An Essay on the Author of the 'Christian Year'* (Edinburgh: Edmonston & Douglas, 1866), 96.

for instance, refers to his 'weak heart' as 'she' and 'my sweet one', in poems which measure his distance from its (or her) concerns.[24]

These shifts in the conception of the heart meant that while the 'woman's heart' remained a commonplace, it became more difficult to assess the differences between masculine and feminine heart-behaviour, and, in terms of poetry, to separate the domain of male poetry from female, personal, heart-centred verse. 'Oh! man has power | Of head and hand,—heart is a woman's dower', wrote L.E.L. in the 1820s, her throwaway line voicing a standard assumption of the time.[25] By the end of the 1840s, however, this neatly divisive platitude was becoming increasingly dubious. When Tennyson writes in *The Princess*:

> Man with the head and woman with the heart:
> Man to command and woman to obey;
> All else confusion, (V. 439–41)

he recognizes these sentiments as outdated clichés by putting them in the mouth of the King, the patriarchal holder of traditional family values whose advice is blatantly ignored by his son and heir. Representative of a younger generation, the Prince realizes that in order to win Ida he must simultaneously persuade her to abandon her overly masculine stance and assume a feminized position himself. The androgynous ideal he holds out is of:

> The single pure and perfect animal,
> The two-celled heart beating, with one full stroke,
> Life. (VII. 288–90)

Man and woman here act and work together in an image situating them as co-sharers in the heart. The feminine heart is one of the gendered concepts which *The Princess* unsettles. 'And all thy heart lies

[24] 'So I, as boyish years went by, went wrong' (published 1865), 3–5, and 'Fearless over the levels away' (unpublished), 5. *The Poems of Arthur Hugh Clough*, ed. F. L. Mulhauser, 2nd edn. (Oxford: Clarendon Press, 1974).

[25] Letitia Landon (L.E.L.), 'The Rose', from *The Golden Violet*, in *The Poetical Works of L.E.L.*, ed. William B. Scott (London: Routledge, 1873), 173.

open unto me' (VII. 168), for instance, which borrows a common trope of early nineteenth-century women's poetry, is set in a lyric probably written by a male poet but read by Ida with the Prince as her auditor. For Tennyson, such ambiguities are productive, although his attitude towards those of his speakers (including his own persona in *In Memoriam*) who appear to have an overly sensitive, feeling heart is not wholly commendatory.

For women writers, these confusions over whether and how the heart was gendered created a specific set of problems. The increasing use of the heart as a synecdoche for the desiring body, a way of expressing the physical effects of sexual desire in a poem without (in theory) overstepping the boundaries of morality, is a case in point. The perceived closeness of women to the body and the perception that women wrote primarily of their own feelings meant that women poets had to write with the consciousness that such descriptions of the heart in physical terms—throbbing, pulsating, spasming—might be read onto their own physiology, much more so than was the case for male poets. Emotional 'self-revealings' and accounts of felt desire, even when attached to a fictional character, risked incurring charges of indecency. L.E.L.'s career provided several instances. Her heroines frequently describe their sensations of love with 'exhibitionist fluency',[26] as in 'The Improvisatrice':

> My pulses throbbed, my heart beat high,
> A flush of dizzy ecstasy
>   Crimson'd my cheek; I felt warm tears
> Dimming my sight, yet was it sweet,
> My wild heart's most bewildering beat,[27]

These lines are breathless, hurried on by the reversed feet of 'Crimson'd' and 'dimming', and they describe how the speaker's body is put on display, external signals (tears, blushing) mirroring inner 'ecstasy'. L.E.L. spent much of her career dogged by scandal (though

---

[26] Angela Leighton, 'Introduction' to L.E.L.'s poems, in Leighton and Margaret Reynolds (eds.), *Victorian Women Poets: An Anthology* (Oxford: Blackwell, 1995), 41.
[27] Landon, 11.

recent evidence suggests that at least some of the rumours were justified), and the extreme emotions of her heroines carried over into perceptions of her own actions, and vice versa.[28] Victorian women writers clearly did not have licence to write freely of physical pleasures and desires. But the problem was that they *were* expected to write 'from the heart', and that heart-centred imagery was becoming associated with passionate and pathological desires and emotions. As the critic Mary Ann Stodart argued in 1842, the ideal subject matter for the woman poet was 'the workings of the stronger passions of the human heart' precisely because 'the peculiarities of her own heart' were the source of her poetic knowledge.[29] The consequences of this kind of affective poetics, however, might be fatal to the reputation and the health of the female poet, not to mention her heroines.

For women writers, writing from the heart was also challenging because it involved negotiating between the private sphere of the emotions and the public sphere of literary publishing. As we have already seen, the heart was frequently represented as the most private, inward, and exclusive part of the individual. Exposing it to others, in the manner of Kingsley's Shelley, can be shameful. When the quiet, religious sister in Coventry Patmore's *The Angel in the House* shows the hero her poems, he writes, 'She, offering up for sacrifice | Her heart's reserve, brought out to show | Some verses', an image indicating the pain her modesty suffers from 'publishing' her work, even in the exclusivity of the family circle.[30] Dobell, in an 1858 letter to his sister, describes women's authorship as:

> A temptation which bids fair to stain with ink the sweetest sanctuaries of life, and taint with the inevitable evils of every unnatural and abnormal gratification three-fourths of the 'women of England' ... there are nobler vocations in this

[28] See Cynthia Lawford's argument that L.E.L. had several illegitimate children by her editor William Jerdan. 'Diary', *London Review of Books*, 21 Sept. 2000, 36–7.

[29] Stodart, 88, 83.

[30] Coventry Patmore, *The Angel in the House: The Betrothal* (London: John W. Parker, 1854), 36.

world than writing books, and a truer womanhood than that which wears its heart on its sleeve.[31]

The idea of 'staining' hints at some unease about the possibilities that fluids (blood, perhaps) will escape the woman's pen and actually defile or 'taint' all that they touch. The heart—in a familiar saying made suddenly admonitory—is escaping the body and being vulgarly exhibited. 'Temptation' and 'unnatural gratification', moreover, might hint at pleasures from writing that are equivalent to sexual temptations.

If the woman writer was engaged in 'printing the secrets of her inmost heart ... for the benefit of all who can pay for them',[32] this suggests a prostitution of the emotions, and given that the heart is so often represented as embodied, it gestures towards prostitution of the body as well. Nineteenth-century writers often discussed the implicit link between woman writer and prostitute in terms of selling or displaying the heart, precisely because it both courted and averted associations with selling the body.[33] L.E.L., Hemans, and other female contributors to the popular annuals, journals, and keepsake books of the 1820s and 1830s were aware that they were marketing ideals of love and romance and that poems focusing on extreme emotional suffering and heartfelt revelations would be popular with their target audience, primarily middle-class female readers (though romantic young men, like the young Edward Bulwer-Lytton, also apparently indulged in reading this genre of women's verse). Yet this high valuation of the emotional and personal in women's poetry created a fraught issue. Those poets who did genuinely seem to be writing from the heart could be accused of exchanging their moral

---

[31] Cited in Emily Jolly (ed.), *Life and Letters of Sydney Dobell*, 2 vols. (London: Smith, Elder, 1878), ii. 120.

[32] Geraldine Jewsbury, *The Half-Sisters*, ed. Joanne Wilkes (Oxford: Oxford University Press, 1994), 214.

[33] On the imaginative association of the woman writer with the prostitute see Angela Leighton, ' "Because Man Made the Laws": The Fallen Woman and the Woman Poet', *Victorian Poetry*, 27 (1989), 109–29 and Catherine Gallagher, '*Daniel Deronda*: The Prostitute and the Jewish Question', in H. Aram Veeser (ed.), *The New Historicism Reader* (London: Routledge, 1994), 124–40.

worth, which rested on the privacy of feelings, for hard cash; while those whose feelings were not perceived as 'real' were engaged in a kind of emotional labour, exploiting the heart in order to earn a poetic living.

This sense of the exploitation of the heart and its status as a commodity was enhanced by its use as a marketing tool, a recurrent image in popular art and artefacts. The resurgent poetic interest in the heart coincided with the golden age of Valentines, for instance, widely available and immensely popular in the decades between 1820 and 1870.[34] Dickens's Sam Weller purchases a Valentine depicting two flaming hearts to send to his beloved, while one of Aurora Leigh's female fans sends her a heart-shaped note.[35] The familiar heart-shape actually appeared on relatively few Valentine's cards, but was common in the form of lockets, pendants, and other trinkets. One miniature gift-book largely authored by L.E.L., the *English Bijou Almanac*, even came in a gilded heart-shaped case.[36] Adelaide Procter, the most popular woman poet of the mid-century, wrote several poems which turn on the difference (or lack of difference) between the heart as commodity and the feeling lover's heart. In 'A Love Token', she adjures a male lover to 'Take a Heart of virgin silver, | Fashion it with heavy blows', carve letters of love on it and set it with gems, then offer it to his lady:

> Should her mood perhaps be gracious—
> With disdainful smiling pride,
> She will place it with the trinkets
> Glittering at her side.[37]

[34] See Ruth Webb Lee, *A History of Valentines* (London: Batsford, 1953).

[35] Charles Dickens, *Pickwick Papers*, ed. Mark Wormald (Harmondsworth: Penguin, 1999), 431. See J. Hillis Miller, 'Sam Weller's Valentine: Dickens', in *Topographies* (Stanford, Calif.: Stanford University Press, 1995), 105–33. *Aurora Leigh*, III. 213–14.

[36] Cynthia Lawford, 'Bijoux beyond Possession: The Prima Donnas of L.E.L.'s Album Poems', in Isobel Armstrong and Virginia Blain (eds.), *Women's Poetry, Late Romantic to Late Victorian: Gender and Genre 1830–1900* (Houndmills: Macmillan, 1999), 102–14 (p. 104).

[37] Adelaide Procter, *Legends and Lyrics, together with A Chaplet of Verses*, introd. Charles Dickens (London: Oxford University Press, 1914), 100.

Procter's haughty *femme fatale* turns the tables by making the male lover's heart into a commodity. More commonly, it is women who are associated with the trope of the heart as merchandise. In 1867 Dante Gabriel Rossetti painted a young woman coyly displaying the jewelled heart on her necklace to the observer. His title, 'Joli Cœur', is ambiguous, as it may either refer to the jewel or to the girl herself: she might either be proudly displaying the gift of a lover's heart (as in 'A Love-Token'), or a woman wearing her own heart on her sleeve. If the latter, the jewelled heart is potentially a metaphor for the woman's body and sexuality as commodity.

Anxiety about this commodification, fears of the expression of sexuality by women, and concerns about women writers in the marketplace combine to ensure that mentions of the heart in women's poetry of this period and in criticism of that poetry are frequently charged, oscillating between the innocuous and the indecent. From one perspective, the heart is an utterly conventional image for women poets to use, occurring with monotonous frequency. In this sense it might operate as a disabling cliché, hindering women's poetry, particularly in the sentimental tradition, from being taken seriously.[38] In her influential and important study *Victorian Women Poets: Writing against the Heart*, Angela Leighton has argued persuasively that women poets sought to overcome the Victorian dissociation of poetry from worldly affairs—money, sex, power—by writing 'not from, but against the heart', that is, they attempted to move beyond the personal and emotional and to reject standard assumptions about the content and beliefs of women's poetry.[39] Inasmuch as the heart stands for a set of ideas summed up in its association with romantic love, this is undoubtedly true, and provides a helpful way of considering how women poets had to negotiate with the discourse of the heart in order to shape a new poetic. But as a key word and

---

[38] On the restrictive and damaging potential of clichéd descriptions of women in this period, see Helena Michie, *The Flesh Made Word: Female Figures and Women's Bodies* (Oxford: Oxford University Press, 1987), 88–102.

[39] Angela Leighton, *Victorian Women Poets: Writing against the Heart* (Hemel Hempstead: Harvester Wheatsheaf, 1992), 3.

image in Victorian women's poetry, the heart also exposes on a small scale what Isobel Armstrong has identified as the 'doubleness' of this poetry, in which 'its ostensible adoption of an affective mode, often simple, often pious, often conventional' is combined with a strategy of questioning, investigating, and reworking these conventions.[40] Heart imagery which seems clichéd, this suggests, could actually be more disturbing than expected, especially when set in the wider context of the culture of the heart in this period.

Armstrong writes, paraphrasing the standard nineteenth-century attitude held by Barrett Browning's Romney Leigh, that:

> The woman poet has only this individualized feeling, feeling as an end in itself . . . only pity as a substitute for analysis, only the rhetoric of the heart instead of the ethical and social understanding which engenders structural change in society.[41]

She then argues convincingly, however, that 'feeling' does not stand apart from 'ethical and social understanding', but can be part of a politics of affect. I want to suggest that this wider argument about the political implications of affective poetry works specifically with regard to the heart, that heart imagery might serve in some ways as a model for how affect becomes politicized. The rhetoric of the heart, as Barrett Browning repeatedly demonstrates, is difficult to separate from wider discourses of nationalism, politics, the gendered body in society, and the role of poetry. The remainder of this chapter will show how she used the heart to think through the difficulties of being a woman poet famed for her romantic life as well as for her daring poetry, focusing particularly on her extended meditation on the possibilities of combining love and writing in *Aurora Leigh*. Barrett Browning, among others, exploits the emergence of a new culture of the heart in mid-Victorian Britain in order to expand the scope of cardiac metaphor and question whether the heart fits into a

---

[40] Isobel Armstrong, *Victorian Poetry: Poetry, Poetics and Politics* (London: Routledge, 1993), 324.

[41] Id., 'Misrepresentation: Codes of Affect and Politics in Nineteenth-Century Women's Poetry', in Armstrong and Blain, 3–32 (p. 7).

model of female poetics. *Aurora Leigh* and its use of the heart should be read in relation to the poems of the 1850s discussed elsewhere in this book, but it does engage more intensely with questions of the gendered heart than any comparable poem of the period. Aurora struggles to reconcile the poet's and woman's heart, and to deal with the physical and sexual connotations of writing from that (or these) hearts at a moment when there was much at stake, personally and in terms of poetics, for all Victorian poets in the concept of 'writing from the heart'.

'A poet's heart', asserts Aurora Leigh, 'Can swell to a pair of nationalities | However ill-lodged in a woman's breast' (VI. 50–2). The poet's heart has special qualities, sympathetically expanding to incorporate national feeling in the widest sense. Aurora boldly suggests that poets might possess a dual allegiance, competing loyalties reconciled in the heart. But if the poet's heart can include both English and Italian aspects, can it also 'swell' to include aspects of both sexes? That 'ill-lodged' makes Aurora's tone hard to identify—is she defiant, bitter, or simply accepting? Barrett Browning's heroine repeatedly refers to the woman's heart, and her own heart in particular, dismissively. The difficulty lies in identifying to what degree such references are ironic, or whether Barrett Browning writes Aurora as a woman aware of or even believing in the accepted limitations of the woman's heart; limitations not just culturally but biologically prescribed. The poet's heart, this quotation implies, is not organically part of Aurora's female body but placed there almost accidentally, even, 'lodged' might suggest, temporarily. It could thus be gendered male, in a reversal of the trope of the female heart within the male poet. Like many other anxious poetic speakers of the period, she will not say '*my* poet's heart' or 'my heart' here, speaking of herself and her poetic career in the third person.

In Barrett Browning's letters and poems, as seen in previous chapters, there is always something oddly literal about her descriptions of the heart, a conscious blend of the actual, physical organ with the metaphorical and spiritual. While this holds true for her imagery in general, in that her metaphors tend to draw on the body and the physical world, it is particularly notable with regard to the heart because it shows how she draws upon and rewrites standard poetic tropes. Although she writes much more daringly than many of her contemporaries (both male and female) about the embodied heart in the writing and reading of poetry, this means that she tends to ignore the effects of physical, heart-based desire on the individual. The heart suffers in her work because of its involvement in poetry—its throbs or spasms are rarely personal in the sense of being caused by love or desire. Her poems also stop short of formally representing the heart's shocks and palpitations. Aurora, for example, boldly describes the world as a female body and poetry in terms of the heart's blood, yet neither here nor in the rest of Barrett Browning's poems is there anything like the detailed physiological description of internal or external effects (blushing, palpitating) experienced by the heroine that was endemic in other Victorian poems of the period. Aurora refuses, or perhaps cannot afford, to accept these models.

Barrett Browning's interpretation of the trope of writing from the heart is to represent the choice of a poetic career as an extreme physical surrender of body and blood. In one of her last poems, 'My Heart and I', she writes:

> You see we're tired, my heart and I.
> We dealt with books, we trusted men,
> And in our own blood drenched the pen, (8–10)

The separation of 'heart' from 'I' here is an example of simultaneous distance from the heart and sympathetic alliance with it, a stance common throughout Barrett Browning's work. The full stop at the end of the first line gives it an air of finality. Dealing with books and with men—writing and love, presumably—is equally disillusioning. Later in this poem, it becomes clear that it is a dramatic monologue about lost love, but these lines, which apparently represent the speaker as an ageing female poet, suggest a possible identification with Barrett Browning herself. 'Drenched' is typically hyperbolic: how could a pen 'drenched' in liquid still write? Does this suggest that the speaker's emotions, like Balder's gush of blood on the page, were too excessive for the writing of poetry? Moreover, the image of a sudden rush of blood is uncomfortable because it recalls medical descriptions of the 'flooding woman'; this blood might be linked to the womb, to menstrual blood, as well as to the heart.

'My Heart and I' apparently accepts the standard association of women's poetry with sexualized suffering, common in the works of Hemans and L.E.L. It stands out from Barrett Browning's earlier poems on poetic self-sacrifice, however, because prior to *Sonnets of the Portuguese* and *Aurora Leigh*, all her poet-figures are male. The self-sacrificing female artistic figures which preoccupied her predecessors, in such poems as Hemans's 'Properzia Rossi' or L.E.L.'s 'The Improvisatrice', are conspicuous by their absence. Most notably, in Barrett Browning's ambitious statement on the role of poetry, 'A Vision of Poets' (1844), the narrator has a vision of a young male poet who learns through a mystical quest that his poetic vocation will involve giving up his heart to God. He is taken by a Sibyl-like guide to a mysterious church which itself seems almost like an organic body, as its aisles 'shoot and interlace', mist rises from it 'throbbingly', and its arches 'bend and slacken' (220–650). It is filled with statues of famous poets:

> All, still as stone and yet intense;
> As if by spirit's vehemence
> That stone were carved and not by sense.

> But where the heart of each should beat,
> There seemed a wound instead of it,
> From whence the blood dripped to their feet (424–9)

Barrett Browning writes in iambic tetrameter (the metre believed to approximate most closely to the pulse) throughout the poem. Statues are an image frequently used in women's poetry, as the poet-heroine becomes frozen into a work of art: Hemans's eponymous Properzia Rossi, for example, creates a statue to tell her lover of her affection after her death, infusing its 'veins' with her heart and soul.[42] Barrett Browning conflates this image with its reverse—the passionate, bleeding body. These statues seem held in suspended motion, 'intense' rather than cold and unmoving. An angelic figure tells the poet that their missing hearts form the pedals of a great organ which plays celestial harmonies. But whenever this organ falls silent the sound of dripping blood breaks the stillness, a passive and almost horrifying bodily action: 'the blood which fell | Again, alone grew audible, | Tolling the silence as a bell' (508–10). The angel describes the sacrificed hearts as 'consummating while they consume' (579). This is, crucially, self-consumption, an apotheosis of painful pleasure. These hearts have been absolutely surrendered to the service of God's poetic work.

At this point in the poem a group of worldly poets, imitating and perverting the dignity of the dead poets, arrive offering 'hand and lip service':

> 'Thou, certes, when thou askest more,
> O sapient angel, leanest o'er
> The window-sill of metaphor.
>
> To give our hearts up, fie! that rage
> Barbaric antedates the age;' (652–6)

These lines bring the difference between the literal and metaphorical heart into the poem and thereby make it clear that Barrett Browning's vision *does* demand a literal sacrifice. By saying, in another curiously physical metaphor (difficult to visualize without a trace of the comic), that the angel's demand 'leanest o'er | The window-sill of metaphor' (653–4), the speakers suggest that it leans towards the rhetorical, that the angel's injunction to sacrifice the heart is half-in, half-out of the figurative. But the poem argues that rhetorically and figuratively devoting the heart to poetry is not enough. It is the fulfilment of the heart in real blood and suffering that makes a poet. These worldly poets echo contemporary gloom about the 'unpoetic' character of 1830s and 1840s Britain when they suggest that their age is not

---

[42] 'Properzia Rossi', in *Works*, v. 162.

one in which this is possible, that it is a 'barbaric' custom. Yet the young and enthusiastic poet, when the others have been blasted out of sight, eagerly accepts his painful role:

> 'I only would have leave to loose
> (In tears and blood if so He choose)
> Mine inward music out to use;' (706–8)

Poetry is the 'inward' becoming outward. 'Loose' suggests a letting go, a pouring outward of the forces of the body. Perhaps ominously, it has to be read as 'lose' to rhyme neatly. 'I only would be spent—in pain | And loss, perchance' (709–10), the poet continues, introducing the idea of poetry as sexual release, 'spending' in poetry figured as a substitute for the other spending of the self in love:

> 'Only embrace and be embraced
> By fiery ends, whereby to waste,
> And light God's future with my past.' (715–17)

This embracing again hints at the physical and human only to burn it away. There is some ambiguity in 'waste': the poet is accepted, and dies in a blaze of sanctity, wasted away in the service of this religious poetic, but there may be a sense in which this is a waste of his passion and talent.

Tricia Lootens argues that the poetic company in 'A Vision of Poets' accept a 'potentially feminine' form of suffering, a judgement which she makes chiefly on the basis of their sacrifice of their hearts.[43] Rightly, however, she (like Barrett Browning), is cautious about the implications of classing this masochism as entirely 'feminine': in *Aurora Leigh*, Aurora hotly contests Romney's casual assertion that women's hearts relish personal suffering (II. 183–98). The poets in 'A Vision' and in 'A Musical Instrument', in which Pan extracts the 'pith, like the heart of a man' (21) from a reed to create a poet, are certainly subjected, in some sense physically, to the male will

---

[43] Tricia Lootens, *Lost Saints: Silence, Gender and Victorian Literary Canonization* (Charlottesville: University Press of Virginia, 1996), 124.

of God. Yet this might only be acceptable because the poets are not actually female. Barrett Browning's language, and indeed the concept of surrendering the heart itself, would immediately verge on the indecent if applied to a woman. Describing the sensations of male heroes allows her to be more extreme, and lets her emphasize that gender divisions are not, in her vision, summed up by statements like 'Men and women make | The world, as head and heart make human life' (II. 132–3), as Romney impatiently tells Aurora, because men in these poems are also subject to and engaged with their hearts.

Where the self-surrender practised by these male poets does come into play with regard to women is in Barrett Browning's representations of the heart in romantic love. Both she and Browning take stock romantic notions of possessing the lover's heart, or sacrificing the heart to a lover, and twist them into a commentary on the fine line between submission and authority and on the ways in which a conventional romantic image can become disconcerting when taken more literally. *Sonnets from the Portuguese*, written in the 1840s during their courtship, is concerned with the physiology of the woman poet and lover and filled with imagery of female bodily weakness. The speaker repeatedly laments the difference between her heart and that of her lover:

> Thou canst prevail against my fears and fling
> Thy purple round me, till my heart shall grow
> Too close against thine heart, henceforth to know
> How it shook when alone. (XVI. 3–6)

Here, as elsewhere in the *Sonnets*, love stabilizes the heart. The speaker represents her heart as weak and failing and the male lover's heart as secure and confident. The shakiness in the rhythm of the first part of line 6 'How it shook when alone', which seems to shift from an iambic to an anapaestic beat, makes this instability register affectively. These stereotypical qualities of the male and female body are to some extent exploited by the female speaker, who demands a closeness that can momentarily seem too much—'My heart shall grow | Too close'—until the next phrase concludes the sentence.

The lovers' bodies are confidently imagined blending together. One of the more overtly self-abasing sonnets, 'Go from me' (VI), contains a similar ambiguity at the octet, where the speaker tells her lover:

> The widest land
> Doom takes to part us, leaves thy heart in mine
> With pulses that beat double (VI. 8–10)

Earlier images have the speaker standing in her lover's shadow, but here his heart is potentially incorporated into her body (in a reverse echo of Romney's 'Lay thy fecund heart in mine'), and she is implicitly in control. This is the moment when the sonnet, in its stance of self-surrender, twists upon itself. Which lover is possessed, and which possessing?

Heart imagery in Robert Browning's poetry of the 1840s and 1850s is similarly charged with possessiveness, a form of surrender which implies dangerous excess. 'Two in the Campagna', discussed in Chapter 2, is an exception in these poems because it is the male speaker who desires to regulate his heart by his lover's. Elsewhere, female speakers follow the trope of yielding the heart to a lover proclaimed by Barrett Browning in the *Sonnets*, but do it with such knowing abandon that it starts to seem suspect. The speaker in 'In a Gondola' puts words in her lover's mouth, telling him to state:

> 'This woman's heart and soul and brain
> Are mine as much as this gold chain
> She bids me wear.' (12–14)

'Heart and soul' are a romantic cliché, but the odd addition of 'brain' introduces a jarring note, and might make us perceive the throwaway 'heart and soul' as more serious, and more physical, than the phrase might seem. This ventriloquism is uncomfortable. Is she asking, masochistically, to be owned, or pointing the fact that such ownership might be a typical male pose? In addition, 'she bids me wear' simultaneously indicates that the power might belong to the woman and hints at the commodification of her heart and soul, as in Procter's poems. Constance, in Browning's other dialogue poem, 'In a Balcony', similarly declares to Norbert when he appears to question her commitment to him:

> I am not his—who change into himself
> Have passed into his heart and beat its beats
> Who gave my hands to him, my eyes, my hair. (20–2)

It is interesting that she uses 'his' rather than 'yours' despite the fact that she is addressing her lover directly, creating a sense that this is a deliberately performative statement. Again, the strange combination of hands, eyes, and hair makes a stock romantic phrase ('gave my hand' would have 'hand in marriage' associations) disturbingly literal, takes it to logical and possibly ridiculous extremes. Constance jokingly emphasizes the surrender of her visible body even while suggesting her own possession, in both senses, of his heart. She could be lost in him, but she could equally be taking him over.

Finally, the speaker of 'Any Wife to Any Husband', whose voice hovers between assurance and paranoia in this meditation on how her loving husband will behave after her death, informs him:

> I have but to be by thee, and thy hand
> Will never let mine go, nor heart withstand
>   The beating of my heart to reach its place. (7–9)

If the personal pronouns were switched here ('You have but to be by me, and my hand') this could be a moving romantic statement of devotion, resembling some made by Barrett Browning in her sonnets. As it is, it is unclear whether the speaker welcomes her husband's attachment, boasts of it, or scorns it. 'Withstand' is important because it implies the possibility of resistance, and hence suggests that the speaker's heart is stronger and more determined than her husband's. As in each of these female speakers, the unity of two hearts in love starts to slide into the inevitable domination of one by another: and it is the woman's heart, here, which does the dominating. The interchangeability of the lovers' bodies in these poems blurs gendered differences even while the speakers ostensibly uphold them.

The Brownings' poems about love manage to question the clichés surrounding the heart, particularly in terms of gender, as well as using them sincerely. Similarly, Barrett Browning's political poems, notably *Casa Guidi Windows*, play on the discourse of the political heart (thinking about such commonplaces as the heart of the nation, hearts of oak, hearts beating as one) and interlace personal and political events. They demonstrate that she sees the heart in terms of nationalism and politics as well as romantic love and poetics. In *Casa Guidi Windows* Barrett Browning exploits the idea that her poem is subjective and heartfelt, yet she also intends it as a powerful intervention in Italian affairs through the affect which the poem might have upon its readers' hearts. *Casa Guidi Windows* uses the heart as an image for the kind of sympathy the reader and poet should have for the cause of Italian liberation, and also attempts to stir up the hearts of the Italian people in order to foster revolution:

> [T]he heart of man beat higher
> That day in Florence, flooding all her streets
> And piazzas with a tumult and desire.
> The people, with accumulated heats,
> And faces turned one way, as if one fire
> Both drew and flushed them, left their ancient beats,
> And went up toward the palace-Pitti wall,[44]

In the first lines of this passage the increased heartbeat initially seems to fill Florence with blood, as though the city streets are a circulatory network. The 'flood' then becomes a rush of active people, like molecules of blood, perhaps, whose 'accumulated heats' cheat the reader of the word 'hearts' while invoking it. Substituting 'hearts' might suggest too much individuality for this passage, where 'the heart of man' gives the people only one, united heart. 'Left their ancient beats' has a dual meaning: physical movement through the streets, away from usual haunts, is synonymous with a change in the periodical movements within the body. Barrett Browning hopes that

---

[44] Part I (1848), 451–7. *Casa Guidi Windows*, ed. Julia Markus (New York: Browning Institute, 1977). Further references are given in the text.

this impassioned moment, which makes her own heart 'beat with
exulting love' (445), is 'The first pulse of an even flow of blood' (468)
which will permanently alter the people's heart, leaving their weaker
'beats' behind. Reynolds notes that the heart is a constant image in
Casa Guidi Windows, which 'is a poem which aims, not to "lull the
throbs of pain" but to amplify them, and it does that by making
the pulse of the verse beat loudly'.[45] But just as the body cannot
sustain an over-strong pulse, the Italian nation cannot maintain it.
The failure of the nation's heart to subside from feverish excitement
to 'even flow' means that in Part II of Barrett Browning's poem
the heart is subdued or exhausted, its 'full beat' 'dropped before the
measure was complete' (II. 6).

In terms of women's poetry about political events, Barrett Browning's evident influence here is Hemans, whose highly influential
nationalistic poems also used the rhetoric of heart for affective ends.
When Hamet, the hero of Hemans's 'The Abencerrage', addresses
his troops, 'Still while he speaks, each gallant heart beats high, |
And ardour flashes from each kindling eye' (ii. 33). The love of men
(and women, in several of these poems) for their country makes war
into a strangely passionate enterprise, and the field of combat, as in
Barrett Browning, produces symptoms of desire:

> There swell those sounds that bid the life-blood start
> Swift to the mantling cheek, and beating heart.
> The clang of echoing steel, the charger's neigh,
> The measured tread of hosts in war's array. ('The Abencerrage', ii. 19)

The odd word here is 'cheek', a word more generally used in descriptions of women, which brings these physiological effects to the
surface and suddenly highlights the physical bodies of these soldiers.
Even a blush, here, can be a masculine call to arms. Hemans's poems
map the excited physiology of the body onto the external world,
sounds 'swell' as the heart distends with feeling, the wild 'tide' of
battle echoes the rushing of blood in the body, and the 'measured

---

[45] Matthew Reynolds, 95. On the heart in *Casa Guidi Windows*, see also pp. 89–103.

tread' of the hosts contrasts with the rapid pulse. She portrays men at war as well as women in love in terms of rushing blood, pulsation, and flows: her language both feminizes these soldiers, to a certain extent, and masculinizes the sensible heart. The difference between this and the imagery of *Casa Guidi Windows*, however, is that Hemans focuses on the individual body and its personal responses but never on her own body, whereas Barrett Browning both leaves the actual body implicit while using physicalized language and imagery and constantly hints at the involvement of her body, the body of a woman poet, in the events she describes. Marlon Ross argues that in Hemans's poetry 'What women must learn is that heart-knowledge cannot protect them from the demands of public life … What men must learn is that heart-knowledge is the basis for all their public actions.'[46] This blurring of the male/female divide, with regard to the heart, simultaneously criticizes and endorses the standard view of 'heart-knowledge' as an intimate, emotional, female response. Ross's comment applies equally well to Barrett Browning, perhaps particularly to *Aurora Leigh*, because Romney is forcibly made to recognize the problems that stemmed from his purely intellectual attitude towards his social goals. Aurora, on the other hand, does not need to learn the lessons of Hemans's heroines, because as a poet her heart is already engaged in 'public life'.

The ambiguities and contradictions in Barrett Browning's treatment of the heart reach their apotheosis in *Aurora Leigh*, where she uses her fictional heroine to explore the issue of fusing the poet's and woman's heart—and, to a lesser extent, the English and Italian heart—in one. It is a difficult task, involving negotiating between confidence and impropriety for both Aurora and her creator. *Aurora Leigh* is the poem of Barrett Browning's most noted (by both her contemporaries and twentieth-century critics) for its use of bodily imagery. F. T. Palgrave recalled Tennyson saying that it and Dobell's

---

[46] Marlon B. Ross, *The Contours of Masculine Desire: Romanticism and the Rise of Woman's Poetry* (Oxford: Oxford University Press, 1989), 275.

'Balder' 'might be defined as "organizable lymph" '.[47] This might just be interpreted as a compliment, as it recognizes the flow of verse and associates it with the physical flow of bodily fluids, a characteristic connection in Barrett Browning's poetry. But it was most likely intended as an insult. 'Lymph' is not blood, it is a colourless fluid, and a 'lymphatic' person is likely to be, in Victorian terms, sickly and effeminate. Describing *Aurora Leigh* as bloodless suggests that it does not quite hit its mark, and is not perhaps as rich, as sustaining, as an equivalent man's poem. Not everyone would have agreed with Tennyson's casual assessment, however. James Russell Lowell, in an essay on Swinburne, argues that *Aurora Leigh* is the worst example of the 'physically intense' school of modern poetry of the late 1850s and 1860s.[48] In a more positive account of Barrett Browning's physicality, Gerald Massey writes, characterizing Barrett Browning but tacitly referring to Aurora:

> And so she goes at her work with brimmed eyes, and hungering lips, and beating heart. On, on she goes, with great bursts of feeling and gushes of thought ... Look not for the calm and finish of a Greek statue from such an attitude of mind, and such a woman's work. It is not a statue, for it is shaped out of human flesh and blood. You see the heart heave within a form vital from top to toe: there is fire in the eyes, breath between the lips, the red of life on the cheek; it is warm with passion, and welling with poetry, in the double-breasted bounteousness of a large nature and a liberal heart.[49]

Massey's 'bursts', 'gushes', and 'welling' imply a lack of control over this emotional outpouring. In the contrast between living being and Greek statue he might be borrowing Barrett Browning's own

[47] *Memoir*, ii. 506. For a recent commentary on *Aurora Leigh*'s physicality, see Herbert Tucker, 'Glandular Omnism and Beyond: The Victorian Spasmodic Epic', *Victorian Poetry*, 42 (2004), 429–50 (pp. 443–6).

[48] James Russell Lowell, 'Swinburne's Tragedies', in *My Study Windows* (London: Sampson Low, 1871), 157–68 (p. 158).

[49] [Gerald Massey], 'Last Poems and Other Works of Mrs Browning', *North British Review*, 36 (1862), 514–34 (p. 531).

terms from her essay on 'The Greek Christian Poets', where she criticizes Gregory Nazianzen for his formal correctness and lack of passion: 'What though the Italian poet be smooth as the Italian Canova—working like him out of stone—smooth and cold, disdaining to ruffle his dactyls with the beating of his pulses—what then?'[50] This expresses her rejection of cold formality (and of regular, non-organic metre) and, by implication, of the image of poet both as sculptor and as statue. Massey's 'double-breasted bounteousness' also picks up on Aurora's imagery of the natural world as mother's breasts and transfers it to the author. He thus appears to be reading the text not just as a body but as the body of the woman poet. This is complicated, however, by his use of exactly the same phrase in a poem on the royal wedding of 1865, which includes this tribute to the late Prince Albert:

> His was a heart that nobly beat to bless,
> And heaved with double-breasted bounteousness
> Like very woman's.[51]

The heart is presumably 'double-breasted' in its two chambers, which might also stand for the male and the female—Massey, an inveterate borrower from Tennyson, probably has the ending of *The Princess* in mind. While the cross-referencing between his two works would doubtless have been obscure to most readers, it is clear that he regards the possession of such a female, heaving, heart as a high grace, and in using the same phrase, intentionally or not, of Barrett Browning and Prince Albert, he hints at the political force of Barrett Browning's 'liberal' woman's heart and her work as well as its poetic virtues.

Tennyson's grouping of *Aurora Leigh* with 'Balder' reminds us that Barrett Browning's poem was published only two years after W. E. Aytoun's caricature *Firmilian* (1854) had discredited spasmodic poetry so thoroughly that it had become more an object of

---

[50] First published in *Athenaeum* (1842). Reprinted in *The Complete works of Elizabeth Barrett Browning*, ed. Charlotte Porter and Helen A. Clarke, 6 vols. (New York: AMS Press, 1973), vi. 168–239 (p. 175).

[51] Massey, 'A Daughter of the Sea-Kings', in *My Lyrical Life: Poems Old and New*, 2 vols. (London: Kegan Paul, Trench, 1889), i. 57.

critical derision than acclaim.[52] The Brownings have been cited as
forerunners of the poetic 'spasmodism' of the 1850s, and *Aurora
Leigh* was a serious candidate for the label at the time because,
like the poems discussed in the last chapter, it is a contemporary
blank-verse tale in which the hero strives to become a poet while
engaging, to a greater or lesser extent, with the social problems of the
time. As already noted, spasmodic poets are remarkable for their use
of physical imagery, and in their poems the anguished, throbbing
heart enjoys a revival; indeed, it becomes a prerequisite for the kind
of poetry these poets wish to produce. When Aurora sees her poetry
in terms of her heart and pulses she is thus writing herself into
a fashionable tradition—or perhaps even setting herself up as an
advocate of its renewal—rather than necessarily providing 'a radical
alteration of tradition'.[53]

Spasmodic poets gain their inspiration from a heartfelt connection
with the universe. As Bigg's Alexis declaims:

> The life of all that is, pulses and throbs
> Like subterranean music in their hearts
> And the great universe streams through their souls.[54]

Aurora Leigh incorporates similar imagery, as when Aurora exhorts
the poet to catch,

> Upon the burning lava of a song
> The full-veined, heaving, double-breasted Age:
> That, when the next shall come, the men of that
> May touch the impress with reverent hand, and say
> 'Behold,—behold the paps we all have sucked!

---

[52] See Mark A. Weinstein, *William Edmonstoune Aytoun and the Spasmodic Controversy*
(New Haven: Yale University Press, 1968).

[53] Joyce Zonana, 'The Embodied Muse: Elizabeth Barrett Browning's *Aurora Leigh*
and Feminist Poetics', reprinted in Angela Leighton (ed.), *Victorian Women Poets: A
Critical Reader* (Oxford: Blackwell, 1996), 53–74 (p. 64). On Barrett Browning and the
spasmodics, see Tucker (2004).

[54] J. Stanyan Bigg, *Night and the Soul: A Dramatic Poem* (London: Groombridge,
1854), 130.

> That bosom seems to beat still, or at least
> It sets ours beating. This is living art, (V. 215–20)

'Living art' takes its motion from the 'living heart' of the age. Aurora imagines a communal poetic heart set beating, as in Dallas's theories, in time with the time itself. Poetry creates pulsation, and texts, here as in other spasmodic poems, throb sympathetically with their readers. Aurora earlier feels a book 'beat' under her pillow (I. 841–2). Similarly, in Smith's 'A Life-Drama' Walter describes how he and a friend 'hung | O'er the fine pants and trembles of a line', while in J. Westland Marston's 'Gerald', a forerunner of 1850s spasmodism, the hero recalls how poetry made him 'quiver with an awful, vague delight, | And find my heart respond'.[55] The difference between this imagery and that used by Aurora, however, is that in the passage cited above the body is indisputably female. As such, her description is more shocking. It links blood and mother's milk, it permits the reader to visualize a heaving bosom, and in 'touch'—a word not quite negated by 'reverent'—and 'sucked' it places men (used as a generic term, but also taking on gendered connotations) in physical contact with these breasts, contact which might produce sexual as well as poetic excitement.

Throughout *Aurora Leigh*, Aurora struggles with the issue of how to exploit and incorporate her poet's heart and body when they are also female, and inevitably cannot be discussed or represented without implications of shameful exposure. Even when she initially seems unaware of this issue, her writing contains tensions which might stem from it:

> But the sun was high
> When first I felt my pulses set themselves
> For concord; when the rhythmic turbulence
> Of blood and brain swept outward upon words,
> As wind upon the alders, blanching them

[55] Alexander Smith, *Poems* (London: David Bogue, 1853), 52–3. J. Westland Marston, *Gerald: A Dramatic Poem, and Other Poems* (London: C. Mitchell, 1842), 11.

By turning up their under-natures till
They trembled in dilation. (I. 895–901)

The poet is passive, the pulses apparently acting without any agency
on her part, and in an almost mechanical way. 'Set themselves'
looks to Browning's 'set my heart' ('Two in the Campagna'), but
Aurora's pulses are set to the rhythm of poetry, not to her lover's
heart. 'Rhythmic turbulence' sums up the contrasting needs to
maintain a steady pulse and to let the heart flow freely. There is
little turbulence in the rhythm of this passage, though, as Aurora
preserves the evenness of metre even while describing its disruption.
Words, as in 'The Student', become possessed with the 'dilation' of
the heart when they are brought into sympathetic contact with it,
but again this dilation, the opening out of the heart, is described
rather than shown in any formal effects. The image of alder leaves,
which might contain an occluded association with book-leaves and
writing, sweeps the reader away from the body towards a mental
picture of 'outward' rather than internal effects. These words, rather
than the poet, reveal themselves and expose their hidden nature. In
the same passage, Aurora writes of the poet: 'The palpitating angel
in his flesh | Thrills inly with consenting fellowship' (I. 912–13).
To insert the word 'angel' into this description seems an attempt to
avoid or divert the close conjunction of 'flesh' with 'palpitating'. It
is a vain effort to retain the exciting physical and sensational effects
of poetry while denying that they have such effects on the body of
the writer. She again specifies that the poet is male, and after the
suggestiveness of 'thrills', quickly adds 'with consenting fellowship',
perhaps in case another and less fellow-feeling might cause such
thrilling.

Despite these instances of uncertainty in Aurora's poetics, in the
first books she still describes how she 'spends' her heart's blood on
poetry with reckless, 'unlicensed' exuberance: 'My heart beat in my
brain. Life's violent flood | Abolished bounds' (I. 961–2). 'Life's',
not 'my'—she is generalizing, averting a potentially dangerous
personal reading even while 'My heart beat in my brain' points

towards the pathological implications of determined blood and the idea of a 'violent flood' in relation to the female circulation. She removes the barrier of her gender by asserting her participation in a wider poetic community:

> And so, like most young poets, in a flush
> Of individual life I poured myself
> Along the veins of others. (I. 971–3)

The 'we' she uses in this first book stands for all aspiring poets. Her comments are again general. 'Flush', for instance, is not a localized, physical blush of desire, not individualized but related to the vague 'individual life'. But Romney's proposal in book II, marking Aurora's entry into womanhood and including lengthy animadversions on the appropriate actions and behaviour of women, makes it painfully clear to her that she is automatically suspect as a poet. Poetry, in Romney's phrase, 'defiles | The clean white morning-dresses' (II. 95–6). Such stains, recalling Dobell's inkstains, seem clearly related to sexual defilement, and could possibly be bloodstains, traces of the heart or of the womb. Aurora specifically tells Romney that she rejects heart-ache, which he genders as a female complaint, in favour of headache, that peculiar disease of male poets (including Robert Browning):

> Here, if heads
> That hold a rhythmic thought, must ache perforce,
> For my part, I choose headaches—(II. 106–8)

Recognizing the link between poetry and suffering, it may be that there is some sarcasm here, if she also recognizes, as we saw in Chapter 1, that poetic headaches ('My blood beat in my brain') are caused by the heart.

In Book III, Aurora is chastened. Like the hero of 'A Vision of Poets', she now associates art with personal suffering. Yet as she lives and works in London, her poetry improves, and it also starts to use more female-centred metaphors for the act of creation:

> I ripped my verses up,
> And found no blood upon the rapier's point;

> The heart in them was just an embryo's heart
> Which never yet had beat, that it should die;
> Just gasps of make-believe galvanic life;
> Mere tones, inorganized to any tune.
> And yet I felt it in me where it burnt,
> Like those hot fire-seeds of creation held
> In Jove's clenched palm (III. 245–53)

'Galvanic' suggests spasmodic, reflex action, and 'make-believe' suggests the insincerity of these actions. This is not a real poetic heart but an imitation. Perhaps showing Aurora's 'fall' into womanhood, the language here has shifted from connecting heart and brain to heart and womb. The woman's act of giving birth, however, effectually slides into the man's act of providing seed: the poet's 'seed' fertilizes the blank pages to give birth to poetry. Aurora's poetry is shaped in a slow process of engendering, rather than one act of creation, or an easily released flow of verse. She works at pouring her heart into verse and, as we have seen in other writers, this has a negative effect on her physical health: 'my pulse | Would shudder along the purple-veinèd wrist' (III. 27–8). Such effort does, however, eventually create the 'true' model of heartfelt poetry:

>   I felt
> My heart's life throbbing in my verse to show
> It lived, it also—certes incomplete,
> Disordered with all Adam in the blood. (III. 338–41)

'Felt' suggests that Aurora is taking the pulse of the poem, physically responding to it. 'All Adam' is a phrase which hints at original sin, the natural man, and thus might hint at sexuality. This may be a casual figure of speech, but it does also imply the presence of a male force within Aurora's poetry and her poet's blood.

By the point when Aurora uses her image of mother's breasts in Book V, she has become capable of defying convention by writing of (and from) the heart-centred woman's body. Yet she shies away from writing of her own heart and body in relation to love and desire. The negotiation in the extracts above, extracts where Aurora uses strong physical imagery, is between the heart and poetry, not the heart and love. While her body infuses itself into the poem's form, indeed, according to her descriptions it *is* the form of her poems, she is very resistant to moments when her own form becomes the object of attention. Aurora has taken Romney's comment on women's failure to generalize, his accusation that their 'quick-breathed hearts' can only sympathize on an individual scale (II. 184–5), so much to heart, so to speak, that it sometimes seems that all she can do is generalize, rejecting personal motions or effects of her own body unless they relate to her poetic career. She boldly discusses 'sexual passion' in connection with the outer world, and to a lesser extent with her poetry, but will not allow it into her body. Within the poem, Lady Waldemar seems to represent the kind of objectified, self-revealing female sensuality which Aurora fears:

> How they told,
> Those alabaster shoulders and bare breasts,
> On which the pearls, drowned out of sight in milk,
> Were lost, excepting for the ruby clasp!
> They split the amaranth velvet-boddice down
> To the waist or nearly, with the audacious press
> Of full-breathed beauty. If the heart within
> Were half as white! (V. 618–25)

The 'milk' hints at the maternal function of these displayed breasts, a function denied here. Lady Waldemar's body 'tells', it is active, it splits and presses against restraints in a near striptease. Despite this display of the breast, rising and falling with the breath and heartbeat, Aurora argues that the real heart is not on show, therefore implying that what the body tells, how it affects others, is not the truth. Lady Waldemar's crime here is to be too open and too aware of her own charms, as she is when she boldly comes to tell Aurora about her love for Romney. She confesses to having a 'Warm, live, improvident, indecent heart' (III. 462)—precisely the kind of shamefully exposed, unfeminine heart that gives women a bad name. In contrast to these displays, Marian Earle's heart and body (inasmuch as the two are distinguishable) are like the poet's in that their actions are described and seen subjectively. Marian relates her pregnancy, for instance, in these terms:

> Through all the heaving of impatient life
> Which threw me on death at intervals,—through all
> The upbreak of the fountains of my heart
> The rains had swelled too large: (VII. 52–5)

Her 'swelling' heart is like her womb, expanding to take in new life.[56] Despite the violence of this imagery Marian retains her innocence, because she uses it without consciousness of her own sexuality. She assures Aurora that when she was enticed away from Romney 'The blood of mine was still, except for grief!' (VI. 756) and that no son could have a mother with 'chaster pulses' (760). At no point has desire agitated her heart.

This seems to be one of the reasons why Aurora admires Marian. Her pale unearthliness and physical innocence contrast with Aurora's blood, which is never 'still'—and not simply because of the disruptions of writing poetry. When Aurora's aunt accuses her of loving Romney, for instance, she is 'devoured' by another blush, a reaction she describes ironically as 'Most illogical' (II. 701). 'After all,' she continues bitterly, 'We cannot be the equal of the male, | Who rules his blood a little' (704–5). The tone here seems both defensive and resentful, the latter perhaps because Aurora dislikes having to use physiology as an excuse for her regretted self-exposure, or because she is bitter about what she (and her creator) see as a genuine physiological truism. It is hard to tell whether these comments, like her statement on the 'ill-lodged' poet's heart, should be read as sarcastic. Written by the young Aurora, they might express inculcated views, which she spends a great deal of the poem growing out of; written in retrospect, they might read as grim humour.

---

[56] On the repeated analogy between heart and womb in *Aurora Leigh*, see Margot Louis, 'Enlarging the Heart: L.E.L.'s "The Improvisatrice", Hemans's "Properzia Rossi" and Barrett Browning's *Aurora Leigh*', *Victorian Literature and Culture*, 26 (1998), 1–19.

Whenever Aurora does speak of her own heart and blood in terms of love and desire, the confidence of her declarations on poetry disappears and her tone becomes similarly evasive. In Book VI, upset by hearing Marian's story, and about to write to Lady Waldemar, she announces:

> If, as I have just now said,
> A man's within me,—let him act himself,
> Ignoring the poor conscious trouble of blood
> That's called the woman merely. (VI. 229–32)

'Trouble of blood' is also potentially metrically troubled, as is the opening line of this passage, hinting at Aurora's confusion or embarrassment. 'Of blood' is a deliberately awkward choice of phrase (as opposed to 'troubled blood'). This passage once more hints that Aurora, as a female poet, might be inhabited by a male spirit, one she opposes to the treacherous behaviour of her own body. She tells Romney, again in confusion after having inadvertently revealed her love for him:

> Have you learnt
> No more of women, 'spite of privilege,
> Than still to take account too seriously
> Of such weak flutterings? Why, we like it, sir,
> We get our power and our effects that way. (VIII. 188–92)

'Power' and 'effects' could potentially apply to poetic effects as well as impact on a lover. Again, the question is whether Aurora is scornful of women, including herself, for having hearts which are unavoidably, naturally, weak and fluttering; or scornful of the cultural and medical attitudes which attempt to enforce this physiological assumption. Once more, there is a dual move here: to persuade Romney that her own emotions are shallow and should not be interpreted as love, and to demand that he change a view of womanhood which would give them credence. Angry with herself for falling victim to such 'flutterings', she is even angrier because she knows that she has revealed herself. Her lack of control over physical impulses, represented in disjointed breath and speech, tears, and a quickened pulse, has been seen and noted. Aurora wants the text to be like her body, not her body like a text. To survive as a woman artist in a world where she is constantly being read personally as well as textually demands the acquisition of a hardened heart:

> O heart,
> At last we shall grow hard too, like the rest,
> And call it self-defence (V. 1061–3)

This move I am tracing, in which Aurora calls attention to her woman's body in order to reject it, can equally be seen in rhythm. Critics have agreed that, as Matthew Campbell puts it, 'Aurora authenticates her utterance through a sounding of the rhythms of her own body'.[57] It is this which has provided one link between the poem and feminist theory, as in Cixous's comment on writing: 'So for each text, another body. But in each the same vibration: the something in me that marks all my books is a reminder that my flesh signs the book, it is *rhythm*.'[58] This certainly holds true to some extent, yet in the passages cited above where Aurora discusses her poetry, she rather writes that she used the rhythm of her heart than actually uses it. The text of her poem 'The Hills', specifically described in affective terms, is not given, and from the perspective of *Aurora Leigh* Aurora is supposed to have developed a style that controls the infusion of the heart:

> And so, through forced work and spontaneous work,
> The inner life informed the outer life,
> Reduced the irregular blood to a settled rhythm. (I. 1057–9)

Aurora's desire for regulation links this passage to the poetic theories of Wordsworth, Keble, and others, in which a 'settled

---

[57] Matthew Campbell, *Rhythm and Will in Victorian Poetry* (Cambridge: Cambridge University Press, 1999), 43. For another statement of this view, see Zonana.

[58] Hélène Cixous, 'Coming to Writing', in *'Coming to Writing' and Other Essays*, ed. Deborah Jenson, introd. Susan Suleiman, trans. Sarah Cornell et al. (Cambridge, Mass.: Harvard University Press, 1991), 1–58 (p. 53).

rhythm'—as opposed to spasmodism—in both poem and physical body indicates health and morality. Blood is unusually part of the 'outer life' here, rather than the inner (spiritual?) consciousness. Although the rhythms of this passage are not quite 'settled', with the iambic pentameter coming undone on 'irregular blood to a', Aurora claims to work towards repressing the metrical presence of the heart, even while writing about the need to incorporate it in her poem. Those moments where the rhythms of her speech are disturbed tend to be, like the blushes and 'flutterings' above, described in retrospect. Her aunt accuses her of speaking in 'convulsions' (II. 731), for instance, when she tries to deny her love for Romney:

> As my blood recoiled
> From that imputed ignominy, I made
> My heart great with it. Then, at last, I spoke,
> Spoke veritable words but passionate,
> Too passionate, perhaps. . ground up with sobs
> To shapeless endings. (II. 718–23)

Marshalling her resources here to speak from the heart, she discovers that the poetics of the body can lead to broken and fragmented speech. The hiatus in line 722 is a pause for doubt about the value of passionate language, but also a moment where the flow of verse threatens to become 'shapeless'. From the calmer perspective of writing, she later judges this as 'too passionate'. On finding Marian in Paris, she notes that her writing becomes disjointed, hurried, 'My hand's a-tremble as I had just caught up | My heart to write with' (VI. 415–16). But once again, this is something which needs to be brought under control, not a welcomed irruption into the text.

Aurora will not acknowledge her own heart's actions fully until assured that they are not solely the result of her 'weak' femininity, signs of heartsickness and a gendered instability. When Romney, chastened and blinded, arrives at her home in Italy as a supplicant, his confession of weakness allows Aurora to recognize that 'He mistook the world; | But I mistook my own heart' (IX. 709–10) without fear that this will immediately reduce her to a sentimental heroine, subject to love. Similarly, Romney admits his own failure to rule his blood, asking for forgiveness, 'If once or twice I let my heart escape | This night' (IX. 463). In this reversal of their relative positions, Aurora finds the assurance that, as Linda Peterson notes of Barrett Browning, the need for love affects both male and female artists and so the desiring heart is not necessarily gendered.[59] Leighton argues that earlier in the poem Aurora 'learned to write because she has learned the insignificance of being loved'.[60] Here she finally learns the significance of love, and the difficulty of sustaining the self without it. Throughout *Aurora Leigh* both hero and heroine devoted their hearts to social and political aims, in the widest possible sense, with Aurora seeking to write world-changing poetry and Romney devoting his energy to the poor. But in the conclusion Barrett Browning has them realize that without appreciating their own, individual, hearts (and this means also appreciating the role of love and passion in life), it is useless to sacrifice them to public and social ends. It is the same lesson that Tennyson's Princess Ida had to learn. Thus, while the heart does have a role in society and in the poetry that Aurora believes will change society, this should be complementary to, rather than a replacement for, the heart of the individual.

While Aurora comes to appreciate the 'value and significance of flesh' not only in the abstract but also in her own person, Romney realizes not only the importance of body (those working-class bodies which he has clothed and fed) but of heart.[61] In the conclusion the bodies of Aurora and Romney, like their hearts, have become equal and interchangeable:

---

[59] Linda H. Peterson, 'Rewriting "A History of the Lyre": Letitia Landon, Elizabeth Barrett Browning and the (Re)construction of the Nineteenth-Century Woman Poet', in Armstrong and Blain, 115–34 (p. 128).

[60] Leighton (1992), 91.

[61] Robert Browning, 'Fra Lippo Lippi', line 268.

> [W]ere my cheeks
> Hot, overflooded, with my tears, or his?
> And which of our two large explosive hearts
> So shook me? That, I know not. There were words
> That broke in utterance .. melted, in the fire. (IX. 716–20)

'Large' and 'explosive' give both hearts masculine strength and violence: the language is 'geological . . . like an earthquake, a volcano and a flood all at once'.[62] This is one of Barrett Browning's metaphors that cannot quite be physically apprehended, recalling similar moments in spasmodic poetry. Romney's blindness means that this encounter is not couched in terms of the gaze but of touch, shaking, the wetness of tears, and hearing. The rhythms of this passage (with another pause where language breaks down) are disjointed, but seem deliberately and triumphantly so. Earlier, Aurora described how the true poet 'shakes the heart | Of all the men and women in the world' (I. 906–7). Now she can submit to be shaken herself, and not through the medium of a text but in physical human contact. In this she has a confidence lacking in spasmodic poetry and in Barrett Browning's earlier speakers. Rather than the two-celled heart of *The Princess*, or the assertive possessiveness of the speakers in *Men and Women*, these lovers retain their own hearts but they become androgynous or indistinguishable. Barrett Browning's apocalyptic ending is not wholly celebratory, given that it is achieved at the expense of Romney's blindness and Aurora's agreement to marry him and join his work.[63] Yet in terms of heartfelt poetry, it does open the possibility that Aurora will be able to write from the heart without rejecting the personal pleasures of love and desire. It also suggests that just as male poets incorporate the 'feminine' heart into their

[62] Simon Avery and Rebecca Stott, *Elizabeth Barrett Browning* (Harlow: Longman, 2003), 139.

[63] Deirdre David, for example, forcefully objects to Aurora's apparent willingness to devote her art to patriarchal aims (whether those of Romney or God). See *Intellectual Women and Victorian Patriarchy: Harriet Martineau, Elizabeth Barrett Browning, George Eliot* (Houndmills: Macmillan, 1987).

work, so Aurora can incorporate a more 'masculine' heart, of assertive passion and force, into hers, without a sense of self-conscious shame or fear of exposure. Barrett Browning thus provides an ideal for women's poetry, and perhaps writing from the heart in general, to aspire to.

4

'The old unquiet breast': Matthew Arnold, Heartsickness, and the Culture of Doubt

Of all the poets in this study, Matthew Arnold was probably the one most anxious about the state of his 'starting, feverish' heart. His father died of angina pectoris, and the account of his sudden death as recorded by Latham became the classic case study of this disease, frequently cited in medical textbooks. Angina was a disease which was represented as both organic and sympathetic, which meant that it was potentially hereditary but could also be induced (or heightened) by nervous problems or emotional upset. It was the heart disease which required the sufferer to take the most care with regard to his or her heart, in terms of avoiding feelings and situations which might induce an attack. Since it involved the heart acting without warning or control, it was also classified as a 'spasmodic' disease. Henry Clutterbuck, in 1840, ascribes it definitely to 'a sudden spasm of the heart', while Charles Williams, more cautiously, blames it on 'exalted sensibility of the nerves of the heart', an odd phrase, since 'exalted' usually implies religious ecstasy or high emotion.[1] Matthew Arnold, as a poet and the son of a victim (who was also of course a literary man), was doubly susceptible. The younger Thomas Arnold remarked in an obituary of his brother that in

---

[1] Henry Clutterbuck, *On the Proper Administration of Blood-Letting for the Prevention and Cure of Disease* (London: S. Highley, 1840), 56. Charles Williams, *The Pathology and Diagnosis of Diseases of the Chest*, 4th edn. (London: John Churchill, 1840), 233.

1846, when Matthew was 24, 'he knew that he was in a certain sense doomed—an eminent physician having told him that the action of his heart was not regular, and that he must take great care of himself'.[2] When Arnold's own son was born, he wrote to his mother:

> I had my own doubts about his dear little heart having constantly remarked its singular agitations at times. But I should not be the least surprised if Brodie or whoever sees him pronounces it only to be an infantine irregularity, and that there is no structural defect.[3]

The picture of Arnold leaning over his son's cradle anxiously watching his heartbeat suggests the extent of his worry about inherited cardiac problems. The reassurance here is not entirely confident: Arnold has already called in an expert on the heart to examine his baby son. He writes to his sister in 1856 that the sympathetic alarm occasioned by his son's illness has also 'nearly developed in me the complaint he is said to have' because it caused 'a fuller beating of the heart than I like'.[4]

In the light of these fears, the emphasis in Arnold's poems on the 'vainly throbbing', 'teased, o'erlaboured' heart and the 'feverish blood' may have specifically personal as well as cultural and poetic implications.[5] Arnold is preoccupied with the idea that the heart, the source of feeling, is inaccessible and unresponsive. While one reason for this is found in his focus on the weaknesses of the individual heart, he also uses the alienated heart as a general image to represent the failure of affect, the sense that poetry has ceased to convey healthful sympathy, morality, and reassurance and is instead transmitting disease and uncertainty—inasmuch as it succeeds in transmitting anything at all. The isolation which is a central motif

---

[2] *Manchester Guardian*, 18 May 1888. Cited by A. Dwight Culler in *Imaginative Reason: The Poetry of Matthew Arnold* (New Haven: Yale University Press, 1966), 61.

[3] To Mary Arnold, 25 Nov. [1852], Lang, i. 248.

[4] To Jane Forster, 6 Dec. 1856, ibid. i. 348.

[5] 'A Summer Night', 24; 'The River', 17; 'Stanzas in Memory of the Author of "Obermann"', 94.

in many of Arnold's poems is presented as a lack of heart-to-heart communication. His interest in the state of his own heart doubtless informs some of this imagery, but he equally tends to evade the personal and describe heartsickness as endemic, a condition of the age and of modern poetry. Arnold's major poems of the 1850s ('Empedocles on Etna' in particular) share many of the concerns of spasmodic writing and of the poems by Barrett Browning and Tennyson examined elsewhere. But Arnold came from a slightly younger generation than Tennyson and the Brownings, whose poetic careers were more or less firmly established by 1850, and was separated by class, education, and religion from the spasmodic poets who were his near contemporaries. His poetic experimentation is intriguing in the light of developments around mid-century because he effectively rejected these developments by cutting 'Empedocles on Etna' from his 1853 collection, criticizing Clough's experiments in form (in *The Bothie of Tober-na-Vuolich* and *Amours de voyage*), refusing to read Alexander Smith, and expressing distaste for *Maud* and for Barrett Browning, whom he described in 1858 as 'hopelessly confirmed in her aberration from health, nature, beauty and truth'.[6] Arnold came from a different poetic background. His family linked him to Wordsworth and to John Keble, his education to Rugby, where ideals of Christian manliness were being formed under the influence of his father, and to Oxford, which he attended at the height of the conflict over Tractarianism. The culture of the heart which he experienced and assessed in his poetry, drawn from these backgrounds, was in many respects distinct from that encountered by other poets in this study.

While earlier chapters located the heart in relation to medicine, poetics, and gender, this chapter places Arnold's poetry in the context of the religious heart, and more precisely in relation to High Anglican values. Arnold stands at the meeting point of three traditions in Victorian Christianity: his father's Broad Church faith, which had some points in common with Evangelicalism and involved

---

[6] To Frances du Quaire, 9 Feb. 1858, Lang, i. 383.

a liberal toleration for other creeds and denominations; the High Church religion of Tractarian Oxford, represented by his godfather John Keble; and the doubt and loss of faith which became an increasing topic of discussion after mid-century, and which affected many of his contemporaries and friends, including Clough. Arnold's poetry is hesitant about subscribing to any one doctrine, but it draws its agonizing over feeling and affect from a combination of the high valuation of emotion—located and experienced in the heart—found in each of these traditions, and the fear that such emotion is now lost. His poetry asks questions about faith, feeling, and faith in feeling which contemporary religious thinkers were debating. Should faith be based on an emotional heartfelt apprehension rather than intellectual assent? Where do our emotions and feelings come from and can we trust them? If faith is reliant upon feeling, how can it be expressed and conveyed to others, or is it necessarily personal and incommunicable?

The heart has of course always been a significant religious symbol, representing the location of God and of faith within the human body, and during the nineteenth century these traditional connotations became increasingly important as the rational and intellectual framework of Christian belief crumbled. The heart (if it could be trusted) seemed to offer a bulwark against doubt by providing comprehensible proof of faith on an individual level. The individual's felt experience of God's presence in his or her heart could not be easily challenged. Evangelicalism gave added impetus to the religious and biblical tradition of the feeling heart by emphasizing it as the site of a regenerate faith and the medium for a personal relationship with Christ. William James, in his classic work on religious faith, used a case study of Stephen Bradley's Evangelical conversion from 1829 to illustrate the role of emotional excitement in religious belief:

> At first, I began to feel my heart beat very quick all on a sudden, which made me at first think that perhaps something is going to ail me, though I was not alarmed for I felt no pain. My heart

increased in its beating, which soon convinced me that it was
the Holy Spirit from the effect it had on me.[7]

Palpitation is initially taken here as a potential symptom of sickness, before the reading shifts to a religious interpretation. Physical
responses, which seem to take place in the heart independently of
the rest of the body and the mind, are a signal of God's presence; for
this speaker, it seems self-explanatory that such heartfelt effects must
be spiritual in origin. Isaac Taylor, brother of the popular Evangelical children's poets Jane and Anne Taylor and himself a widely
read Evangelical writer, argued in his *Natural History of Enthusiasm*
(also from 1829) that 'Divine energy' manifested itself in two ways,
corresponding to mind and body, and that:

> As the one kind of Divine energy does not display its presence
> by convulsive or capricious irregularities, but by the unnoticed
> vigour and promptitude of the functions of life, so the other
> energy cannot, without irreverence, be thought of as making
> itself felt by extra-natural impulses, or sensitive shocks upon the
> intellectual system; but must rather be imagined as an equable
> pulse of life, throbbing from within and diffusing softness,
> sensibility and force throughout the soul.[8]

The first kind of energy, felt in the body, corresponds to the
healthy motions of heart and lungs, processes which ensure the
continuation of life and operate without conscious thought. Taylor's
book contrasts with Bradley's account in that it sets out to counteract
the valorization of excessive emotion and sensibility as symptoms
or products of faith, in a deliberate response to the trend towards
'enthusiasm' in the early nineteenth century. His metaphor of faith
as a steady and calming pulse is common in devotional writings and

---

[7] William James, citing Bradley, in *The Varieties of Religious Experience*, introd.
Reinhold Niebuhr (New York: Simon & Schuster, 1997), 161.

[8] Isaac Taylor, *Natural History of Enthusiasm* (London: Holdsworth & Ball, 1829),
63. Tennyson (and Hallam) were also familiar with Taylor's works. Eleanor Mattes
discusses Taylor's influence on Tennyson in *In Memoriam: The Way of a Soul* (New
York: Exposition Press, 1951), 40–3.

hymns of the period. 'Speak to my warring passions: Peace! | Say to my trembling heart: Be still!', wrote Charles Wesley in the late eighteenth century. [9] William Cowper, on the other hand, begs for an access of feeling:

> O make this heart rejoice, or ache;
>   Decide this doubt for me;
> And if it be not broken, break,
>   And heal it, if it be.[10]

Wesley and Cowper follow a standard Biblical trope whereby feelings of doubt and fear are displaced onto the heart, which is then accused of hindering the whole man. The heart is the aspect of the body, or self, on which God acts directly. Cowper's 'doubt' is ambiguous: either doubt of God's presence, which would be resolved by any sense of Him in the heart, doubt as to whether the speaker's heart deserves to be made to rejoice or to ache, or perhaps doubt as to whether the heart itself is capable of feeling. Such 'introspective, physically intimate' language, describing the relationship between Christ and the speaker in terms of body and blood, became gradually unacceptable in mainstream churches as the century progressed, if still popular outside them.[11] Christopher Wordsworth, brother of the poet and a High Church Anglican, later summed up this attitude when he described Evangelical language such as 'Let me to thy bosom fly' as 'inexpressibly shocking', a comment which suggests that his shock is related to the implication that God or Christ possesses a physical body, a 'bosom', and could be embraced.[12]

If nineteenth-century Evangelicalism introduced the discourse of the feeling heart from the 'low' branch of the Church, from the other extreme came an increased concentration on the heart in Roman

---

[9] *A Rapture of Praise: Hymns of John and Charles Wesley*, selected by A. M. Allchin and H. A. Hodges (London: Hodder and Stoughton, 1966), 111.

[10] W. Cowper and J. Newton, *Olney Hymns* (London: [n.p.], 1779), 81.

[11] Susan Tamke, *Make a Joyful Noise unto the Lord: Hymns as a Reflection of Victorian Social Attitudes* (Athens: Ohio University Press, 1978), 140.

[12] Christopher Wordsworth, *Thoughts on English Hymnody: or, Preface to 'The Holy Year'* (London: Rivington, 1865), p. xxxi.

Catholicism. The Society of the Sacred Heart was officially founded in 1800 and granted a mandate from the Pope in 1826. In 1856 the Feast of the Sacred Heart was extended to the whole Church.[13] The subsequent emphasis on Christ's wounded, fleshly heart doubtless contributed to Anglican writers' anxiety about dwelling on the heart in their own writings. Henry Manning, who had moved from Evangelicalism to Tractarianism before converting, wrote in 1873 that '[T]he heart of Jesus is a heart of flesh—a heart taken from the substance of His Blessed Mother—a symbol, indeed, because it best symbolizes and manifests the eternal love of God; but it is more than this, it is also a reality'.[14] The heart is a means of summing up Christ's humanity, and so its flesh and blood materiality needs to be stressed. Hopkins, another Tractarian convert, was more anxious to play down the naked physicality of Christ's heart, defensively arguing that:

> The heart, I say, is agreed to be one of the noble or honourable members of the body. There would no doubt be something revolting in seeing the heart alone, all naked and bleeding, torn from the breast; but that is not in question here: Christ's heart is lodged within his sacred frame, and there alone is worshipped. And considered as within the breast, who is there however truly or delicately, however even falsely or affectedly modest who ever thought it shame to speak of the human *heart*?[15]

Hopkins uses the heart's status as a literary and cultural symbol to argue that it is more than a physical organ and hence can be discussed without a shameful focus on the body itself. 'Revolting' introduces a sense of distaste for the physical heart even as Hopkins attempts to

---

[13] See Margaret Williams, *The Society of the Sacred Heart: History of a Spirit 1800–1975* (London: Darton, Longman and Todd, 1978).

[14] Henry Manning, *The Divine Glory of the Sacred Heart* (London: Burns and Oates, 1873), 12–13.

[15] *Sermons*, 102. On Hopkins's anxiety about the unity of body and soul in Christ, see the Conclusion, 303–4.

deny it. There is an air here of protesting too much, as he apparently implies that discussing the heart *could* be immodest.

The heart's all-purpose currency as a religious image also meant that it could be used by those who were not necessarily Christian, in Establishment terms, to express a more secular and generalized faith. 'Feel it in thy heart, and then say whether it is of God! This is Belief, all else is Opinion,' wrote Carlyle at a climactic moment of *Sartor Resartus* (1833–4).[16] In a note from his time at Cambridge, possibly addressed to Tennyson, Arthur Hallam commented: 'With respect to prayer, you ask how am I to distinguish the operations of God in me from motions in my own heart? Why should you distinguish them, or how do you know there is any distinction?'[17] Susan Shatto and Marion Shaw note that in the original manuscript draft of the *Memoir* there are quotation marks around 'from motions in my own heart', suggesting that these might have been Tennyson's own words, and therefore implying that he had expressed doubt about the link between God and the heart which Hallam supports here.[18] Hallam's response and Carlyle's contemporary assertion both give feeling and emotion, located in the heart, the status of religious acts. These extracts give the impression that the writer is testing the motions of their heart to see whether they are sufficiently Christian. But this assumes that he or she is capable of making such a distinction. Hallam's comment once again implies that God could be present in the physical self, not simply metaphorically located in the heart as a spiritual site. He may then be guilty of the transgression warned of by the philosophical and medical writer William Newnham, in his discussion of the responsive heart:

> It can scarcely be necessary to caution the unwary or the captious reader against the *abuse* which may be made of this physical agency, so as to *mis*-represent the operations of the

---

[16] Thomas Carlyle, *Sartor Resartus* (London: Chapman and Hall, 1896), 155.

[17] Cited in *Memoir*, i. 44.

[18] *In Memoriam*, ed. Susan Shatto and Marion Shaw (Oxford: Clarendon Press, 1982), 284.

Holy Spirit of God ... as blended with, or equivalent to, the mere impulses of *animal feeling.*[19]

Casual correlations of God and 'my own heart', Newman suggests, might be dangerous, in associating spirituality with a fallible, undependable human organ and thus privileging individual feeling over external authority.

The heart was the basis of appeal when rational proof of Christianity seemed lost. 'All my conviction is but faith, and it proceeds from the heart, and not from the understanding', wrote the influential German philosopher and alleged atheist Johann Fichte.[20] The heart underpins Ludwig Feuerbach's controversial *The Essence of Christianity* (1841), in which he argues for sympathy, a religion of love, and identification with Christ as human; just as it also serves as an important image in the secular humanism of George Eliot, his translator. Feuerbach's imagery again suggests that he is considering the actual physical heart as well as the heart as spiritual symbol:

> As the action of the arteries drives the blood into the extremities, and the action of the veins brings it back again, as life in general consists of a perpetual systole and diastole; so is it in religion. In the religious systole man propels his own nature from himself, he throws himself outward; in the religious diastole he receives the rejected nature into his heart again.[21]

The pulsation of the heart and movements of the circulation provide a parallel for religious feeling. As in studies of poetic rhythm, this links physical, human processes to the Divine. Feuerbach sums up his argument about the significance of human feeling and emotion

---

[19] William Newnham, *The Reciprocal Influence of Body and Mind Considered* (London: J. Hatchard, 1842), 578.

[20] Johann Fichte, *The Destination of Man*, trans. Mrs Percy Sinnett (London: Chapman, Brothers, 1846), 74. This book expresses Fichte's liberal opinion that faith cannot be objectively assessed or defined. He was accused of atheism in Germany in the 1790s.

[21] Ludwig Feuerbach, *The Essence of Christianity*, trans. George Eliot (1841), introd. Karl Barth (New York: Harper and Row, 1957), 31.

in religion by stating, 'The truly religious man unhesitatingly assigns his own feelings to God.'[22] This again implies that religion is purely a matter of personal feeling; there can be no external check on whether God is inspiring the individual or not. Following these continental thinkers, Francis Newman (John Henry Newman's brother) wrote in *Phases of Faith* (1850), his defence of rationalism and historical criticism of the Bible, that the prerequisite for faith was '*the heart's belief in the sympathy of God with individual man*'.[23] Personal feelings and perceptions of sympathetic warmth, located in the heart, could not be disproved—which produces a dichotomy wherein the heart is simultaneously an unassailable and an unstable basis on which to rest religious belief.

Such use of the heart to defend what would have appeared to members of the Anglican Establishment as infidelity and near-heretical questioning of tradition and authority provides some reason why High Church poets and theologians, including those writers who influenced Arnold most strongly in his youth, were deeply suspicious of discussing the heart and of appearing to rely on it as a guide, in either poetry or religion. For the leading poets and theologians of the Oxford Movement—Keble, John Henry Newman, Edward Pusey, and Isaac Williams—the heart remains essential to faith, but only if it is shaped and disciplined by God and the Church rather than dictating faith itself. While recognizing their own debts to Evangelicalism (the childhood faith of many Tractarians) it was precisely the kind of interpretation of and reliance upon physical and emotional experience offered by Cowper's hymns and in accounts such as Stephen Bradley's that these writers deplored. Edward Pusey complained in 1838, in a letter on Dr Arnold, that the false ingredient in Arnold's liberal Broad Church theories was the Evangelical tendency to look to the feelings 'as something in themselves, something to be analysed, used as a criterion of the

---

[22] Feuerbach, 55.
[23] Francis Newman, *Phases of Faith*, introd. U. C. Knoepflmacher (Leicester: Leicester University Press, 1970), 133.

spiritual state'.[24] Newman expanded on this in his comments on Evangelicalism:

> There is a widely, though irregularly spread School of doctrine among us, within and without the Church, which aims at and professes peculiar piety as directing its attention to the heart itself, not to anything external to us, whether creed, actions or ritual. I do not hesitate to assert that this doctrine is based upon error, that it is really a specious form of trusting man rather than God.[25]

Rather than allowing 'heart' to encompass a vague and nebulous realm of feeling, Newman emphasizes that the heart is intrinsically human ('the heart *itself*') and is therefore, in his terms, unreliable. While 'certain dispositions of the heart', as Isaac Williams put it, are necessary for the reception of faith, these dispositions are formed by church duties, which create an appropriate framework for experiencing and understanding feelings, rather than being naturally part of the heart, whether the latter is considered as a physical or spiritual site.[26]

Clough, writing to a friend in 1838 about being at Oxford at the height of the Tractarian movement, remarked:

> And it is no harm but rather good to give oneself up a little to hearing Oxford people, and admiring their good points, which lie, I suppose, principally in all they hold in opposition to the Evangelical portion of society—the benefit and beauty and necessity of forms—the ugliness of feelings put on unnaturally soon and consequently kept up by artificial means, ever strained and never sober.[27]

[24] E. B. Pusey, 20 Aug. 1838, in *Spiritual Letters of E. B. Pusey*, ed. J. O. Johnston and W. C. E. Newbolt (London: Longmans, Green, 1898), 41.

[25] J. H. Newman, 'On the Introduction of Rationalistic Principles into Revealed Religion', in *Essays: Critical and Historical*, 2 vols. (London: Basil Montagu Pickering, 1872), i. 30–101 (p. 95).

[26] 'Religious doctrines and articles of faith can only be received according to certain dispositions of the heart; these dispositions can only be formed by a repetition of certain actions.' Williams, 'On Reserve in Communicating Religious Knowledge' (Part 2), Tract 87, *Tracts for the Times 1838–1840* (London: J. G. & F. Rivington, 1840), v. 58.

[27] To J. P. Gell, 8 May [1838], *The Correspondence of Arthur Hugh Clough*, ed. F. L. Mulhauser, 2 vols. (Oxford: Clarendon Press, 1957), i. 71.

Clough accurately defines the oppositional stance of Tractarianism, its attempt to stem the flood of 'feelings' in religion. As he notes, Tractarians saw this appeal to feeling as 'strained', false, even embarrassing, an unpardonable giving way to sentiment. 'Check every rising feeling at once,' Pusey bluntly advised a correspondent in 1844.[28] The use of 'forms' restrains feeling by incorporating it into a traditional structure, just as poetic form contains in this sense the emotions of a poem. Clough and his correspondent, J. P. Gell, were debating at this point whether the exposure of feeling in poetry could ever be justified. Gell asserts, defensively, that poets have 'a certain manliness, which takes away from their public display all that unpleasant appearance of sophistication'. 'Sophistication' might well be equivalent to keeping up feelings 'by artificial means'. The question of whether (male) poets should write from and of personal feeling is, Gell writes, 'linked to that of "relating experience" in religious affairs'. [29] He associates the writing of poetry with religious self-expression, and implies that both might be incompatible with manly Christian reserve. Excessive religious feeling or enthusiasm was (as we have seen with other forms of intense feeling) tainted with effeminacy, creating another potential source of anxiety or embarrassment about heartfelt revelation.

Charlotte Yonge's anecdote about Keble's correction to her novel *Heartsease* is well known: 'The chief alteration I remember was that a sentence was erased as "coarse", in which Theodora said she really had a heart, though some people thought it was only a machine for pumping blood.'[30] Keble might have objected to the description of the heart as mechanism, but it seems more probable that he was alarmed by a female character referring directly to her physical heart. The smallest association of the heart with physicality is still assumed to verge on indecency. Over-hasty discussion of the heart's feelings, Keble's censorship suggests, could shock the reader,

---

[28]   Pusey (1898), 25.

[29]   J. P. Gell to Clough, 13 July 1838, Clough, ed. Mulhauser (1957), i. 77.

[30]   Charlotte M. Yonge, *Musings over the 'Christian Year' and 'Lyra Innocentium'* (Oxford: James Parker, 1871), p. xxxvi.

besides exposing the writer to the shame of having shared what should be private. To insist on the heart's emotion is impolite and unfeminine. Keble's correction to Yonge's work also fits with the key Tractarian doctrine of 'Reserve', associated both with Keble's theories and with his personal actions and habits. Reserve, a concept codified by Isaac Williams in his two tracts on the subject, initially referred to the process by which religious revelation is withheld until the individual is prepared to receive it. As a general idea, however, it came to be interpreted in terms of the need for self-control and caution in personal expression. The difficulties of expression, plus the possibility that emotional self-revelings could become out of control, were such that it was preferable to exercise reserve in describing feeling, particularly though not exclusively when that feeling related to religion.

Reserve was frequently imagined in terms of preventing the heart from eluding the control of mind and will. As Pusey wrote in a sermon on the vacillations of faith: 'The heart may, and must, rise and sink; we can, by God's grace, control it, hold it down, keep it outwardly still, hinder it from having any wrong vent; we cannot hush its beatings.'[31] 'Still' here does not mean 'motionless'—the heart cannot be still except in death—but is used in the archaic sense of 'soft, subdued', like the 'still small voice' speaking through the storm in 1 Kings 19: 12. 'Outwardly' is also important. Pusey does not imply that strong emotion can be avoided but that it should be repressed lest it become visible to others. This extract beautifully sums up a widespread Tractarian attitude. It is not that the heart should not play a part in faith—this is impossible, if man 'cannot hush' it—but that this part must be controlled. Pusey continues by assuring his listeners that once the heart is under God's command: 'Thy heart will still rise and sink; but it will rise and sink, not restlessly, nor waywardly, not in violent gusts of passion; but, whether rising or sinking . . . resting in stillness on the ocean of the Love of God.'[32]

[31] E. B. Pusey, *Parochial Sermons*, 2 vols. (Oxford: John Henry Parker, 1853), i. 96.
[32] Ibid. 96.

The heart is a wilful organ needing to be disciplined by God, lest it become prey to dangerous passions. Keble's immensely popular book of religious verse *The Christian Year* (1827) similarly uses repeated imagery of the wayward heart being calmed or comforted by God's will. The 'untuned heart' the poet brings to God in his opening 'Dedication' is gradually tuned in the course of *The Christian Year*, as the speaker subjects himself to God and asks Him to provide peace for body and mind: 'The languid pulses Thou canst tell, | The nerveless spirit tune.'[33] Keble shares Pusey's view that the excitable, throbbing heart is something to be avoided rather than sought. Addressing the heart in 'Seventh Sunday after Trinity', he writes:

> Sweetly thy sickening throbs are ey'd
> By the kind Saviour at thy side;
> For healing and for balm e'en now thine hour is come. (16–18)

'Sickening' potentially disturbs the metrical pattern if it is not elided. Such throbbing is 'sickening' because it might create heartsickness, Keble suggests, but there is also a sense that observing or feeling the heart's palpitation is distasteful. Anything other than a sobering and steady pulsation is regarded with misgiving. Later in the poem, Keble writes of 'The curse of lawless hearts, the joy of self-control' (56). As I have argued elsewhere, the process of regulating the heart in time with God's will in Keble's writing takes place through rhythm as well as content, as each poem underlines its conservative sentiments by returning to a reassuringly controlled beat.[34] Clough, who, like Arnold, was very familiar with Keble's poetry, echoes this outlook and that of Pusey in an unpublished poem: 'But thou, O human heart of mine, | Be still, contain thyself, and bear' ('In a London Square', 7–8). It also recurs throughout the poetry of Christina Rossetti, in which the heart is repeatedly admonished and instructed in calmness

---

[33] John Keble, 'Dedication', line 7 and 'Second Sunday after Epiphany', lines 51–2, *The Christian Year, Lyra Innocentium and Other Poems* (Oxford: Oxford University Press, 1914). All further references given in the text.

[34] Kirstie Blair, 'John Keble and the Rhythm of Faith', *Essays in Criticism*, 53 (2003), 129–51.

and self-discipline. Diane D'Amico, for instance, has noted that in Rossetti's copy of *The Christian Year* she chose to underline many of Keble's references to the heart and its sufferings, suggesting that she felt these had some personal relevance to her, as a High Church advocate, a poet, and perhaps particularly as a female poet.[35]

To examine how the principle of exercising reserve with regard to the heart operated in poetry, I want to turn to two contrasting sonnets, one by Richard Trench, written in 1838 after he had adopted High Church principles, and one by Frederick Faber, an Oxford Movement poet who later converted to Roman Catholicism, from his 1840 collection. Trench's sonnet strongly expresses the need for caution in revealing the heart:

> A wretched thing it were, to have our heart
> Like a broad highway or a populous street,
> Where every idle thought has leave to meet,
> Pause, or pass on as in an open mart;
> Or like some road-side pool, which no nice art
> Has guarded that the cattle may not beat
> And foul it with a multitude of feet,
> Till of the heavens it can give back no part.
> But keep thou thine a holy solitude,
> For he who would walk there, would walk alone;
> He who would drink there, must be first endued
> With single right to call that stream his own;[36]

Making the heart, the most private and intimate organ, into a marketplace has connotations of prostitution, besides those of simple buying and selling, as does the image of a pool fouled by animals. The heart's blood is soiled and muddied, perhaps, because vice could (as humoral theory attested) alter the constitution of the blood. Trench's sonnet ends with an exhortation to the reader:

---

[35] Diane D'Amico, 'Christina Rossetti's *Christian Year*: Comfort for the "Weary Heart"', *Victorian Newsletter*, 72 (1987), 36–42 (p. 39).

[36] Richard Chenevix Trench, 'Sonnet', in *Poems, Collected and Arranged* (London: Macmillan, 1865), 37. Trench served as curate to Hugh James Rose, one of the original leaders of what came to be known as the Oxford Movement.

> Keep thou thine heart, close-fastened, unrevealed,
> A fenced garden and a fountain sealed. (13–14)

This imagery, drawn from the lover in the Song of Solomon, suggests parallels between virginity or celibacy and the preservation of the heart's privacy. The heart should be withdrawn from the world, guarded. In this sonnet it is the set form itself, the 'nice art' of the sonnet, which does the guarding, fencing the heart in. The act of keeping the heart 'close-fastened', however, might also create tension in the writing of poetry. Keble argued in his influential lectures as Oxford Professor of Poetry that poetry provided a 'safety-valve' for feelings that might otherwise be mentally and physically dangerous, including religious feeling:

> [N]othing takes such entire possession of the human heart, and, in a way concentrates its feeling, as the thought of God and an eternity to come: ... nothing so powerfully impels it, sadly and anxiously, to look round on all sides for remedy and relief. As a result of this, Religion freely and gladly avails itself of every comfort and assistance which Poetry might afford.[37]

For Keble, the heart inevitably seeks release from oppressive feeling, and it is in the regulated form of poetry that this release is best found. Poetry can reassure the poet (and implicitly the reader) of the secure promise of Christianity, removing doubt and fear. While it stems from the heart, however, it must still, as Trench's poem advises, maintain a stance of dignity and self-control: it is both expressive and carefully managed.

Written only two years after Trench's poem, Faber's sonnet 'The Confessional' exposes the difficulties of this position and the tensions between reserve and expression in Tractarian poetics. The poet agonizes about his revelation of his heart to an intimate male friend:

---

[37] *Keble's Lectures on Poetry, 1832–1841*, trans. E. K. Francis, 2 vols. (Oxford: Clarendon Press, 1912), i. 55, ii. 480.

Now thou hast seen my heart. Was it too near?
Didst thou recoil from the o'erpowering sight;
That vision of a scarred and seamed soul?
Ah! yes: thy gentle eyes were filled with fear
When looks and thoughts broke out from my control,
Bursting themselves a road with fiercest might—
Wide-opening secret cells of foulest sin,
And all that lurks in that dark place within!
Well, be it so, dear friend! It was but right
That thou shouldst learn where blossoms yet may bless,
And where for ever now there must be blight
Riven with burning passion's torrent course,
Shattered and splintered all with sin's mad force—
Thou saw'st my heart, and did not love me less.[38]

'Heart' is used here as synonymous to 'soul', but the imagery of 'cells', rushing 'torrents', and the dark places within has physiological resonance, suggesting the depths of the body. The hint of something sinister lurking at the heart is similar to Coleridge's comment in *Aids to Reflection* (and Trench's early letter on that subject), although Faber takes this rhetoric to exhaustive extremes.[39]. There are, as in Trench's poem, clear implications that the release of the heart's forces is connected with the exposure of passion—passion which, in this imagery, looks suspiciously sexual. Faber, an extreme partisan of Catholic Anglicanism who converted to Roman Catholicism in 1845, was unsurprisingly regarded with some hesitation by its more restrained leaders, and himself demonstrated fears that his poems to his young male friends would be misinterpreted when he revised and cut them from later collections.[40] 'The Confessional' manages to abandon reserve entirely while agonizing over it. The speaker claims to fear self-revelation, and expects that it will induce distaste,

---

[38] Frederick William Faber, 'The Confessional', in *The Cherwell Water-Lily and Other Poems* (London: J., G., F. and J. Rivington, 1840), 68.

[39] See below, p. 182.

[40] For details of these revisions and a longer study of 'The Confessional', see Kirstie Blair, 'Breaking Loose: Frederick Faber and the Failure of Reserve', in *Victorian Poetry*, 44 (2006).

even while being incapable of restraining himself from it. But the poem does react to Tractarian ideals of constraint, order, and self-repression despite its excesses in that it is 'ruled' to some degree by its formal qualities, the regular rhyme scheme and metre. It flirts with the idea of containment through the sonnet structure and the iambic pentameter, yet uses a rhyme scheme (*abcacbddbebffe*) that does not fit into any established sonnet form. In the irruption of a rhyming couplet which does not rhyme with any other line ('Riven with burning passion's torrent course | Shattered and splintered all with sin's mad force') into the final quatrain, for instance, this sonnet is partially 'splintered', forced out of shape.

Faber's emphasis on the 'blight' at his heart might also have some bodily correlation in his own anxieties about his health. In 1842, he wrote to a close friend: 'I have had some frightening work at my heart, but medical exam. seems to have ascertained that there is no disease (structural) but that it was a confinement of mind caused by nervous excitement and overwork.'[41] Like Mark Pattison, Faber perceives himself as falling prey to the 'nervous excitement' caused by the fervid religious atmosphere of Oxford controversies. Note also how he recognizes the difference between 'structural' and sympathetic disease: further evidence that the distinction was commonly known and discussed. Such comments feed into Faber's statements about his wayward heart and its lack of appropriate behaviour. Always concerned about his over-emotional disposition and propensity towards violent feeling, he commented after his conversion that the strictness of Roman Catholicism might help to tame the heart: 'The red cross on my rough habit must keep that little beater down, and bid it beat, not less ardently, but for Jesus only.'[42] As both Trench's and Faber's poems show, the focus on heartfelt emotion in Anglican-inflected religious discourse led to intense interest in it, and ambiguous responses whereby the revelation of emotion clashes with its containment. Whether Faber's poem 'gives healing relief to

---

[41] To J. B. Morris, 27 Sept. 1842. Unpublished letter, London Oratory Archives.

[42] Cited in John Edward Bowden, *The Life and Letters of Frederick William Faber* (London: Thomas Richardson, 1869), 303.

secret mental emotion, yet without detriment to modest reserve: and while giving scope to enthusiasm, yet rules it with order and due control', as Keble prescribed, is uncertain, to say the least.[43] The heart has implicitly defied these prescriptions.

In an unpublished poem, 'Whence are ye, vague desires', Clough sums up the ambiguities surrounding the conjunction of the spiritual heart with the physical, material organ by asking whether these desires are:

> A message from the blest
>   Or bodily unrest;
> A call to heavenly good
>   Or fever in the blood. (20–4)

As in Hallam's comment or Newnham's warning this suggests the difficulty of separating religious impulses from the pathological. Clough's poem is both light and serious, for the different possibilities of interpreting these 'vague desires' would lead to very different ends. By the 1840s, the decade when Clough and Arnold attended Oxford and published their first poems, the influence of the Oxford Movement was fading, with a large number of high-profile conversions to Roman Catholicism (Newman and Faber among them), and the rise of doubt as an 'observable and much-discussed cultural phenomenon', perhaps best exemplified by the publication of J. A. Froude's *The Nemesis of Faith* in 1849 and its subsequent burning in Oxford.[44] A poem from the same year by Clough, implicitly addressed to God, asks: 'Be thou but there,—in soul and heart, | I will not ask to feel thou art' ('υμνος αυμνος' ('A hymn, yet not a hymn'), 39–40). Although this initially seems to indicate confidence in God's presence, there is some ambiguity about the speaker's motives, one of which might be the fear that if he did make this

---

[43] Keble (1912), i. 22.

[44] Frank Turner, 'The Victorian Crisis of Faith and the Faith that was Lost', in Richard Helmstadter and Bernard Lightman (eds.), *Victorian Faith in Crisis* (Houndmills: Macmillan, 1990), 9–38 (p. 10).

request, he would be unable to feel, too hardened to recognize the sensation of faith. By not requiring a response from God, moreover, the speaker hints at his anxiety that there might be no answer to his demands. If God's presence is not felt, experienced as a reality, what is the difference between faith and doubt? And even if God's presence is felt, Clough's poems suggest, we might not be able to trust our own sensations.

Both Clough and Arnold's poems written during and after their Oxford years circle around these issues, featuring heroes who are afraid to trust their emotional responses or bemoan their inability to feel, whether in relation to faith or romance. Arnold's poems in particular stage a series of laments for the loss of feeling in his age, a loss which he associates with the inaccessibility and insensibility of the heart and its potential sickness. The 'fierce necessity to feel' ('Iseult of Brittany', 124), Arnold's poems argue, painfully remains, while the power which would enable feeling—a power strongly associated with poetry itself—has been taken. In 'Memorial Verses', written on Wordsworth's burial in 1850, Arnold recalls a time when poets were physicians to the human condition: Goethe diagnosed its ills and Wordsworth's poetry soothed and 'loosed the heart' (47), in the cathartic relief identified by the poetics of Keble and others. This time, however, is past and no new poet has arisen with the same capacities: 'Others will strengthen us to bear - | But who, ah! who, will make us feel?' (66–7). As he remarks in a notebook entry:

> The misery of the present age is not in the intensity of men's suffering—but in their incapacity to suffer, joy, feel at all, wholly & profoundly—in their having their susceptibility eternally agacée by a continual dance of ever-changing objects.[45]

Throughout the notebooks and the poetry Arnold discusses 'feeling' obsessively but with great ambiguity, as something his poems both long for and shrink away from. In 'The New Sirens', for example, he writes:

[45] *Matthew Arnold: The Yale Manuscript*, ed. S. O. A. Ullmann (Ann Arbor: University of Michigan Press, 1989), 145.

'Come', you say, 'the brain is seeking,
  While the sovran heart is dead;
    Yet this gleaned, when Gods were speaking,
  Rarer secrets than the toiling head.

'Come', you say, 'opinion trembles,
  Judgment shifts, convictions go;
    Life dries up, the heart dissembles—
  Only, what we feel, we know. (77–84)

The dichotomy between brain and heart, seen in many Victorian poems, is frequently stated in this way in Arnold's poetry. That is, he writes that the heart would be and has in the past been the preferred guide, but is now dead or at least impotent and has therefore given way to the head. Allott supplies the note: 'Arnold never subscribed to the extreme Romantic view of the "new sirens" that "Only, what we feel, we know" (l. 84), but he believed with many Victorians that it was a mistake to exalt "head" over "heart".'[46] 'Only, what we feel, we know', however, is potentially ironic, for if the heart 'dissembles' how can we trust in the truth of feeling? Arnold attempts to draw together affect and intellect, but if the heart is dead or lying there is no obvious location for affect. Moreover, the comma after 'Only' suggests a possible reading of 'we' as exclusive rather than inclusive, referring to the Sirens, 'what *we* feel, *we* know'. The succeeding lines, 'Hath your wisdom felt emotions? | Will it weep our burning tears?' (85–6), would then tempt (or taunt) the speaker of the poem by remarking on the inability of modern man to experience the emotional charge that the New Sirens offer, perhaps because he has become too intellectual. 'Your wisdom' and 'it' (rather than 'you') is distancing, and the combination of 'wisdom' and 'emotion' (concepts usually placed in opposition) itself seems to mock the physical/spiritual uncertainties and ambiguities of the rhetoric of feeling. 'Feeling' is the temptation held out to poets by these dubious representatives of passion and Romanticism, but the suggestion in 'The New Sirens'

---

[46] Allott and Super, 52 n.

is that to accept it would mean alienating oneself from the modern world, where feeling is not tenable—a tantalizing impossibility.

Arnold's poetry of the 1850s takes the heart as the organ of feeling and then laments the subject's inability to access, trust, or rely upon it. He seems to seek the security and reserve offered by Tractarian poetics, but is also fascinated by the poetry of sensation and affect, of spasms and palpitations, advocated by Hallam and practised by Keats, Shelley, Tennyson, and the spasmodic poets, among others. As a child, Arnold was taught to repeat lyrics from *The Christian Year*, and the influence of Keble's poetry, in which adherence to set principles and a steady beat is paramount, is clear in his own.[47] Arnold's conception of metre, as expressed in the 'Preface to *Merope*' (1858), maintains the need for metre as a restraining force:

> Powerful thought and emotion, flowing in strongly marked channels, make a stronger impression: this is the main reason why a metrical form is a more effective vehicle for them than prose: in prose there is more freedom, but, in the metrical form, the very limit gives a sense [of] precision and emphasis. The sense of emphatic distinctness in our impressions rises, as the thought and emotion swell higher and higher without overflowing their boundaries.[48]

The function of metre here is apparently not to damp down emotions but to enhance them, something like Wordsworth and Coleridge's accounts. A greater impact is made by the contrast between form and freedom than by freedom itself. Form is the passage or channel through which liquid feelings and thoughts can flow and by which they are controlled. This imagery might be related to Arnold's

---

[47] Park Honan, *Matthew Arnold: A Life* (London: Weidenfeld & Nicolson, 1981), 12. Honan suggests that 'The Buried Life' is the poem closest to Tractarian poetics (p. 227). On Keble's influence, see Daniel Kline, '"For rigorous teacher seized my youth": Thomas Arnold, John Keble and the Juvenilia of Arthur Hugh Clough and Matthew Arnold', in Kirstie Blair (ed.), *John Keble in Context* (London: Anthem, 2004), 143–58.

[48] Allott and Super, 682–701 (p. 697).

constant description of the hidden interior life as a river or stream, partly reminiscent of the circulation of blood in the body. The confidence with which Arnold states this theory in the late 1850s, however, is not quite borne out by his earlier poetry. Limits, in many of his poems, are both sought and rejected, form is simultaneously unsteady and carefully controlled, and the containment of emotion leads to its dissipation as often as its strength. An unfinished poem from his notebooks, in which the speaker considers retiring from the world, asks:

> Say, my father, does the tired
> Restless heart in this retreat
> Learn to know what it desired,
> Knowing, clasp it and securely beat? ('To Meta: The Cloister', 29–32)

The trochaic measure, falling to a graceful conclusion in the final extra foot of the last line, and the confident rhymes, indicate the safety which the heart is offered. Yet the metre is not regular tetrameter—each line ends on a stressed syllable, meaning that either the final beat is missing, left implicit, or the lines awkwardly consist of two or three trochees and an amphibrach. The beat here is not quite secure. The 'father' addressed is a monk, and this passage acts as a homage to Arnold's poetic and religious fathers: Keble, his godfather, and Newman, whom he described as one of the greatest influences on his life. But Arnold cannot quite share the Christian conviction that makes the renunciation of the world and of emotion in exchange for confidence and security worthwhile. The poem questions (in rhythm as well as content) rather than accepts. In 'The Second Best', he writes:

> Moderate tasks and moderate leisure,
> Quiet living, strict-kept measure
> Both in suffering and in pleasure—
> 'Tis for this thy nature yearns. (1–4)

Measure here is indeed more strictly kept, as, assuming an elision on 'moderate', the first three lines follow a trochaic tetrameter pattern.

The poem continues by advocating that man reject thinking and reading in favour of obedience to an 'impulse, from the distance | Of his deepest, best existence' (21–2). 'Impulse' hovers between suggesting a physiological basis, a 'pulse' of feeling, and a religious or moral drive, perhaps stimulated by God. In 1873, Arnold argued in *Literature and Dogma* that 'native, instantaneous, mechanical impulses' should be controlled and regulated by 'Conduct'. Describing an impulse as both 'native' (presumably in the sense of 'natural') and 'mechanical' recalls language used to discuss the heartbeat. Arnold attempts to combine the mechanical and organic concepts of bodily impulses in one. Given that he associates the control exercised by 'Conduct' with the very 'object of religion', then the aim of religion becomes to some extent the regulation of impulses.[49] Yet his earlier poetry is again deeply divided over whether this is something to be sought or rejected. The pointed title of 'The Second Best' leaves it open to debate whether the 'second best' option is the 'moderate' life which the poet feels he should espouse, or more generally the compromise the modern world demands from him, in that he yearns for a world of passion and sensation while recognizing the impossibility and undesirability of achieving it.

Many of Arnold's best-known poems represent this by simultaneously celebrating and rejecting a surrender to 'impulse'. In 'Isolation: To Marguerite' the speaker laments his heart's lapse into feeling:

> Farewell!—and thou, thou lonely heart,
> Which never yet without remorse
> Even for a moment didst depart
> From thy remote and sphered course
> To haunt the place where passions reign—
> Back to thy solitude again! (13–18)

The 'remote' course is equivalent to the distanced perspective Arnold advises for the poet in 'Resignation', where his vision of the poet suggests withdrawal from earthly affairs:

---

[49] *The Complete Prose Works of Matthew Arnold*, ed. R. H. Super, 11 vols. (Ann Arbor: University of Michigan Press, 1960–77), vi. 179, 174–5.

The poet, to whose mighty heart
Heaven doth a quicker pulse impart,
Subdues that energy to scan
Not his own course, but that of man. (144–7)

Arnold here follows the common notion that the poet's heart is more sensitive, but no sooner has he introduced this idea than he turns, at the line-ending, to the definite assertion that this pulse is 'subdued'. The poet's energies are thus turned outwards rather than inwards, possessing a wider scope than individual feeling. In order to fulfil the correct conditions of poetic creation, this suggests, the speaker of 'Isolation' would necessarily have to return to his 'solitude'. But while he commands and berates the 'lonely heart' and its 'conscious thrill of shame' (19) at stooping to this level, there is also a sense of loss and regret in 'Isolation', as the heart's failure to find a reciprocated love confirms the speaker's solitude. Human sympathy is fallible and in this poem at least there is no alternative source of sympathy in God.

Even while Arnold repeatedly rejects the 'quicker pulse' and 'passions' of human feeling, the fact that his poems constantly return to such imagery and emphasize the speaker's failure to subdue his heart might suggest that he recognizes this struggle is itself 'poetic'. Several of his poems hint at a cautious adherence to the idea that great poetry necessarily stems from the heart, from passionate, restless feeling. In 'A Summer Night' the poet is asked (or asks himself):

Hast thou then still the old unquiet breast,
Which neither deadens into rest,
Nor ever feels the fiery glow
That whirls the spirit from itself away,
But fluctuates to and fro,
Never by passion quite possessed
And never quite benumbed by the world's sway? (27–33)

These lines are uneasy in their distribution of stresses, shifting between tetrameter and pentameter lines, and the rhythm becomes seriously unsteady in the truncated line 'But fluctuates to and fro', where 'fluctuates' disturbs the beat because it adds the possibility of an extra syllable. These lines are also unsettled because of the recurrence of two unstressed beats at different points within the line, e.g. 'Néveř bў pássioň', 'bў thě wórld's sẃay'. Such fluctuation is the reverse of the calm mind and body of the ideal Anglican religious poet. 'You are too content to *fluctuate*,' wrote Arnold to Clough in 1853, perhaps accusing him of a failing which he himself feared.[50] The lines vacillate because, it seems, Arnold is again unsure of the answer which is being sought—should the poet seek to have an 'unquiet breast', or reject it? Which is preferable, passion or numbness? The middle ground which Arnold seeks in such poems as 'Resignation', where the poet can calmly withdraw from individual passions to a clear vantage point, no longer exists. As in many of Arnold's poems, the poet's passion here is described from a spectator position, in the second person, not as if it inhabited the speaker's body. Arnold's 'fiery glow', 'spirit', and so forth are not obviously physical. Whereas Barrett Browning's ability to surprise (and sometimes scandalize) the reader comes from the lurking possibility that her images can be read literally and in physical terms, Arnold's imagery eschews a literal reading. The passage thereby seems more detached. It is as though Arnold introduces this passage into the poem to assure the reader that he is suffering the agonies and ecstasies of the poet, while avoiding the necessity to express them or own them himself. The description of the 'unquiet breast' is contained because it is voiced by an external force, and in the final line, it turns out to be more controlled than is apparent. 'Possessed' looks back to 'rest', and the world's 'sway' is a pun: while it seems to fit with 'fluctuates', 'sway' equally suggests stern command. What seemed wavering suddenly appears, in another light, rigidly fixed.

In common with many of the poets discussed earlier, Arnold's poems gesture towards symptoms of heart disease in that the heart as represented here inevitably veers between oversensitive palpitation and acute sensation and coldness and hardness—all potentially signs of either organic or sympathetic disease. He is uncertain, however,

[50] To Clough, 30 Nov. 1853, Lang, i. 28.

whether viewing a disturbed heart as a valuable poetic gift is possible, and invariably discusses the heart in a curiously remote tone of mingled desire, anxiety, and envy. A. Dwight Culler notes a comment in a letter to Clough, in which Arnold paraphrases Hamlet: 'but thou'dst not think, Horatio, how ill it is here—'.[51] 'Again the dash', Culler comments, 'to indicate that, if the reader wishes to supply the words "about the heart" he may, but the writer himself would be embarrassed by so direct a reference to that palpitating organ.'[52] Culler is right to identify embarrassment as a force here. Arnold is, almost coyly, shying away from overt self-revelation, evincing the kind of reticence shown by Keble's editing of Yonge's novel, as opposed to the self-dramatization of a poet like Byron, whom Arnold describes as displaying 'the pageant of his bleeding heart' throughout Europe ('Stanzas from the Grande Chartreuse', 136). But Arnold's hesitation to mention the heart also dramatizes his stance of distance from it: the quotation trails off before it can definitely indicate the heart's problems. Of course, this serves to draw attention to the heart's absence and so gives it an important imaginative presence.

Critics have considered the 'buried life', a concept which Arnold repeatedly returns to in his poems of the 1850s, as something without a specific location or frame of reference, an ambiguous 'hidden ground within' or an empty linguistic construct, a reference to concealed desire.[53] Arnold is writing in a tradition, however, where the void within the breast is an established literary trope connected to heartsickness and the inability to feel, and his recurring imagery of the hidden interior self is closer to this tradition than has been noted. It seems clear from his poems that the buried life not only has a definite imaginative location in the heart, but is itself analogous to it. At first, for example, 'The Buried Life' avoids using the word 'heart':

---

[51] [*c*.15 Dec. 1849], ibid. i. 167.   [52] Culler, 57.
[53] See David Trotter, 'Hidden Ground Within: Matthew Arnold's Lyric and Elegiac Poetry', *ELH* 44 (1977), 526–53. Trotter briefly discusses Keble's interest in the buried life in relation to Arnold's (pp. 546–7).

> But there's a something in this breast,
> To which thy light words bring no rest,
> And thy gay smiles no anodyne. (6–8)

In the same way as Arnold's reference to Hamlet, the odd phrase '*a something*' highlights this avoidance, because the indefinite article points towards one object, something material. The phrasing might hint that the poet's heart is so far removed that he can no longer even confidently identify it as such, or state that he possesses a heart at all. Meanwhile, the iambic tetrameter pulses steadily behind his words. 'Anodyne' is a term Arnold also uses of Tennyson's *In Memoriam* in 'The Scholar-Gipsy' (190), and which he associates with the (futile) attempt to produce affective poetry. 'The Buried Life' continues:

> Alas! is even love too weak
> To unlock the heart, and let it speak?
> Are even lovers powerless to reveal
> To one another what indeed they feel? (12–15)

The slight jar to the metre caused by the extra syllable in 'unlock', requiring readers to perform their own elision ('T'unlock'), could signal the resistance of the heart to being opened. The addition of an extra foot in the last two lines here, with the qualifiers 'even' and 'indeed', moves away from the four-beat rhythm and into a more varied measure, as the line lengths of the poem and the iambic pulse begin to waver and stumble. Arnold denies the commonplace that lovers understand each other's hearts, a denial that means that all men and women, no matter how intimate, are banned from comprehension of another and self-revelation. Poetry, as Keble argued, should provide an outlet. Yet in 'The Buried Life' the lack of communication seems to refer to the act of writing the poem itself. Arnold as poet cannot convey what he feels, he can only discuss the general impossibility of feeling. For Keble and Newman, in addition, God's sympathy for and understanding of men's feelings serves as a replacement for human comprehension and a higher good; whereas for Arnold the lack of human sympathy equals the removal of the only possible outlet for feeling. David DeLaura convincingly argues that Arnold secularizes

Newman's idea of 'inwardness', faith dwelling in the heart, which means that religion is no longer available, in this poem, as an external frame of reference into which the inward life can be absorbed.[54]

The four references to the heart (plus that 'something') in the first twenty-eight lines of 'The Buried Life' naturally suggest the possibility that the 'unregarded river of our life' (39) that runs 'through the deep recesses of our breast' (38) is akin to the blood and the circulation. The dual movements of 'eddying' and 'driving' on in this poem could relate to the pulsation of the heart as well as the motion of the stream. Physiological texts commonly use similar imagery. The medical writer H. M. Hughes, for example, deploys an extended metaphor of streams and rivers throughout his lengthy discussion of the circulation.[55] Arnold equates tracking man's 'true, original course' with:

> A longing to inquire
> Into the mystery of this heart which beats
> So wild, so deep in us—to know
> Whence our lives come and where they go.
> And many a man in his own breast then delves,
> But deep enough, alas! none ever mines. (51–6)

The solution to all life is to be found in the beating heart, but again it recedes from knowledge. This seems slightly stilted and generalized, 'us' and 'his' rather than 'me' and 'mine'. The rhythm of these lines eddies, indicating restless enquiry rather than conclusion. Discovering the heart corresponds to finding the origins of the self and discovering the potential of truthful self-expression, the power not only to feel but to make words correspond with feelings:

> A bolt is shot back somewhere in our breast,
> And a lost pulse of feeling stirs again.

---

[54] David DeLaura, *Hebrew and Hellene in Victorian England: Newman, Arnold, and Pater* (Austin: University of Texas, 1969), p. xi.

[55] H. M. Hughes, *A Clinical Introduction to the Practice of Auscultation* (London: Longman, Brown, Green and Longmans, 1845), 204–6.

The eye sinks inward, and the heart lies plain,
And what we mean, we say, and what we would, we know. (84–7)

Line 84 recalls the literal 'doors' or valves of the heart (which, in a diseased heart, threaten to become corroded and stop the circulation). The passive tense ('is shot back') gives no sense of how (or by whose agency) this release happens. The metre here becomes more regular, although the variation from iambic measure on 'Ănd ă lŏst púlse' suggests a slight disorder in pulsation, and line 87, longer by an extra foot and slowed down by the pauses created by the punctuation, is left uncertainly hanging on without a rhyme.

Arnold's use of rhythm echoes the uneasiness he feels about the heart. William Oram suggests, on 'The Scholar-Gipsy': 'What sets it off from most Romantic myths of self-division is its insistence that the loss of contact with one's deepest self is a means of protection', an insight which suggests that Arnold's denial of the buried life—of contact with the heart—may be a deliberate strategy.[56] In the light of his own fears about cardiac disease, for instance, dissociating the self from the heart's actions might be sensible. Trotter writes that 'Arnold hopes that the "buried life" of men could pace itself, could find respite from the insistent, jarring rhythms of the modern world.'[57] But Arnold's refusal to 'pace' his own lines steadily, in the rhythmical cross-currents of 'A Buried Life', indicates a partial rejection of this hope. It could also show that for Arnold it is less a hope than a fear, in that a rhythmically steady interior life would be devoid of the shocks and starts which form the poetic impulse. Assuming that he chooses his measures carefully, there is something almost defiant in his refusal to keep to a steady beat, his resistance to harmonious conclusions.

This is particularly evident in 'Empedocles on Etna', Arnold's long poem of 1852, which he later cut from the 1853 volume. His decision to do so was doubtless in part based on his worry that 'Empedocles'

[56] William A. Oram, 'Arnold's "Scholar-Gipsy" and the Crisis of the 1852 *Poems*', *Modern Language Quarterly*, 45 (1984), 144–62 (p. 149).
[57] Trotter (1977), 526.

would be read as a 'spasmodic' poem. It certainly shares many of the characteristics of Smith and Dobell's work, featuring a godlike speaker suffering from passion and near-insanity who laments his alienation from the world, a mixture of genres and forms, and a tendency to use or describe irregular measures. The 'jarring rhythms' of Empedocles' long speech to Pausanius are a good example:

> And we feel, day and night,
> The burden of ourselves—
> Well, then, the wiser wight
> In his own bosom delves,
> And asks what ails him so, and gets what cure he can. (I. ii. 127–31)

Or:

> Once read thy own breast right,
> And thou hast done with fears;
> Man gets no other light,
> Search he a thousand years.
> Sink in thyself! there ask what ails thee, at that shrine! (I. ii. 142–6)

The short quatrains seem self-contained and measured, reasoning, before the final line of each stanza disrupts the pattern. These long lines pivot back on themselves, requiring the reader to search the previous stanza for a rhyme. They create a sense of expansion, urgency in the alliteration and haste of phrases such as 'gets what cure he can', which is immediately succeeded by constraint as the lines are held back, checked. The trimeter of the quatrain and hexameter of the long lines reject both common measure and the straightforward iambic pentameter. Empedocles uses the rhetoric of the heart with scorn and bitterness, mocking the idea of heart as 'shrine' and as cure. His imagery of 'delving' in the bosom recalls 'The Buried Life', an allusion which ironizes Empedocles' reference by suggesting that there is little cure to be found, because 'deep enough, alas! none ever mines'. Both poems imagine the 'breast' as a subterraneous region ('sink in thyself') of caverns, rivers, and veins of ore, dark and dangerous.

Empedocles used to be a healer, as Pausanius sadly remarks:

He could stay swift diseases in old days,
Chain madmen by the music of his lyre,
Cleanse to sweet airs the breath of poisonous streams, (I. i. 115–17)

The affective healing power of Empedocles' music also makes him a model for the poet. Pausanius, himself a physician, links Empedocles' malady with the evil state of his times, but more so with 'some root of suffering in himself, | Some secret and unfollowed vein of woe' (I. i. 151–2). From having the power to cure, Empedocles has become trapped in an impotent interior life. He 'hears nothing but the cry of the torrents, | And the beating of his own heart' (II. 213–14). Over-attention to the heart's sounds and motions is, of course, a symptom if not a cause of disease, and even these 'torrents' could be an externalized representation of rushing blood. Empedocles' disordered circulation, 'the veins swell, | The temples tighten and throb there—' (II. 215–16), and pleas for more air have been compared to Arnold's own fears of heart disease. One medical writer notes that in angina pectoris, 'any exertion at once produces so anxious a desire for more air as can be expressed by no fitter term than the *air-hunger* of the Germans'.[58] Arnold wrote to Clough: '*congestion of the brain* is what we suffer from—I always feel it and say it—and cry for air like my own Empedocles.'[59] 'Congestion' is (as we have seen) an illness stemming from a rush of blood to the affected part, comparable to 'determination'. It is perhaps significant, too, that the historical Empedocles, who wrote on physiology as well as philosophy, argued that respiration and circulation were intimately linked, and that the heartbeat caused the motions of the lungs in breathing.[60]

---

[58] George W. Balfour, 'Clinical Lectures on Diseases of the Heart', *Edinburgh Medical Journal*, 19 (1873–4), 1058.

[59] 12 Feb. 1853, Lang, i. 254.

[60] Gweneth Whitteridge summarizes Empedocles' views in William Harvey, *An Anatomical Disputation Concerning the Movement of the Heart and the Blood in Living Creatures*, trans. and introd. Gweneth Whitteridge (Oxford: Blackwell, 1976), 23 n.

Empedocles is thus sick at heart both actually and metaphorically. He traces man's progress in terms of the heart's decay, from the happiness of 'youthful blood' (I. ii. 352) to 'Our shivering heart is mined by secret discontent' (I. ii. 366), to:

> We pause; we hush our heart,
> And thus address the Gods:
> 'The world hath failed to impart
> The joy our youth forebodes,
> Failed to fill up the void which in our breasts we bear. (I. ii. 372–6)

'Our heart' makes it seem that men share one communal heart, unless Empedocles is regally referring to himself in the third person, avoiding personal reference to his own heart. The speaking or clamouring heart in the first line is replaced by a void in line 376. 'Bear' can mean either to carry, or to suffer. 'Mining' the heart will only produce evidence of a prior loss and emptiness: while man sought to 'delve' into its riches, it has already been undermined. 'Once read thy own breast right | And thou hast done with fears' is in this sense ironic. What man discovers in his breast is a lack, an incapacity to feel and so an inability to fear—the kind of inability that leads to suicide. Empedocles' leap into the volcano is a surrender to this void, and hence to the passions inside himself, given that the volcano's flames and eruptions are themselves an established image of feelings warring within the self.

In Empedocles' account of man's ailments and attempted cures, one of the causes of sickness is, crucially, the frustration of being unable to choose one's own rhythm:

> Born into life!—we bring
> A bias with us here,
> And, when here, each new thing

Arnold could have known of Empedocles' medical fame from his reading of several lives of Empedocles and Simon Karsten's *Philosophen Graecorum Veterum Operum Reliquiae* (1830), a copy of which he owned. See C. B. Tinker and H. F. Lowry, *The Poetry of Matthew Arnold: A Commentary* (London: Oxford University Press, 1940), 289.

Affects us we come near;
To tunes we did not call our being must keep chime. (I. ii. 192–6)

'Affect', Empedocles states, is outside man's control; we have no choice about how we are influenced. Two apparently contradictory responses to the world—instinctive and controlled—are juxtaposed here in a manner which once more recalls poetic debates about organic versus mechanical rhythm. But they turn out not to be contradictions, in that man is affected against his will, forced to react in certain ways, so that native impulses and even affect itself are part of a wider regulatory scheme, whether this is natural (physiological) or supernatural. While man seeks to impose his will on the world, 'Limits we did not set | Condition all we do' (I. ii. 184–5). The question that Empedocles cannot answer is, who did set these limits? Does their apparent existence prove the presence of the gods, or God?

Arnold wrote in his list of projects for 1849: 'Empedocles—refusal of limitation by the religious sentiment.'[61] One aspect of this refusal is the rejection of harmonious rhythm, the desire not to be contained by the measure of a possibly non-existent deity. Empedocles holds out the seductive possibility of accepting defeat: 'Man's measures cannot mete the immeasurable All' (I. ii. 341). Assuming an elision on 'th'imm-', this is one of the more harmonious long lines of this section. But he immediately counteracts, contemptuously, 'Fools!' (I. ii. 347). As there is no firm evidence that the gods exist, man's measure does not have a sure reference point or analogy and hence cannot be steady or peaceful, but is instead reflected in pointless physiological spasms and fluctuations. 'Nor does being weary prove he has where to rest' (I. ii. 351), Empedocles concludes, in a line which awkwardly rejects the iambic measure, demonstrating its own lack of restfulness. As in 'The Buried Life', the possibility of a respite from broken, hesitant rhythms is claimed as a comforting illusion, which the modern poet has perforce to reject. The end of 'Empedocles on Etna', however, does not even allow the reader to

---

[61] Arnold, ed. Ullmann, 114.

have confidence in this rejection, because after Empedocles' agonized suicide the final lines of Callicles' hymn are perfectly rhymed and exactly equivalent in metre:

> The day in his hotness,
> The strife with the palm;
> The night in her silence,
> The stars in their calm. (II. 465–8)

Does this harmony, continuing without Empedocles' disruptions, simply show the limitations of Callicles' outlook on the world, or might it indicate that Empedocles was wrong to reject the gods, that something persists below or around the broken rhythms of man? This is the question that Arnold's poems often seem to circle round, never quite providing a final answer.

Arnold's rejection of 'Empedocles on Etna' as 'morbid', offering no hope or comfort, seems to suggest that he saw this vision of heartsickness and suicide as overly extreme. His preface famously argues that the purpose of poetry is to create pleasure, and through this morality.[62] This and his later criticism gives poetry a vital role in culture and civilization, but, as has often been remarked, there is a strong divide between the principles stated in the prose and those embodied in the earlier poems, with their repeated failures of sympathetic communication. His poetry of the 1850s strongly suggests that poetic affect and sympathy are fruitless and that the incapacity to feel anything healthy or good, any sense of connection to others—represented in the distant and diseased heart—is an inescapable component of modern life. The decay of religious belief means that Christianity cannot quite offer the desired security for the heart, and even if it did, this security might be stultifying rather than inspiring. Form as well as content contributes to the resulting oscillation between passionate involvement and extreme detachment in Arnold's poems. When in 'Stanzas from the Grande Chartreuse' he recalls the passions of Shelley and Byron, he suggests that these

---

[62] 'Preface to Poems (1854)', in Allott and Super, 589–609. See especially pp. 591–2.

have faded without trace and that time has not proven their worth. 'Have restless hearts one throb the less?'(144) because Shelley lived and sung? Arnold seems to invite a negative answer. His poems are the most expressive of all Victorian poetry in their descriptions of the poetic crisis which so many believed in, a crisis of endemic heartsickness, in which a culture of feeling seemed destroyed and the loss of faith provided no trustworthy external authority.

5

'Raving of dead men's dust and beating hearts': Tennyson and the Pathological Heart

For the Cambridge Apostles in the 1820s and 1830s, the years when Tennyson began to publish his poetry, the heart and circulation were imagined at the centre of a poetic theory of affective influence. John Kemble wrote to William Bodham Donne of invigorating England:

> By a higher and a holier work, by breathing into her the vigorous feeling of a Poet, and a Religious man, by pouring out the dull and stagnant blood which circulates in her veins, to replenish them with a youthful stream, fresh from the heart: yea so be it, even must the cost be my own life-blood.[1]

The roles of the poet and the religious man, envisaged in quasi-physiological terms, are here equivalent. This is at once a national, religious, and artistic aim, which connects to Romantic imagery of streams and fountains, to imagery of the body politic, and to biblical rhetoric. The idea of pouring breath and blood into a feminine England also has fertilizing, sexual overtones. Like Barrett Browning's martyr-poet, Kemble imagines spending his own blood to aid others. His assertion echoes (or seeks to fulfil) the words of Keats's sonnet to Haydon:

[1] Cited in Peter Allen, *The Cambridge Apostles: The Early Years* (Cambridge: Cambridge University Press, 1978), 100.

These, these will give the world another heart
And other pulses.[2]

The submerged allusion to the new heart of the New Testament gives
religious colour to Keats's vision of a redemptive poetic generation
who will cause the nation's heart to feel once more. Tennyson's
early poetry, which, along with that of Keats and Shelley, Hallam
dubbed the 'poetry of sensation', is a significant part of this Apostolic
enterprise because it is both poetry which describes sensation and
affective poetry, altering the reader's heart. Yet despite the confident
pronouncements on the poet's superior sensibility and the importance of literature in Hallam's famous review of *Poems, Chiefly Lyrical*,
both Tennyson's poetry and that of his contemporaries reveals the
same preoccupation with heartsickness and the difficulties of affect
that we have seen in Arnold and others.[3] R. C. Trench, another of
the Apostles of Hallam and Tennyson's generation, wrote to Donne
in 1831: 'Literature will not do for me . . . there is always the central
hollowness, the cold black speck at the heart, which is spreading
and darkening, and which must be met by other arms than those
which Letters supply.'[4] Citing Coleridge, and recalling Hallam's very
similar letter of a year earlier (see p. 51), Trench leaves it ambiguous
whether this 'central hollowness' is felt in the self, in society, or
both. Tennyson's early poems express similar nagging doubts. They
are frequently divided as to whether the heart is a valuable source
of feeling and emotion or a threateningly volatile part of the self.
They tend to envisage extreme situations in which sensitivity has
become almost pathological in intensity, and has led to a dangerous
abandonment to sensation, as in 'Fatima':

> My heart, pierced through with fierce delight,
> Bursts into blossom in his sight (34–5)

---

[2] 'Addressed to the Same ['Great spirits']', lines 11–12. *The Poems of John Keats*, ed.
John Barnard, 3rd edn. (Harmondsworth: Penguin, 1988). All further references are to
this edition.

[3] A. H. Hallam, *Englishman's Magazine*, 1 (1831), 616–28. Reprinted in John Jump
(ed.), *Tennyson: The Critical Heritage* (London: Routledge, 1967), 34–49.

[4] Cited in Allen, 125.

or, alternatively, scenarios in which the heart is numbed to all sensation, 'frozen', incapable of feeling at all ('The Two Voices', 422). By 1834 (the year after Hallam's death), when Tennyson refers to the 'new heart' of Keats and Kemble in a letter on Henry Taylor's preface to *Philip Van Artevelde* (1834), a work heavily critical of the poetry of sensation, he is increasingly negative:

> I close with him in much of what he says of modern poetry though it may be that he does not take sufficiently into consideration the peculiar strength evolved by such writers as Byron and Shelley, which however mistaken they may be did yet give the world another heart and new pulses—and so are we kept going.[5]

The criticism of Byron and Shelley as 'mistaken' signals the distance Tennyson has come from Apostolic beliefs. Through the implicit reference to Keats he draws attention to the fact that Keats's comment is no longer new, itself a cliché. While agreeing in essence with Keats's sonnet, then, he contrives to make it sound weary and repetitious. Instead of being rejuvenated we are 'kept going'. The heart that is worn out is replaced, but the sense is that Tennyson would almost have liked to stop. As the speaker of 'Nothing Will Die' asks, 'When will the heart be aweary of beating?' (6), in a question which might sound hopeful as well as nervous.

Tennyson is the Victorian poet who makes greatest play with the physical heart and with the culture of heartsickness, in that there is almost always an edge of pathology to his use of heart imagery. Moreover, he integrates form and content in his heart-centred poetry more successfully and consistently than any other poet of the period: his most famous poems published in the 1850s, *In Memoriam* and *Maud*, both incorporate the pulse in their rhythms, though to very different ends. While Tennyson's poetry from his earliest publications to the end of his career shows a consistent interest in heart-centred imagery, these two poems are, I argue, the finest examples of how the

---

[5] To James Spedding, Oct. 1834, Lang and Shannon, i. 120.

culture of the heart infiltrated Victorian poetics. It is not so much that Tennyson used the heart, pulses, and circulation in radically different ways from other writers, as that his work reflected upon and to some extent influenced all the discourses already discussed. He was aware of new developments in physiology and medicine and was himself something of a hypochondriac with regard to the heart; he wrote poems which reflected upon gendered and religious poetics; he was a major influence on spasmodic writing (and borrowed from this genre himself in *Maud*) and, while he never formulated a metrical theory, those who did invariably used his poetry to furnish examples of experimentation and innovation.[6] The poetics of the heart in the nineteenth century are fundamentally Tennysonian. His poems, I suggest, are intensely engaged with the transmission of affect from heart to heart and, like many examples we have seen, are divided on whether this sympathy will create health or disease.

The heart in *In Memoriam* and *Maud*, the subjects of the rest of this chapter, stands in ambiguous relation to the speakers of these poems because it is unclear whether it works with them or against them, possessing a will of its own. The heartbeat is both what they are reduced to and what they are sustained by. In both poems the individual speaker tries to find ways in which the heart within the body can be connected to wider processes, to seek a context, whether social, religious, or political, in which personal feelings will be meaningful. Rhythm is one of the agents in effecting this sense of connection, and I argue here that the pulse is the basis of the metrical patterns underpinning each poem. If the heartbeat is the primary impetus behind rhythm, however, the question is again one of agency—does the speaker dictate its beats, or is the pulse or whatever motive force dictates it (a force which could of course be associated with God) effectively in control? *In Memoriam* and *Maud* are poems about the heart's progress, or otherwise, from sickness to health. But while the former represents the attempt

---

[6] George Saintsbury, for instance, takes Tennyson as the key exponent of prosodic developments in the mid-century in *A History of English Prosody*, 2nd edn., 3 vols. (London: Macmillan, 1923), iii. 296.

to integrate the heart into a healing religious and poetic scheme of regeneration before it becomes permanently diseased, the latter presents a striking example of the entirely pathological heart, and a case study of a sufferer from nervous heart disease. Reading *Maud* and *In Memoriam* through the heart shows the speakers of both poems struggling to come to terms with their lack of poetic command, their inability to separate the metaphorical from the literal, and their helpless consciousness of underlying heartsickness.

In Memoriam, since it indisputably sprang from Tennyson's personal grief, was read by his contemporaries as truly 'written from the heart'. James Stirling, for example, comments: 'Here, if ever . . . is a human heart nakedly given us, and we may not reject the lesson.' Although 'nakedly' sits uneasily here (note that it refers to the style of presentation rather than the heart itself) Stirling implies that the moral and religious impetus behind the poem is sufficient to excuse this self-revelation. Moreover, he reads Tennyson's poem as designedly universal, or at least national: 'For us, it shall not be the heart of the poet, but the broken heart of the century that wails here in an absolute music.'[7] Edward Tainsh writes, in his assessment of Tennyson in 1868:

> To thousands, this is a sort of sacred book, and it dwells in their hearts in a place quite by itself. Deeper than all praise or fame, is the glory of having stirred the hearts and quickened the spirits of thousands of men to whom not many of the words spoken in their ears at present stand for much. This our poet has done in this his greatest poem.[8]

'Hearts' and 'spirits' here might either be synonymous or opposed: *In Memoriam* touches body and mind. This was the poem that made Tennyson 'our' poet (not least by making him poet laureate), that

---

[7] James Stirling, *Jerrold, Tennyson and Macauley, with Other Critical Essays* (Edinburgh: Edmonston & Douglas, 1868), 94, 95.
[8] Edward Tainsh, *A Study of the Works of Alfred Tennyson* (London: Chapman and Hall, 1868), 140.

furthered, in William Howitt's phrase, his 'access to the bosoms of the multitude'.[9] As this suggests, it is the heart, not the intellect, that will be altered in the experience of reading.

Such responses are not facile or atypical. Recurring again and again in contemporary reviews of *In Memoriam* is the idea that Tennyson's poem literally affects the hearts of its readers, creating feelings, 'stirring', 'quickening', that will result in an improved moral—and even physical—life. F. W. Robertson, literary critic, social reformer, and an acquaintance of Tennyson's, took *In Memoriam* as the exemplary poem in his argument, written in 1852, on the healing and relieving attributes of poetry. Advising working men on the need to read poetry, he gives it a vital political role in defusing feeling: 'For it is a mistake to think that Poetry is only good to nurse feeling. It is good for enabling us to *get rid* of feeling for which there is no available field of action. It is the safety-valve to the heart.' Robertson might almost be citing Keble's lectures here. Repeatedly praising Tennyson for his 'large, human heart', he argues that the dry hearts and jarred nerves of the working population could be soothed by reading him.[10] By the 1860s, as Pat Jalland notes, *In Memoriam* was increasingly replacing Keble's *The Christian Year* as the consolatory literature of choice.[11] Alexander Macmillan, one of many who wrote to express gratitude for the poem, told Emily Tennyson in 1859 that when his brother-in-law (the critic George Brimley) had lost his faith 'under the influence of a fatal and most painful disease', reading *In Memoriam* proved a 'blessed influence', at once reconciling him to suffering and reviving his religious belief. He also read the poem with his brother as he too was dying.[12] Most famously, Queen Victoria was comforted

[9] William Howitt, *Homes and Haunts of the Most Eminent British Poets*, 2 vols. (London: Richard Bentley, 1847), ii. 465.

[10] F. W. Robertson, 'Two Lectures on the Influence of Poetry on the Working-Classes' (1852), in *Lectures and Addresses on Literary and Social Topics* (London: Smith, Elder, 1858), 93–202 (pp. 180, 152). Stephen Prickett associates Robertson's theories with Keble in *Romanticism and Religion: The Tradition of Coleridge and Wordsworth in the Victorian Church* (Cambridge: Cambridge University Press, 1976), 118.

[11] Pat Jalland, *Death in the Victorian Family* (Oxford: Oxford University Press, 1996), 282.

[12] 29 Sept. 1859, Lang and Shannon, ii. 242–3.

after Albert's death by reading Tennyson. In a draft letter to Princess Alice at the time, Tennyson tentatively suggested that *In Memoriam* might prove helpful because 'I continually receive letters from those who suffer telling me how great a solace this book has been to them.'[13] One of the most widely cited texts in contemporary sermons and religious writing, it might be considered on a par with religious verse or hymns in its potential to reintegrate readers into a community.

In Memoriam's affective power substantially rests on its constant invocations of the heart and on the embodiment of the pulse in metre, creating a flexible yet insistent beat which operates on poet as well as reader. Tennyson is fundamentally engaged here with the measure of the heartbeat in relation to the sick heart, and with how the duration of life might relate to the lasting beat of metre. One medical writer remarks, on grief:

> The only purely sedative passion is sorrow—and sorrow only in so far as it is unmixed with any impulse, whether of anger or even despair. It is only that kind of sorrow which is absolutely aimless, that retards and relaxes the contractions of the heart . . . Yet it is not incorrect to speak of any of the active passions as depressing, when long continued. For any desire or longing, when it possesses the mind for a lengthened period, although at first it excites the contractions of the heart, ends by exhausting and weakening it.[14]

The speaker of *In Memoriam* dreads that he suffers from 'aimless' sorrow, and hence emotion that would make the heart beat 'low' (IV. 8), 'muffled' (XLIV. 15), and faint, yet fears simultaneously that he suffers from the active and exciting passions of anger and despair, and that his heart is over-beating and palpitating. The question of the physical heart in *In Memoriam* is all the more acute, moreover, because it is a poem about an actual heart—Arthur Hallam's—that now only exists in the figurative, through the medium of Tennyson's

[13] [23 Dec. 1861], ibid. 290.
[14] J. Burdon Sanderson, *Handbook of the Sphygmograph* (London: Robert Hardwicke, 1867), 46.

poetic discussion. For a poem founded, as Samantha Matthews notes, on a 'passionate imaginative attachment to the body', identifying the nature of both Hallam's and the poet's sickness is vital.[15] Tennyson could hardly have failed to appreciate the significance of Hallam's apparent death from disease of the heart and circulation, not least in relation to his own fears of illness as a hereditary and occupational hazard. With his documented interest in medical and physiological research, he would also have been aware that intense grief was often cited as a leading cause of functional heart disease.[16] As his poem moves slowly from despair to tentative hope, it considers whether the poet's heart is 'too far diseased' to recover. Moreover, it poses the question of whether Hallam's heart still feels and acts, still influences others, now that the organ within the body is dead. Is the material heart all there is, or can the heart exist as a meaningful and affective presence if it is not embodied?

The rhythm of *In Memoriam*, in its regular four-beat tetrameter pattern, asks to be read as the heartbeat, but this underlying pulse is not entirely reassuring for either speaker or reader. Indeed, Tennyson, as speaker of this poem, seems at times bitterly to resent the measure which he deploys, as though the rhythm works on, through, and despite him. *In Memoriam* V reveals a tension between morbid and curative poetry, mechanical and organic rhythm:

> But, for the unquiet heart and brain,
> A use in measured language lies;
> The sad mechanic exercise,
> Like dull narcotics, numbing pain. (V. 5–8)

'Unquiet' is literally so, as an awkward two-syllable word and because the trochaic substitution and comma after 'But' slightly disturb the metre. In contrast, the metre then settles into exactly measured

---

[15] Samantha Matthews, *Poetical Remains: Poets' Graves, Bodies and Books in the Nineteenth Century* (Oxford: Oxford University Press, 2004), 237.

[16] 'I used, from having read in my father's library a great number of medical books, to fancy at times that I had all the diseases in the world,' Tennyson told Hallam Tennyson (*Memoir*, i. 269). For details of these medical books see Nancie Campbell (ed.), *Tennyson in Lincoln*, 2 vols. (Lincoln: Tennyson Society, 1971).

iambic tetrameter for the central couplet. Measured language here does not release pain, as Robertson believed, but dulls it temporarily. In this stanza, the speaker refuses to give any indication of agency, so that it is left ambiguous whether he has actively chosen to use measured language or not. His use of the term 'mechanic' could imply that metre is more a reflex action than an intellectual decision. Edward FitzGerald famously remarked that *In Memoriam* had 'that air of being evolved from a Poetical Machine of the highest order'.[17] If the heart mechanically produces poetry based on its pulse, it would resemble a 'Machine' within the poet's body, acting automatically and doomed to break down eventually. 'Mechanic' suggests the fear that poetry is not a positive means of controlling the unruly heart and giving it a joyful peace, but a tired and tiring process in which pain can only be numbed, never relieved or cured. The pulse of the verse might hence be less a comfort than a dull progression, a wearing out or wearing down. Timothy Peltason reads the first sections of the poem as an 'attempt to live in a perpetual present of grief . . . inevitably frustrated by the mysterious forward momentum of consciousness'.[18] Reading this 'forward momentum' as the everyday beat of the heart, however, it could be seen as a physical reflex, and one at once perpetually present and moving through time. The speaker is thwarted not by his 'consciousness', his mind, but by his body—either by nature or perhaps by God's will working in it and sustaining it. If the heartbeat in the poem maintains steadiness and continuity in the face of the speaker's vacillations, it can be read as holding alive what might otherwise die; but of course the speaker is unsure whether death would be a peaceful release or a terrifying end. The pulse of the verse thus represents simultaneously a reassuring natural or heavenly process that underpins the uncertainties of the poem, and the frail beat of the desperately weakened human heart,

---

[17] To Frederick Tennyson, 31 Dec. 1850, in *Letters and Literary Remains of Edward FitzGerald*, ed. William Aldis Wright, 3 vols. (London: Macmillan, 1889), i. 208.

[18] Timothy Peltason, *Reading 'In Memoriam'* (Princeton: Princeton University Press, 1985), 26.

always threatening to stop, haunted by lingering sympathy with 'The darkened heart that beat no more' (XIX. 2).

For the reader, the general predictability of Tennyson's measures offers security and memorability. But such rhythmic predictability might also induce numbness. Robert Douglas-Fairhurst writes of Keats's Titans from 'Hyperion':

> [T]he most sympathetic response to the Titans could be a measured indifference to their fate, as we discover within the perpetual motion of their blood, fixed into the rhythms of printed verse, an imperturbability in the face of suffering to which they too must reconcile themselves.[19]

The description of the Titans' sufferings, their 'sanguine feverous boiling gurge of pulse' (II. 28), is almost perfectly regular: *measured* indifference is therefore a consciously appropriate description, as the reader's lack of sympathy for the Titans, Douglas-Fairhurst argues, springs precisely from Keats's decision not to embody their pain in rhythm. The poet of *In Memoriam* fears a similar indifference on the reader's part and on his own account, lest he should become indifferent to Hallam's loss. Hence the poem repeatedly and deliberately stages the memory of Hallam's death and its effects on the heart in terms of loss of balance, causing the poet to fluctuate between 'calm despair' and 'wild unrest'(XVI. 2). He writes in LXXXV:

> My blood an even tenor kept,
>   Till on mine ear this message falls, (17–18)

The news of Hallam's death is unexpectedly reported in the present tense, repeating the moment of shock. The poet continually refers back to the initial blow to his heart, as in VII:

> Doors, where my heart was *used* to beat
> So quickly, (3–4) [italics added]

---

[19] Robert Douglas-Fairhurst, *Victorian Afterlives: The Shaping of Influence in Nineteenth-Century Literature* (Oxford: Oxford University Press, 2002), 17.

The pause in the comma after 'Doors', and the two unstressed syllables of 'where my', speed up the line, as Tennyson's heartbeat quickens with anticipation. These doors are again suggestive of the valves of the heart, which shut in shock or pain, altering the regular circulation. Just as they are closed against Tennyson, so his heart is shut into itself, devoid of sympathy. The possible extra stress on 'So' again briefly suggests the tremor of a faster pulse as the metre remembers the effects of Hallam's presence, a presence immediately returned to absence. Even tenor is momentarily jarred, as in the use of the present tense in LXXXV. These moments of metrical or linguistic disturbance, like pangs of grief intruding into the slow, steady pulse, keep the heart embodied in the rhythm alive and responsive, not permitting it to sink into the lassitude of grief even as they are painful and damaging. While the regularity of the four-beat rhythm sets limits to metrical variation, then, the pulse wavers from moment to moment in the poem between over-slow and over-fast, both characteristics of disease.

If the rhythm is read as the pulse, Tennyson's form itself could represent the circulation, in the movements of the verse, the rhyme scheme, and the constant recurrence of themes and images in the larger cyclical pattern of the poem. W. David Shaw describes the action of *In Memoriam* as:

> An opening and a shutting of the hand, the heart, the mind. A motion of dilation, when grief stretches itself almost to the breaking point ... is followed by a contracting motion, when the mourner simply wants to throw his arms around his friend.[20]

The famous *abba* rhyme scheme encourages each stanza to circle back on itself, returning to the starting point. In Michael Wheeler's important discussion of the religious heart in *In Memoriam*, he observes that 'Four line stanzas are often not unlike the four-chambered heart in

---

[20] W. David Shaw, *Tennyson's Style* (Ithaca, NY: Cornell University Press, 1976), 139.

their systolic-diastolic movements.'[21] Eric Griffiths similarly identifies 'swelling and failing' as 'vital motions of the poetry'. He associates these motions with respiration, focusing primarily on the importance of breath and lungs, the physical movements involved in speaking the verse.[22] Beneath the rhythms of the breath and controlling them, however, lies the circulation of the blood and the heartbeat, at least according to Victorian medical opinion.[23]

While the form and rhythm of *In Memoriam* ensure that the heartbeat is a constant presence, the heart itself, though frequently mentioned in the poem, is rarely dwelt on. When the speaker does discuss his heart, he is restrained, restricting himself to brief and generalized mentions of his 'forsaken heart' (VIII. 18); Hallam's 'faithful heart' (XVIII. 14); or a more universalized 'unquiet heart' (V. 5). One explanation for this might be an anxiety about the language of the heart and its value in a poetic climate where such language was in common usage. Isobel Armstrong notes of the lines 'And dead calm in that noble breast | Which heaves but with the heaving deep' (XI. 19–20) that the 'dead language of poetic diction' in 'noble breast' counterpoints the poet's 'living, suffering "heart"'.[24] But Tennyson is, I would argue, more ambivalent about the heart in this particular example than Armstrong recognizes, given that 'heart' itself might easily be perceived as part of the 'dead language of poetic diction'. For this reason among others, *In Memoriam* is deeply concerned about cardiac metaphor. The word 'heart' both carries an immense weight of significance and is used bitterly, at times almost ironically, with the knowledge that this clichéd poetic invocation is

[21] Michael Wheeler, *Death and the Future Life in Victorian Literature and Theology* (Cambridge: Cambridge University Press, 1990), 225.

[22] Eric Griffiths, *The Printed Voice of Victorian Poetry* (Oxford: Clarendon Press, 1989), 106.

[23] 'Respiration's having been placed under the guidance of the motion of the heart, leads to the accomplishment of all its actions more completely than could have been done by any other means' (Joseph Swan, *An Essay on the Connection between the Action of the Heart and Arteries and the Functions of the Nervous System* (London: Longman, Rees, Orme, Brown and Green, 1829), 115.

[24] Isobel Armstrong, *Language as Living Form in Nineteenth-Century Poetry* (Brighton: Harvester, 1982), 189.

all that remains of Hallam's sympathetic heart. In *In Memoriam* VI, for instance, the speaker interrogates the commonplaces of loss:

> That loss is common would not make
> My own less bitter, rather more:
> Too common! Never morning wore
> To evening, but some heart did break. (VI. 5–8)

Tennyson stages the final sentence as a cliché, but the lack of quotation marks make the tone ambiguous. If he is uttering one of the pious condolences he has just rejected, does he do so ironically? Or is he hopeful that by stating this cliché he will confirm its truth in his own case, given that two sections earlier he orders his heart to break? At this point in the poem, he is angered rather than comforted by the thought of a community of loss. Yet by placing a commonplace in his own voice he participates in the linguistic community which he has identified. Susan Shatto and Marion Shaw cite Numbers 16: 29, 'If these men die the common death of all men', as the chief source for this section.[25] Another obvious allusion is to Hamlet's bitterness at Gertrude's soothing commonplace 'Thou know'st 'tis common—all that live must die.'[26] By positioning himself with Hamlet, Tennyson is against commonplace, but by virtually quoting Gertrude's line and Hamlet's caustic response ('Ay madam, it is common'), he acknowledges that his grief is in literary terms already common (though Shakespearian allusion might blur the sense of 'common' as coarse, lower class), and can only be expressed in the language of others. Using a clichéd image of heartbreak is simultaneously a way of integrating himself into a community of writers and readers, and of rejecting it.[27]

---

[25] *In Memoriam*, ed. Susan Shatto and Marion Shaw (Oxford: Clarendon Press, 1982), 167.

[26] *Hamlet*, I. ii. 72. *William Shakespeare: The Complete Works*, ed. Stanley Wells and Gary Taylor (Oxford: Clarendon Press, 1986). Peter Sacks identifies this allusion in *The English Elegy* (Baltimore: Johns Hopkins University Press, 1985), 174.

[27] See Christopher Ricks, 'Tennyson Inheriting the Earth', in Hallam Tennyson (ed.), *Studies in Tennyson* (London: Macmillan, 1981), 66–104. Ricks argues that allusions are an 'honourable seeking of relief in a community of interest' (p. 89).

The worry which seems to coalesce around particular references
to the heart is that if heart-centred metaphors are 'dead' then the
metaphorical reanimation of Hallam's heart in Tennyson's verse, so
that it would survive as symbol, an affective presence if not a living
organ, is an impossibility. Anxiety about the language of the heart
is thus associated both with the threat of Tennyson's heart failing
him and with the question of possible sympathy with Hallam's dead
heart through its poetic afterlife. This is already clear by the extended
image of the heart in IV:

> My will is bondsman to the dark;
> I sit within a helmless bark,
> And with my heart I muse and say:
>
> O heart, how fares it with thee now,
>   That thou should'st fail from thy desire,
>   Who scarcely darest to inquire,
> 'What is it makes me beat so low?'
>
> Something it is which thou hast lost,
>   Some pleasure from thine early years.
>   Break, thou deep vase of chilling tears,
> That grief hath shaken into frost! (2–12)

'With my heart' implies that the poet is thinking 'with' (by means
of) his heart, but the questions here also suggest that 'I' and 'my
heart' are two separate entities estranged within a darkened body.
That the heart is still living could here be ascribed merely to the
fact that it is outside the operations of the paralysed will. Up until
'Break', the tone is close to remote pity, but the disturbing emphasis
on the first syllable in line 11, the irruption of an exclamation into
this questioning, and the certainty of 'hath shaken' (as opposed to
'scarcely', 'something', 'muse') shock the reader. The command is
a shattering contrast to the mild question 'How fares it with thee
now?', as though the poet suddenly loses all patience with gentle
enquiry. This image of the 'deep vase' is the first explicit metaphor
for the heart, changing it from a living organism, possessed of voice
and movement, to a cold and inanimate container.

The fact that Tennyson suddenly moves into metaphor here might suggest that 'Break' cannot be placed in conjunction with 'heart' itself. The speaker desires heartbreak yet shrinks from a direct command. When he later wishes that 'my hold on life would break' (XXVIII. 15), 'hold on life' is similarly substituted for the heart, in a substitution which hints at the possibility that the heart itself represents this 'hold'. In 'Break, break, break', moreover, a poem written under the immediate impetus of Hallam's death, the broken or breaking heart is a potent absence. There is a form of reserve (discussed earlier in a religious context) operating here, as Tennyson turns away from and disguises painful emotions, perhaps because dwelling on the heart's feelings might seem again like immodest self-display. The irruption of 'Break' into IV makes it clear that the speaker cannot dwell on the heart without feelings of grief and anger breaking, dangerously, into his words, without breaking down. Moreover, the evasion of reference to the heart could signal fear that there is nothing living there to respond. Left with 'a void where heart on heart reposed' (XIII. 6), the speaker avoids looking too closely at this empty space. Only by 'scarcely daring to inquire' can the heart hope to survive and the speaker contain his emotion.

From this point onwards in *In Memoriam*, the heart—and Hallam's touch, his breath, and his pulse—tend to be implicated in imagery, diffused through figurative language, rather than openly discussed, perhaps because the failure of dialogue with the heart in IV has induced an anxiety about direct reference. Rather, as in Arnold's 'A Buried Life', Tennyson's language and imagery and of course the form and structure of the poem draw attention to the heart more subtly. Words such as 'beat' in *In Memoriam* have connotations with the pulse, yet allow the speaker to avoid explicitly writing of the heartbeat: the clock which 'Beats out the little lives of men' (II. 8), for instance, 'the life that beat from thee' (VI. 12), or 'At last he beat his music out' (XCVI. 10). In XLIX, the 'muffled motions' which 'blindly drown | The bases of my life in tears' (15–16) might also be associated with the sounds of the pulse in the depths of the body. The vision of Hallam as a 'central warmth diffusing bliss'

(LXXXIV. 6) likewise compares him to a heart, dispensing heat to 'all the branches of thy blood' (8). More externalized references, such as the 'wild pulsation' of the dove's wings in XII, remind us, in a reference to 'Locksley Hall' ('Make me feel the wild pulsation that I felt before the strife' (109)), of the lack of such feeling in the speaker's heart, or at least of his refusal to acknowledge it.

Having resigned the will, however, the heart is the only entity still striving to hold together 'A weight of nerves without a mind' (XII. 7). The continuing pulsation of the rhythm might offer a reassurance that it is still working behind the speaker's fluctuations. Tennyson may try to escape his own heart and body—'I seem to fail from out my blood' he writes in II, seeking to exchange the fallible, changing human frame and the physical insistence of the heart and circulation for the yew tree's 'stubborn hardihood'—but he needs the heart, blood, and circulation to keep going, not merely in order to survive, but in order to cure himself of grief by reaching a point where he can again feel sympathy. The movement in the poem is towards a slow acceptance of the speaker's own heart and the possible uses of figurative language related to the heart. Through his gradual use of heart-centred imagery to indicate recovery he also demonstrates that such language is not worthless cliché or empty rhetoric. Rather, it might have meaningful referents and purposes, one of which would be the transmission of affect. Tennyson is using the heart in this poem to interrogate the value of poetry itself, and through form and imagery he arguably reaches the conclusion that poetry can be affective, not least in remembering Hallam's heart and recreating sympathy with it. His conviction of Hallam's afterlife and resurrection can rest on a feeling of involvement with the 'deep pulsations of the world' (XCV. 40), pulsations at once imaginatively intertwined with and at a remove from the literal beat of Hallam's heart.

By LVIII Tennyson has reached a turning point in his search for sympathy because he has started to appreciate the possibilities of touching other hearts. LVIII describes the affect of his earlier words, which until now were deeply concerned with the survival of his own heart:

As drop by drop the water falls
In vaults and catacombs, they fell;
And falling, idly broke the peace
  Of hearts that beat from day to day,
  Half-conscious of their dying clay,
And those cold crypts where they shall cease. (3–8)

Again 'heart' is found in conjunction with 'broke' but not, we note, as the subject of the verb. 'Vaults' and 'sepulchral halls' seem connected to these crypts so that the words/water-drops, at first falling 'as if' into a grave, now appear to be falling on entombed hearts. The emptiness imagined here is both inside and outside the body, which has been figured in earlier sections as desolate, and associated with imagery of deserted houses, closed gates and doors, cold and silent spaces, 'the chambers emptied of delight' (VIII. 8). Unlike the poet's heart, these hearts live solely in the present ('from day to day') and have no connection to any wider rhythm. The ambiguous tone of Tennyson's reference to these 'half-conscious' hearts (with almost a note of relish in the alliterative 'cold crypts') could signal a longing, like them, to be unaware of his own mortality, but might equally indicate his sense, as a poet, of his own superiority over banal day-by-day existence. It is possible that he intends a slight emphasis on '*they* shall cease'. His heart, fully conscious of its dying clay, might find a means of survival—perhaps through the medium of poetry itself.

The remembrance of earlier poems in LVIII suggests that a change has occurred. 'Idly' implies a lack of thought and responsibility, but now the poet is moving towards a position of agency and a reanimation of the heart. When he resumes his questioning of 'measured language' in LXXV, the measure of verse 'brings myself relief' (2). It is now his own choice. Rather than numbing pain, 'relief' suggests the physical relief of tears and sighs—both of which are associated with releasing the pressure of the distended, swollen heart. Moreover, this suggests that the poet may be open to sympathy and ready to participate in a wider community. In LXVI, shortly after proclaiming 'You thought my heart too far diseased', he writes that grief has 'made me kindly with my kind' (7). This is a triumph of healthy sympathy. 'Today they count as kindred souls' (19), the speaker writes of other mourners in XCIX. Shortly afterwards, he announces:

> I will not shut me from my kind,
>   And, lest I stiffen into stone,
>   I will not eat my heart alone,
> Nor feed with sighs a passing wind: (CVIII. 1–4)

There is a sense of determination here very different from the passivity of the speaker at the start of the poem. 'Kind' in *In Memoriam* does, however, always carry the weight of Hamlet's bitter description of himself as 'A little more than kin, and less than kind' (I. ii. 65), a line which haunts the poet's optimism by raising the question of who exactly counts as one's 'kind'. There are various communities offered within the poem: other mourners; Tennyson's 'kin', his blood family; his readers; and, lastly, the community of the dead. Hallam's heart is described in LXXXV as 'with kindliest motion warm' (34)—akin to him, kind to him, and also kindling him into poetic inspiration. Tennyson plays on the possibility that 'kindness' creates kinship, envisaging a time when all men, like Hallam, will possess 'The larger heart, the kindlier hand' (CVI. 30).

When family and community were mentioned earlier in *In Memoriam* they were associated with loss and death. Yet by CVII, the third Christmas, the family are able to celebrate cheerfully for the first time,

> Bring in great logs and let them lie,
>   To make a solid core of heat;
>   Be cheerful-minded, (17–19)

'Core' and 'heat' both symbolically suggest the renewal of the heart, strongly associated throughout the poem with the 'hearth' in the household, as in XX, 'For by the hearth the children sit | Cold in that atmosphere of death' (13–14). 'Core' recalls the fears of XXXIV:

> My own dim life should teach me this,
>   That life shall live for evermore,
>   Else earth is darkness at the core,
> And dust and ashes all that is. (1–4)

The fires in the centre of the earth, in a metaphor drawn from geology, threaten to go out. In this section Tennyson replaced 'My dark heart shall teach me this' in the first line with 'My dim life'. The first version indicates more strongly, in the relation between 'dark heart' and 'darkness at the core'—two phrases that are practically synonymous—that the heart's illness can be projected outwards onto the world, a world growing colder and darker with passing time. Fire in the heart(h) will annihilate such gloom, as will the company of others, the solid core of Tennyson's family.

In order that his pulses may 'beat again | For other friends' (LXXXV. 57–8) the poet needs to reach the point where he is assured of Hallam's being 'working' (LXXXV. 43) in his own. In other words, rather than being a weight on the heart, the knowledge of Hallam's past love—and his present afterlife—will sustain it. LXXXV recapitulates the whole process of grieving up to this point. The poet again questions ''Tis better to have loved and lost' and explains to an auditor how he is able to love anew despite having a 'widowed' heart (113). In this section Tennyson represents his heart as first 'virgin', then 'married' to Hallam, which suggests that he genders it feminine. Love, whether sexual or not, took the heart's innocence because it has become aware of the desire to be regulated by another heartbeat. The alternative is to dwell alone on loss and sorrow, like the heart:

> That beats within a lonely place,
> That yet remembers his embrace,
> But at his footstep leaps no more, (110–12)

Here the heart 'may not rest | Quite in the love of what is gone'(113–14). The possible pun on 'quite' ('quiet') indicates again that the poet's heart will not rest peacefully but seeks to continue, to

beat on. Indeed, the poet is now actively seeking a replacement for
Hallam's heart, as his own

> [S]eeks to beat in time with one
> That warms another living breast. (115–16)

The nice distinction in 'living' shows that Hallam is not forgotten.
Earlier in this section Tennyson twice uses the line 'My old affection
of the tomb':

> And every pulse of wind and wave
>   Recalls, in change of light or gloom,
>   My old affection of the tomb,
> And my prime passion in the grave: (73–6)

These waves remember the hostile sea of 'Break, break, break'
and suggest that oceanic circulation now recalls positive memories.
Remembering the medical connotations of 'affection' and 'passion',
according to which these terms indicate dangerous illness or infection,
it is tempting to read the 'affection of the tomb' as a statement of
the death of Tennyson's illness; perhaps even a recognition of the
affectations of grief (noting that 'of' not 'in' the tomb). In the
following stanzas this 'affection' takes on Hallam's ghostly voice,
telling the poet to seek a new friendship. Tennyson's reply, 'Canst
thou feel for me | Some painless sympathy with pain?' (87–8),
is crucial since it admits the possibility that sympathy, albeit on a
heavenly plane, *can* be painless. Hallam's healing sympathy from the
grave demonstrates that communication between the dead and the
living heart is possible, and therefore hints at an afterlife dependent
on sympathy felt by the living for the dead and vice versa.

In CXXII, Tennyson imagines how Hallam could be reanimated
in his body:

> If thou wert with me, and the grave
>   Divide us not, be with me now,
>   And enter in at breast and brow,
> Till all my blood, a fuller wave,
>
> Be quickened with a livelier breath. (CXXII. 9–13)

The comparison of blood and pulses to waves, hinted at in LXXV, now suggests a greater acceptance of cardiac metaphor, as the poet becomes more in tune with the motions of his heart. The 'pulse of wind and wave' which is externalized in LXXXV is accepted as a bodily motion, and so the poet's body is interfused with the natural world, no longer alienated. The relation between heart and lungs (and heart and mind, 'brow') is one of mutual cooperation. Thinking, breathing, and pulsing are all human actions which have previously been associated with weariness and despair in the poem, and are now regaining dynamism. Hallam enters the poet's body as into the body of the poem, inspiring more heartfelt poetry. 'If thou wert with me' also harks back to Tennyson's mystical experience of unity with Hallam through the 'deep pulsations of the world' (XCV. 40):

> Æonian music measuring out
> The steps of Time—the shocks of Chance—
> The blows of Death. (41–3)

The implicit presence of a force 'measuring' the shocks and blows under which the poet has suffered suggests that all this suffering has been directed towards some end, and perhaps introduces another sense of measure, that of desert. If the fluctuations within the speaker are perceived as deliberately 'measured out', then the poem's measure *has* been imposed from without; the poet has been resisting its Divine origin. In this moment, cosmic pulsations indicate that there is a use in blood and breath other than to lead to the grave, and remind the poet that physical rhythm in the body can connect the human to the Divine. Hence man is more than 'wholly brain' and more than wholly clay (CXX. 2). For Tennyson it is now imperative that man is not dust, that the processes and motions of the human body are not pointless, as Hallam's presence is thus joyfully envisaged as a quickening of the pulse and the breath, a welcome speeding up of rhythm.

This new-founded hope is also represented in a greater acceptance of circulation and of the processes of nature. When spring arrives for the third time in the poem it awakens in the poet's heart (CXV), in response, perhaps, to the memory of the time when 'all the secrets of the Spring | Moved in the chambers of the blood' (XXIII. 19–20) as he walked with Hallam. Cold and deserted chambers from earlier in the poem, now specifically referring to the heart, are infused with new life and hope. Towards the end of *In Memoriam*, as Alan Sinfield notes, the poet 'consistently rejoices in the processes of nature', which is perceived anew as 'breathing or pulsing with life', effects which are transmitted to the poet's respiratory and circulatory systems.[28] Acceptance of the cyclical movements of the season, and an openness (shown in repeated imagery) to remembering the past, gives the heart in *In Memoriam* the will to carry on. It is sustained by wider movements of circulation, as well as the enduring pulse.

In CXXIV, two sections after this re-energizing of blood and breath, Tennyson writes:

> If e'er when faith had fallen asleep,
>   I heard a voice 'believe no more'
>   And heard an ever-breaking shore
> That tumbled in the Godless deep;
>
> A warmth within the breast would melt
>   The freezing reason's colder part,
>   And like a man in wrath the heart
> Stood up and answered 'I have felt.' (9–16)

The heart counters the force of 'ever-*breaking*' by proving its wholeness. But with 'the' rather than 'my' the heart speaks for itself, not necessarily for the whole body and still less for the mind. 'Freezing', previously an attribute of the heart in IV, is transferred to the reason. The heart, seemingly fully personified, takes over the speaker to provide its own answer—as though finally impatient with the vacillations of the poet's voice, cured, and able to intervene directly and explicitly in the process of the poem. Its actions do still seem beyond the poet's control, but rather than slow weariness it is quick, alive to

---

[28] Alan Sinfield, *The Language of Tennyson's 'In Memoriam'* (Oxford: Blackwell, 1971), 122.

action and response. 'I have felt' is a definitive statement because it is not necessary to say what has been felt. This famous moment seems to demonstrate that 'the heat of inward evidence' (a phrase from 'The Two Voices' (284)) is the final proof of faith. As in Carlyle and Hallam's assertions, cited earlier, the motions of the heart validate belief. Tucker points out, however, that 'the spontaneous language of the heart is quoted speech'.[29] It is distanced by the past tense and by the speaker's failure to say this himself. Moreover, to say 'I have felt' as a religious assertion was almost a cliché in itself by this point, and (as we saw in Chapter 4) one that was treated with suspicion by some religious writers.

The certainty of this passage is modified in succeeding stanzas, but it still provides proof of the necessity of the heart's responses. Immediately afterwards, CXXV describes how Hope will now abide with the poet, until 'this electric force, that keeps | A thousand pulses dancing, fail' (15–16). 'This' force suggests a specific reference, as though by 'this' he gestures towards himself, referring to an internal power which might be aligned with the forceful heart of the previous section. It seems he is now part of the unity of 'a thousand pulses', beating together. The passing of time in *In Memoriam* brings about a resurrection not of but in the body. In the process of beating towards death the pulse has 'Remade the blood and changed the frame' (Epilogue, 11). This is a religious renewal: 'A new heart also will I give you, a new spirit will I put within you: and I will take the stony heart out of your flesh, and I will give you an heart of flesh' (Ezekiel 36: 26). But it is also a physiological remaking. With the appreciation of the constant changes within the body, changes presided over and participated in by heart and circulation, the body does gain a kind of immortality; it is part of the general circulation carried out in nature. Similarly, the pulse is strengthened in its individual beat by the realization of greater rhythmic processes and measures connected to Nature and God and by a sympathetic communication with the

---

[29] Herbert Tucker, *Tennyson and the Doom of Romanticism* (Cambridge, Mass.: Harvard University Press, 1988), 403.

dead. This realization involves an acceptance of the role of a heart and pulse which are not entirely figurative, but not simply literal either: an acceptance that metaphorical implications of the heart can also be trusted and perceived as meaningful. The poet thus gains the heart to carry on. Whatever religious progress is made in *In Memoriam*, the individual progress made by the speaker is from bodily sickness to health, from mourning to consolation. And as the poet finds his heart again and accesses feeling, so the reader experiencing this process might be enabled to do the same: Tennyson's poem eventually does work like the various repetitive and soothing rhythms he initially rejects, to draw the heart into time. Earlier poems and later will return to the sickness; this tentatively approaches the cure.

In the years between 1850 and 1855 Tennyson took up his role as national poet, and many of the poems he composed were marked by an overt engagement with public affairs. *Maud*'s blending of social and personal ills reflects this shift. *Maud* is Tennyson's most sustained effort in the creation of a character and a narrative which are trapped in subjectivity, morbidly aware of sensation, and, in his words, 'constitutionally diseased'. 'Constitutionally' suggests both a disease inherent in (and inherited by) the individual and one caused at least partly by 'the circumstances of the time', the constitution of the country.[30] The speaker of this poem suffers from an illness that is, in medical terms, at once organic and sympathetic, and as in the case studies of physiologists, one informs and worsens the other. If *In Memoriam* can be read as an affective poem in the tradition of curative religious poetry, *Maud* must be read as a sensational, even spasmodic poem, in part a reaction to new writing emerging in the early 1850s—in particular 'Empedocles on Etna', 'A Buried Life', and Smith's 'A Life-Drama'—and in part a return to the concerns of many of Tennyson's early poems. As such, it investigates the possibility which *In Memoriam* eventually rejects—that sympathy

---

[30] 'I took a man constitutionally diseased and dipt him into the circumstances of the time and took him out on fire.' Tennyson to Archer Gurney, 6 Dec. 1855, Lang and Shannon, ii. 138.

could spread not health, but disease. The heart in *Maud* is embedded in the same anxieties and ambiguities as in *In Memoriam*: sickened, subjected to sudden shocks and starts through emotional turmoil, seeking security in love for one person or in sympathy with the community. Yet these poems use the pathological heart for very different ends. The speaker of *In Memoriam*, I have argued, cannot or will not write at length of the heart, but its presence informs much of the imagery, and is a constant (in the sense of faithful, as well as continuous) presence in the metre of his poem. The speaker of *Maud* mentions the heart much more often, dwelling on its symptoms and actions in flamboyantly metaphorical but uncertain terms. The effect of his references, however, is not to concentrate knowledge of the heart but to dissipate it. In *Maud*, there is no formal or rhythmic stability, the heart no longer acts as guarantee for the survival of the self, and a return to health seems largely out of reach.

Organic and sympathetic heart disease manifest themselves in similar symptoms (either hardness, coldness, distension, and a slow pulse, or alternatively burning, throbbing, a rapid pulse, and loss of breath) and lead to similar results. The negotiation between them, however, could be crucial for the speaker in terms of agency. Being sick, particularly having a diseased heart, allows him to claim that his near-madness has physical rather than (or at least as well as) mental causes. If these physical causes, moreover, are due to external factors and 'sympathetic' responses to his environment, then his illness is symptomatic of the age and is beyond his control. Matthew Allen, a well-known doctor and erstwhile friend and acquaintance of Tennyson, directly linked organic disease to the state of society in his treatise on insanity:

> It need scarcely be mentioned, that the present constitution of society is not in a healthy state. It is not bound together by that order and sympathy which should exist, but on the contrary, discord and disseverment prevail to an extent which seems to threaten its decomposition and destruction.[31]

---

[31] Matthew Allen, *Essay on the Classification of the Insane* (London: John Taylor, 1837), 18.

Both 'constitution' and 'state' in this passage (as in Tennyson's use of 'constitutionally') can almost be taken verbatim. The British state itself is 'altered and dangerous'. Writing in 1837, Allen assumes his reader's awareness of the constitutional links between the increase in insanity and the disorders of the state: a fact that the speaker of *Maud* is clearly familiar with. Roger Platizky argues convincingly that *Maud* and several of Tennyson's other poems are heavily influenced by contemporary works on insanity, including the influential writings of George Man Burrows.[32] Tennyson's knowledge of Burrows's work could easily have extended to familiarity with his book on the relation between insanity and heart disease. As noted in Chapter 1, Burrows writes extensively on 'the frequent and intimate relation subsisting between structural changes in the heart and these important cerebral affections'.[33] The emphasis on the deranged heart in *Maud* is therefore important not just as one symptom of incipient madness but as the root which might underlie it, with the initial shock to the speaker's heart inaugurating 'structural changes' that create the mood and even the form, the structure, of the rest of the poem. The speaker of *Maud*, indeed, fits so precisely into the stereotype of the sufferer from nervous heart disease, and has experienced every upsetting cause listed by experts on the condition—the sudden death of a loved one; the failure of a 'vast speculation'; sexual passion followed by disappointment in love; political upsets and disruptions and finally war—that it is difficult to believe Tennyson is not making a deliberate reference to this particular medical discourse.[34] John

[32] Roger S. Platizky, *A Blueprint of his Dissent: Madness and Method in Tennyson's Poetry* (London: AUP, 1989), 36.

[33] George Man Burrows, *On Disorders of the Cerebral Circulation; and on the Connection between Affections of the Brain and Diseases of the Heart* (Philadelphia: Lea and Blanchard, 1848), 122.

[34] Tennyson had experienced most of these causes himself, albeit to a lesser extent than his speaker. Ralph W. Rader explores the connections between them in *Tennyson's 'Maud': The Biographical Genesis* (Berkeley and Los Angeles: University of California Press, 1963). Ironically, Tennyson's depression in the 1840s was partly due to the collapse of Allen's wood-carving scheme, in which he and his family had heavily invested. They only recouped their money on Allen's death from heart disease. See Christopher Ricks, *Tennyson*, 2nd edn. (London: Macmillan, 1989), 164–7.

Williams, who includes all these causes in his revised introduction to *Practical Observations on Nervous and Sympathetic Palpitation of the Heart*, written two years before *Maud*'s publication, states that such sympathetic disorders are most common in men aged 15–25. At 25, then, Tennyson's speaker just falls into this range.[35] If he successfully locates himself within a pathological discourse and represents himself as suffering from an environmental, sympathetic disease, then he can disengage from assuming responsibility for his speech and actions. As James Kincaid nicely remarks, 'He is not angry, but smug,' perhaps because medical theories have neatly provided several excuses for his condition.[36] Platizky suggests that madness in *Maud* is 'a psychotic defence mechanism against having to communicate with others, to share a collective humanity'.[37] Unlike the speaker of *In Memoriam*, who slowly realizes the need for reintegration, the hero of *Maud* spends most of the poem vehemently asserting his lack of kind (and the general lack of kindness) in modern society, and refuses to enter into sympathetic, heart-based communication with others. Linda Shires associates this rejection of community with new ideas of manliness which focused on the inward-looking individual rather than male solidarity.[38] Her argument is also relevant to the speaker's disease because the 'poetic crisis' about manly verse which she identifies led, as we saw in Chapter 3, to anxiety about the feminized heart and its increased likelihood to develop circulatory and nervous disorders. Repeated imagery in *Maud* invariably refers to the heart as something other, alien, regarded with clinical detachment. Even Maud's love, which might have offered redemption and rejuvenation for the speaker's heart, only has the effect of altering the type of symptoms he feels, so that the heart of stone, dead to all feeling, is replaced with the desperately sensitive, violently disordered heart,

---

[35] John Williams, *Practical Observations on Nervous and Sympathetic Palpitation of the Heart*, 2nd edn. (London: John Churchill, 1852), 158.

[36] James R. Kincaid, *Tennyson's Major Poems: The Comic and Ironic Patterns* (New Haven: Yale University Press, 1975), 117.

[37] Platizky, 61.

[38] Linda Shires, '*Maud*, Masculinity and Poetic Identity', *Criticism*, 29 (1987), 269–90 (p. 274).

pulse, and circulation. At the end of the poem, I suggest, the speaker does not regain health but instead manages to incorporate the heart's pathology (rather than sympathy) into a common cause, finding a language and a situation which permit him to surrender the effort of dealing with his heart alone, and which—ironically—make his blood-ridden language appear normal, if not worthy.

Maud was read by contemporaries as another spasmodic poem, and after *In Memoriam* it was widely seen as a regression (a further regression, for those critics who read *In Memoriam* as morbid and self-obsessed) into madness and disorder, a poem that would produce confusion and discord in the reader. 'God makes these morbid, hysterical, spasmodic individuals occasionally', argues Brimley in a defence of the speaker.[39] Joseph Collins has argued that Tennyson influenced spasmodic poems, rather than vice versa, and that most of their salient characteristics can be found in Tennyson's early work.[40] While this is undoubtedly true, the popularity of spasmodism in the early 1850s might have encouraged Tennyson to return to these poetic interests and rework them to further extremes. Weinstein, for instance, points out that what he terms 'the Spasmodic paradox', a hero who claims interest in society yet is wholly subjective in outlook, is entirely relevant to *Maud*.[41] Violent and grotesque imagery, shifts in tone and form, and an emphasis on love as a redemptive force are also characteristic of the genre. Above all, however, what *Maud* has in common with poems of the 1850s by Arnold, Dobell, Smith, Barrett Browning, Westland Marston, and Stanyan Bigg is that they all describe various losses of control that are envisaged as involuntary actions, and they focus with relish on physiological and pathological imagery.

[39] George Brimley, *Essays*, ed. William George Clark (Cambridge: Macmillan, 1858), 78.

[40] Joseph J. Collins, 'Tennyson and the Spasmodics', *Victorian Newsletter*, 43 (1974), 24–8.

[41] Mark A. Weinstein, *William Edmonstoune Aytoun and the Spasmodic Controversy* (New Haven: Yale University Press, 1968), 89.

The opening stanzas of *Maud* introduce the unbalancing 'shock' suffered by the speaker:

> And my pulses closed their gates with a shock on my heart as I heard
> The shrill-edged shriek of a mother divide the shuddering night.
>
> (I. iv. 14–15)

This shock is insistently physical due to the placing of the phrase 'on my heart'—although 'shock' probably refers back to the pulses it appears to act *on* the physical organ, as the gates, the valves of the heart, shut upon it. A shock 'in' the heart would not carry the same implication of a blow falling, a physical jolt to the passive heart. From this destabilizing moment onwards, imagery of heart, pulse, and circulation and rhythmic and formal variation are endemic. Also in the opening sections, for instance, the ruin of the speaker's father is envisaged as a cross between vampirism and leeching: his rival 'Dropt off gorged from a scheme that had left us flaccid and drained' (I. i. 20). 'Us'—the speaker's blood has also been depleted by this family loss. Blood is not specifically mentioned, but the opening lines of *Maud* have set up a 'horror of blood' (I. i. 3), which encourages the reader to expect its presence here. Ernest Jones's 'The Cost of Glory', published in the same year as *Maud* and also sometimes described as a spasmodic poem, contains a strikingly similar image of vampirism, describing the actions of an avaricious lawyer in defrauding the heir to the estate. This lawyer:

> [L]ent to him from whom, 'tis said,
> He once had begged his daily bread:
> Steadily opened pore by pore,
> With a lulling lure and a winning word
> Like the flapping wing of the vampire-bird,
> And sucked—and sucked—till he bled no more;
> Then changed his tune in a single hour;
> He felt, and he let him feel his power,
> Nor one poor drop of gold would fetch
> To slake the thirst of the perishing wretch;

> But when he found he had sucked him dry,
> He turned his back and let him die.[42]

The absence of an object in the first line here (not 'steadily opened *him*') makes the suffering hero appear to consist of his body alone, as if it is his 'pores' themselves which are lulled into quiescence. These actions are narrated from an outside perspective, with a fascination that almost makes Tennyson's equivalent passage seem understated. Both poets take the metaphor of blood as money and the competitor as vampire and make its consequences literally fatal to the victims. This process is also one of emasculation, given that the blood of the weaker and less worldly man in both cases is transferred to the more potent rival.

The dishonour of being left 'flaccid and drained' might explain why in its next appearance in *Maud* the heart is stony, with the emphasis on firmness and assertion, the opposite of flaccidity. 'May make my heart as a millstone, set my face as a flint' (I. i. 31) is the speaker's response to the evils of the 'golden age', an implicit linkage of himself with the Book of Job, where the heart of the monstrous Leviathan is 'as hard as a piece of the nether millstone' (41: 24). The reworking of this in *Maud* moves it from simile towards metaphor: not 'as hard as' but simply 'as'. 'May', however, contradicts this assertiveness because it hovers dubiously between the sense of 'I am able to' and 'I might'. Despite the tentative claim to agency this seems like a cross between defiance and wishful thinking. And even this possibility of negative action has vanished by I. vi. 264, where the world outside has apparently pre-empted the speaker in turning his heart to stone:

> Till a morbid hate and horror have grown
> Of a world in which I have hardly mixt,
> And a morbid eating lichen fixt
> On a heart half-turned to stone. (I. vi. 264–7)

These final four lines return to the *In Memoriam* rhyme scheme for the first time in this section, with the turning inwards of the central

---

[42] Ernest Jones, *The Battle-Day, and Other Poems* (London: G. Routledge, 1855), 5.

lines here reflecting the speaker's paralysing self-regard. Anapaests at the start of each line, rather than the iambic or trochaic foot of *In Memoriam*, hurry the lines onward, before they themselves become 'fixt' in impotence. The archaic spelling of 'mixt' and 'fixt' brings the words up short, emphasizing constraint, as well as adding to the alliterative build-up of 't' and 'h' in the passage (both of which are emphasized in 'heart'). Lichen, like the 'marish mosses' in 'Mariana' (40), is slow-moving but tenacious, as the contrasts of 'eating/fixt' seem to demonstrate. Rather than the speaker eating his own heart, it is being eaten—he tries to transfer his own actions onto something external. 'My heart' has become 'a heart', not even taking the definite article as in *In Memoriam*, and 'may make' has become the passives 'have grown' and 'fixt'.

Initially 'sick to the heart of life' due to the baleful influences of society and grief at his father's death, the speaker's sickness takes a new turn when the pangs of love begin to affect him. The heart '*half*-turned to stone' is immediately followed by:

> O heart of stone, are you flesh, and caught
> By that you swore to withstand? (I. vi. 268–9)

The heart hardened and calcified in political antagonism has apparently melted in the heat of love. But it is now 'you', entirely separate from the speaker. Recalling Othello's (rather premature) assertion to Iago on planning to kill Desdemona, 'No, my heart is turned to stone; I strike it, and it hurts my hand,' the heart of stone now seems intended to signify the speaker's imperviousness to love; an imperviousness which we suspect he is proud of.[43] There is a sense of reproach here, addressed to an unruly organ which is failing the speaker. He transfers his susceptibility to Maud onto the heart and then blames it for his weakness. 'I fear', in the next lines, with the double implication that the speaker is afraid the heart has given in, and afraid of love itself, makes his sensitivity to love explicit:

---

[43] *Othello*, IV. i. 178. Susan Shatto identifies this reference in *Tennyson's Maud: A Definitive Edition* (London: Athlone Press, 1986), 182.

> For what was it else within me wrought
> But, I fear, the new strong wine of love,
> That made my tongue so stammer and trip (I. vi. 270–2)

The speaker's focus has moved from the consideration of the heart's possible reactions to the world outside, to its workings 'within'. Both the heart of stone and the wine are religious images, associated with the new life brought by Christ in the Gospels. The speaker thus emphasizes the intensity of his love, almost verging on blasphemy. Philip Bailey, in his popular spasmodic poem 'Festus', which Tennyson apparently admired, has his hero declaim at a moment of heightened passion:

> And thou, my blood, my bright red running soul—
> Wine of my life, which makest drunk my soul,
> Rejoice thou, like a river in thy rapids![44]

Festus, the Faust-like character, exalts the heart's passions as part of his fall into intellectual pride and sensuality. In Tennyson's lines, the stammer, seen in the pauses around 'I fear', demonstrates that love is already working a change that affects speech and breath. 'Catch not my breath, O clamorous heart'(I. xvi. 567), as the speaker instructs when he is preparing to ask Maud about her feelings. R. J. Mann described this short stanza as 'the one *spasm* of the poem', a comment which again suggests that those parts of the poem where the heart is escaping the speaker's mind and will are the most 'spasmodic'.[45]

The speaker's failure to escape 'heart-free' from his encounters with Maud is explicitly revealed when their eyes meet in church, producing an extreme heartfelt response:

> And once, but once, she lifted her eyes,
> And suddenly, sweetly, strangely blushed
> To find they were met by my own;

---

[44] Philip Bailey, *Festus* (London: William Pickering, 1839), 135. For Tennyson on Bailey, see Lang and Shannon, i. 265.

[45] R. J. Mann, *Tennyson's 'Maud' Vindicated: An Explanatory Essay* (London: Jarrold, 1856), 35.

> And suddenly, sweetly, my heart beat stronger
> And thicker, until I heard no longer
> The snowy-banded, dilettante,
> Delicate-handed priest intone. (I. viii. 305–12)

Suddenly the speaker is thrust into a new role. Although still suffering himself from an inescapable physical response, he becomes aware of the fact that Maud is responding to him as he does to her, an awareness made manifest in the exact repetition in lines 306–8. The lines speed up with his heart, through internal rhymes ('banded/ante/handed') and consonance. It is 'strange' that Maud should blush because all his earlier descriptions of her have stressed coldness and paleness, a lack of blood. Her blush of consciousness places her in a position of weakness. The speaker's heart becomes more manly and forceful—and notably is then 'my heart' again. His mastery is immediately impaired, however, when he too is overcome by the violence of his reactions, to an extent that suggests a case of palpitation: 'From a slight cause the action of the heart will become tumultuous, the pulse accelerated, propelling the blood to the most minute of its arterial ramifications, and laying the foundation of functional disturbance.'[46] Furthermore, there is an uneasy negotiation between 'sweetly', which suggests a feminine delicacy, and 'stronger and thicker'. Later the speaker will delight himself with the thought that he can hold 'dominion sweet' (I. xvi. 548) over Maud's pulse: this is his first sign that such lordship is possible. But 'sweet' also takes on the connotations of a high-pitched, maddening sensibility, as in Keats's 'Endymion':

> His poor temples beat
> To the very tune of love—how sweet, sweet, sweet. (II. 764–5)

W. O. Markham notes that such a loud and rapid pulse can be deceptive. Apparently indicating health, it is actually a symptom of the reverse. A 'hard, sharp and quick impulse', like a hammer-blow, frequently indicates the weakness of the heart. Ominously for the

---

[46] John Williams, 92.

masculinity of the speaker, he continues, 'Such a beat is met with often in weak and excitable females.'[47] In addition, since numerous medical writers associated dangerous palpitations with an excessive interest in love and sex, the possibility is raised that rather than providing an antidote to the world's sickness, the speaker's love for Maud might itself be disturbed. Harmless symptoms of love are exaggerated by the speaker's heart until they border on the pathological, further indicated by the fact that the intonations of church ritual (specifically High Church in this instance), signifying continuity and community, are drowned out by the insistently physical rhythm of the body. Such overwhelming of the affective powers of religion by those of love can be threatening to the lovers themselves, as Poe remarked:

> They fell, for Heaven to them no hope imparts
> Who hear not for the beating of their hearts.[48]

The insistently thumping heart is as symptomatic of danger as the earlier heart of stone.

Even at those moments in the poem when love is reciprocated and the speaker's blood ought to be most healthy, his tranquillity is never allowed to last. A new sympathetic disturbance inevitably arises. At I. xviii. 600, for example, he seems to have 'become aware of his life's flow' and thus reached an Arnoldian 'lull in the hot race' ('The Buried Life', 88, 91):

> And never yet so warmly ran my blood
> And sweetly, on and on
> Calming itself to the long-wished-for end,
> Full to the banks, close on the promised good. (I. xviii. 601–4)

The first line is a steady iambic pentameter, a rhythm rare in this poem. Blood which runs 'freely, in very *dilatable canals*' is a sign of

---

[47] W. O. Markham, *Diseases of the Heart: Their Pathology, Diagnosis and Treatment*, 2nd edn. (London: John Churchill, 1860), 98.

[48] Edgar Allan Poe, 'Al Araaf', concluding lines, Mabbott, i. 94.

good health.[49] But the blood here is not quite calm but 'calming', not quite at the 'good' but approaching it, just as the rhyme of 'blood' and 'good' is close but not perfect. In fact, by the following stanza, the sound of Maud's steps 'shook my heart': he is still at the mercy of his pulses. Similarly, 'Beat, happy stars' (I. xviii. 679) has been cited as representative of the speaker's entrance into cosmic rhythm, as in *In Memoriam* XCV, and is recognized by Mann as 'that variation of rhythmic flow which swells and contracts, like the rise and fall of a melody issuing from ... a passionate human heart'.[50] Critics have been almost unanimous in reading this passage as a sign of positive recovery:

> Beat, happy stars, timing with things below,
> Beat with my heart more blest than heart can tell,
> Blest, but for some dark undercurrent woe
> That seems to draw—but it shall not be so:
> Let all be well, be well. (I. xviii. 679–83)

Observing the night sky 'Throbbing with stars like pulses', however, is a very spasmodic tendency, and therefore probably not the best indication of renewed health.[51] Like the spasmodic heroes cited earlier, the speaker is unable to escape his subjectivity. 'Things below' do not move in tune with the heavens, instead the stars pulsate to human rhythm. By the third line, 'but' creeps in and with it a river that is not calm but dark and threatening: Arnold's 'buried stream'. The change in the commencement of the fourth line, from a firm monosyllable to the iamb 'That seems', marks an ominous irregularity before the stop that jars the music out of time. Just when it appears that all is well it becomes clear, once again, that the heart cannot beat temperately but is subject to unexpected fits and starts. The speaker's dark hints suggest an underlying pathology that he will not reveal and 'shall not be so' and 'let all be well' are firmly

[49] Thomas Burgess, *The Physiology or Mechanism of Blushing* (London: John Churchill, 1839), 59.
[50] Mann, 50.
[51] Smith, 'A Life-Drama', in *Poems* (London: David Bogue, 1853), 4.

conditional. Moreover, it is dubious whether this moment really indicates the underlying harmony of the speaker and the world, as in *In Memoriam*, or whether it is rather an instance of pathetic fallacy, of projection caused by love. As one lover in 'Night and the Soul' comments:

> To those who love, the universe,
> Like a great heart, is ever beating;
> And every strong pulsation keeps
> The one dear loved name still repeating.[52]

Remembering the birds that cry 'Maud, Maud, Maud' to the speaker, it seems that this too could be another instance of subjective rather than objective sympathy.

The final instance of an (apparently) joyous heart is also the most famous, the conclusion to the lyric 'Come into the garden, Maud':

> My heart would hear her and beat,
>   Were it earth in an earthy bed;
> My dust would hear her and beat,
>   Had I lain for a century dead;
> Would start and tremble under her feet,
>   And blossom in purple and red. (I. xxii. 918–23)

'Blossom' refers back to the dream of I. vi, and before that to 'Fatima'. The remarkable repetition of consonants and vowels apparent to both ear and eye (heart/hear/her/beat/earth) and the containment of the first stressed word in the others within the line (heart: hear/beat, earth/earthy) gives this stanza a curiously self-contained, claustrophobic intensity. It is not quite saying 'heartbeat', although the pulse is implicit. There is something decidedly sinister about this romantic assertion, not only, as Ricks points out, due to the irony that becomes apparent in II. v. 239–58 (when the speaker imagines himself dead and buried), but also because both these moments

---

[52] J. Stanyan Bigg, *Night and the Soul: A Dramatic Poem* (London: Groombridge, 1854), 62.

resonate with fears of the heart continuing after death. This was a possibility regarded with fascination, and in some cases horror, by many Victorian commentators. 'The time is at hand | When thou shalt more than die' (II. iii. 139–40), the speaker prophetically tells his heart (reverted to stone on hearing of Maud's death). 'More than die' hints at possible damnation, but also at the potential fate of being buried alive, which is almost what occurs in the next section.

While writing *Maud* in 1855 Tennyson was reading Edgar Allan Poe's poems and tales with great interest.[53] In Poe's short story 'The Premature Burial', thoughts of being buried alive 'carry into the heart, which still palpitates, a degree of appalling and intolerable horror from which the most daring imagination must recoil'.[54] The narrator of this story suffers from syncope, a cardiac disease which physiologists claimed could result in 'living inhumation' because in this condition the pulse may stop for a prolonged period.[55] Poe's story also discusses a French case where a young 'litterateur', Julien, rejected in love, went to the tomb of his lover to steal a lock of hair and was appalled to find her still living: 'She was aroused, by the caresses of her lover, from the lethargy which had been mistaken for death.'[56] The resonance between this short story and the conclusion to Tennyson's 'The Lover's Tale', written in 1869, is striking.[57] Tennyson's rejected lover Julian (only so named in the final part)

---

[53] 'He read some of Edgar Poe's Poems to me two or three evenings, then the beginning of "Maud" & the Mad Song, and one night all "Maud" ' (Emily Tennyson, Feb. 1855). *Lady Tennyson's Journal*, ed. James O. Hoge (Charlottesville: University of Virginia Press, 1981), 42. Shatto notes a connection between *Maud* and 'The Premature Burial' (p. 208). On Tennyson and Poe, see also Gerhard Joseph, *Tennyson and the Text: The Weaver's Shuttle* (Cambridge: Cambridge University Press, 1992), 26–46.

[54] Mabbott, iii. 957.

[55] James Hope, *A Treatise on Diseases of the Heart and Great Vessels* (London: William Kidd, 1832), 500.

[56] Mabbott, iii. 957.

[57] Tennyson said that the final part of *The Lover's Tale*, 'The Golden Supper', was based on an incident in Boccaccio (*Memoir*, ii. 50). Poe also used a source which cited Boccaccio's narrative (Mabbott, iii. 970 n.).

goes to the grave of Camilla for a final kiss. But when he puts his hand on her heart,

> It beat—the heart—it beat;
> Faint—but it beat: at which his own began
> To pulse with such a vehemence that it drowned
> The feebler motion underneath his hand. (IV. 79–82)

Camilla's weak, intermittent pulse and Julian's shock are reflected in the pauses of the first two lines, before Julian's pulse starts again with vehemence. As he kneels in the 'Dust, as he said, that once was loving hearts, | Hearts that had beat with such a love as mine' (IV. 67–8) it is for an unnerving moment as though the lover's wish in *Maud* has come true, with the roles reversed. Moreover, this moment literalizes Julian's earlier image of his inner state (written over thirty years earlier) as 'the deep vault where the heart of Hope, | Fell into dust, and crumbled in the dark—' (I. 90–1). This is another odd cardiac metaphor because 'Hope', an abstraction, becomes related to a physical heart composed like all organs from the biblical 'dust'. The 'handful of dust' (*Maud* II. v. 241) that was Julian's heart is painfully reawakened, and despite Camilla's happy resurrection (she has lain 'three days without a pulse' (IV. 34)), Julian never escapes from the horror of this scene. The narrator finds him 'a skeleton alone | Raving of dead men's dust and beating hearts' (IV. 138–9).

In 1855 Tennyson wrote to Dr Mann:

> Merwood brought me a lump of snake's eggs, and I picked carefully out two little embryo snakes with bolting eyes and beating hearts. I laid them on a piece of white paper. Their hearts or blood vessels beat for at *least* two hours after extraction.[58]

Nineteenth-century physiologists carried out a number of experiments designed to discover whether the heart had its own intrinsic power—if the pulse continued after the death of the brain and destruction of the spinal cord, what made it beat? Could a person seemingly dead still have a beating heart, and could they be

---

[58] *Memoir*, i. 406.

revived by reviving the heart? *The Times*, in 1841, reported the case of a sailor who had been pronounced dead, but whose heart was discovered to be beating four hours later.[59] In the late 1850s the brilliant physiologist Michael Foster, who later proved that a heart cut into fragments would continue to pulsate, was commencing his investigations.[60] Lewes also cites several cases where the heart has continued beating after death, including the famous instance of Vesalius' arrest after a dissection he was performing revealed that the subject's heart was still pulsating.[61] When the speaker in *Maud*, therefore, hyperbolically claims that his heart would respond after 'a century dead' and describes himself in terms of being buried alive ('Maybe still I am but half-dead' (II. v. 337)), he is playing on the common cultural perception that his heart might be a separate and inextinguishable entity, with a beat that will never let him rest. Once awakened from its stupor by Maud, the narrator's heart continues as a maddening inorganic pulse after her death. Rather than the natural and harmonious pulsations of nature he hears the sounds on the roadway:

> And the hoofs of the horses beat, beat,
> The hoofs of the horses beat,
> Beat into my scalp and my brain, (II. v. 246–8)

The line-break emphasizes 'beat into'. 'Into', not 'in': the pulse is fully externalized. The sensitive heartbeat has been replaced by an insistent, infuriating beat, reminiscent of that heard by Poe's narrator in 'The Tell-Tale Heart', where it clearly implies insanity.

In part III, however, the speaker signals his partial recovery:

> 'It is time, O passionate heart and morbid eye,
> That old hysterical mock-disease should die.' (III. vi. 32–3)

---

[59] Inquest on Alla Arab, *The Times*, 25 Dec. 1841, p. 2.

[60] See Gerald Geison, *Michael Foster and the Cambridge School of Physiology* (Princeton: Princeton University Press, 1978), 191–296.

[61] G. H. Lewes, *The Physiology of Common Life*, 2 vols. (London: William Blackwood, 1859), i. 336.

Unlike earlier invocations, this is direct speech—possibly a bad sign, as it might indicate greater detachment from his body. 'That' could either make this statement refer to disease as a general condition ('it is time that') or refer very specifically to the speaker's own disease ('that old thing'). The speaker again lays the blame for his illness on his heart, ordering it to come under his control, but in doing so he recognizes that the heartsickness he suffered from (or suffers from) was hysterical, purely sympathetic as opposed to organic. In other words, it was not quite 'real'. In terms of nineteenth-century discussions of hysterical disease, his enlistment to fight in the Crimean War could provide a cure by removing his agonized concentration on his own breast and inciting him to look outward, to associate himself with a common cause, 'And the heart of a people beat with one desire' (III. vi. 49). A contemporary historian of the war notes: 'It was like a return to the youth of the world when England found herself once more preparing for the field. It was like the pouring of new blood into old veins.'[62] Such imagery might well draw on *Maud* and similar poems. War provided a means of rejuvenating the heart by awakening national pride. Kingsley even suggests, at the end of his disgusted review of spasmodic poetry in 1854, that war might cure the ailments of literature, as well as the general disaffection of the 1850s: 'A general war might . . . sweep away at once the dyspeptic unbelief, the insincere bigotry, the effeminate frivolity which now paralyses our poetry as much as it does our action.'[63]

This belief is strong in war poetry produced around the same time as *Maud* and which uses similar imagery.[64] One of R. C. Trench's war poems concludes: 'Praise the Giver of all good things, praise the Giver of the best, | Of a firm heart firmly beating in a strong resolved

[62] Justin McCarthy, *A History of our Own Times*, 4 vols. (London: Chatto & Windus, 1879), ii. 286.

[63] Kingsley, 'Alexander Smith and Alexander Pope', *Literary and General Lectures and Essays* (London: Macmillan, 1890), 61–102 (p. 98).

[64] For a bibliography of Crimean war poetry and a commentary, see Patrick Waddington (ed.), *Theirs But to Do and Die: The Poetry of the Charge of the Light Brigade at Balaklava, 25th October 1854* (Nottingham: Astra, 1995).

breast.'[65] This manly and determined heart is clearly what is needed to get through the crisis, and Crimean war poetry is full of claims that England has risen to the challenge. John Fletcher, in 'The Battle of the Alma: A National Ballad', asserts that:

> A thousand glorious tokens
> Can prove, by field and flood,
> Time has not touched the English heart,
> Nor blanched the English blood.[66]

Even 'the pulse of passion', in this poem as in Hemans's earlier patriotic, impassioned hearts, becomes noble when it heralds an onslaught on the enemy. Armstrong similarly points out the almost sexual emphasis on blood and guts in Gerald Massey's *War Waits* (1855), where war leads to 'a royal throbbing in the pulse that beat voluptuous blood'.[67] Such poems are also fond of symbolic moments when the hearts of England beat together for once:

> Weep!—but let the thought bring healing
> That a *nation's* heart is feeling.[68]

Or:

> The martial glow in England's sons was kindled to a flame,
> From breast to breast with rapid course the spark electric flew,
> And England's daughters burned in heart to serve their country too.[69]

Patmore, a friend of Tennyson's who shared his early enthusiasm for the war, has his hero in *The Angel in the House* begin a poem with the lines:

---

[65] 'On the Breaking Off of the Conferences at Vienna, June 1855', *Poems, Collected and Arranged* (London: Macmillan, 1865), 350.

[66] *The Battle of the Alma: A National Ballad*, 2nd edn. (London: R. Theobald, 1855), 2.

[67] 'The Fifth of November at Inkermann', *War Waits*, 2nd edn. (London: David Bogue, 1855), 29. See Isobel Armstrong, *Victorian Poetry: Poetry, Poetics and Politics* (London: Routledge, 1993), 271–3.

[68] Anon., 'England's Heroes!' (n.p.: n.p., 1855), stanza XI.

[69] Helen MacGregor, 'The Heroines of Scutari', in *Lays of the Crimea* (London: Longman, 1855), 14.

'The pulse of War, whose bloody heats
Sane purposes insanely work,
Now with fraternal frenzy beats,
And binds the Christian to the Turk.'[70]

This poem was first published in serial form between 1854 and 1856, and so could have been influenced by *Maud*. Patmore's 'sane purposes' and 'fraternal' try to hold back the countercharge of 'bloody', 'insanely', and 'frenzy', without much effect other than creating an unmanageable tension within this verse. The speaker of *Maud* works within this same tension: fraternity which rests on slaughtering brother-men; frenzy which serves a civilized country fighting a civilized war. It certainly seems that he has found a context in which language such as 'the blood-red blossom of war with a heart of fire' (III. vi. 53), even while it refers back to Maud's rose-garden, no longer solely indicates his individual pathology. Enrolment in war here is also an enrolment in the language and imagery of war, language which incorporates the heart and circulation into a context where wildly throbbing hearts and rivers of blood are patriotic images.

When the speaker exclaims, 'We have proved we have hearts in a cause, we are noble still' (III. vi. 55), the switch to 'we' demonstrates his altered sympathies. 'I have felt' (III. vi. 58): at last he assumes agency, in the same words used in *In Memoriam* CXXIV, although we may well question, as Tennyson may have expected his readers to, whether the war is only a new form of hysteria. Many critics have accepted the ending of *Maud* as indicative of the speaker's full recovery, and as a straightforward incidence of patriotic sentiment on Tennyson's part written to accord with popular views but unfortunately published when opinion had turned against the war.[71] On the other hand, J. R. Bennett and Cynthia Dereli, among

---

[70] *The Angel in the House: The Espousals* (London: John W. Parker, 1856), 6.

[71] See James Norman O'Neill, 'Anthem for Doomed Youth: An Interdisciplinary Study of Tennyson's *Maud* and the Crimean War', *Tennyson Research Bulletin*, 5 (1990), 166–82. Elaine Jordan supports the theory of a positive ending in *Alfred Tennyson* (Cambridge: Cambridge University Press, 1988), as do Ricks (1989) and Tucker (1988).

others, have argued that *Maud*, and a number of other contemporary writings on the war, are ambiguous, and that Tennyson's attitude cannot be established from that of his speaker.[72] Even in a climate of public support for the war, its beneficial effects were not universally accepted. In the 'Peace or War' dialogues from *Blackwood's*, which Tennyson almost certainly read, 'Irenaeus' argues that: 'War unites us, it is true, but it checks national improvement and healthy growth, and fixes our minds on an unhealthy and unnatural source of excitement.' His opponent responds by listing the evils of peace, but he does not deny the justice of the comment.[73] Given the awareness of the sick heart throughout this poem, it seems probable that the speaker of *Maud* is deluding himself when he believes that this war will offer relief, rather than social disease on the grand scale. The hopes in *In Memoriam*, which are also hopes for the poetic heart, have little place here, where the heart remains a pathological organ, and one whose figurative connotations are used, in the conclusion, to justify the speaker in his sickness. He might count himself lucky if he escapes from the war without having developed the organic heart disease that was just about to be classified, 'soldier's heart'.[74]

Discussion of *In Memoriam* and *Maud* consolidates the idea that the 1850s were the decade when engagement with the heart, in poetry and poetics, was most intense. Although Tennyson uses the heart as an image throughout his works—indeed, it is one of the most common words in his poetry, and unquestionably the

---

[72] J. R. Bennett, 'The Historical Abuse of Literature: Tennyson's *Maud: A Monodrama* and the Crimean War', *English Studies*, 62 (1981), 34–45. Cynthia Dereli, 'Tennyson's *Maud*: Ambiguity and the War Context', *Tennyson Research Bulletin*, 7 (1997), 1–6.

[73] [G. C. Swayne], 'Peace and War, I', *Blackwood's Edinburgh Magazine*, 76 (1854), 589–98 (p. 595).

[74] 'Soldier's heart' or 'soldier's spot', a weakness caused by the anxiety induced in battle, was not formally classified until the American Civil War but had been discussed beforehand. In 1864, a government commission was set up in Britain to study heart disease in the army, and it remained a serious concern until after the First World War. See P. W. Skerrit, 'Anxiety and the Heart: A Historical Review', *Psychological Medicine*, 13 (1983), 17–24 (p. 19) and Joel D. Howell, ' "Soldier's Heart": The Redefinition of Heart Disease and Speciality Formation in Early Twentieth-Century Great Britain', in W. F. Bynum, C. Lawrence, and V. Nutton (eds.), *The Emergence of Modern Cardiology* (London: Wellcome Institute, 1985), 34–52 (p. 35).

most common form of referencing sensation—these two poems make his earlier representations of heart, pulse, and circulation into central themes. Between them, *In Memoriam* and *Maud* manage to unite the spasms and shocks, palpitations and over-beating of many poems with an Arnoldian anxiety about the heart as alienated and inaccessible, and they do so metrically as well as thematically. As the following Conclusion briefly suggests, Tennyson partly moved away from the considerations of affective, heart-centred verse in his next major enterprise, but he had already produced the two most influential poems in creating and sustaining the culture of the heart in this period.

Conclusion

In the late 1850s, Tennyson turned to a project radically different from the contemporary pathologies of *Maud*: his Arthurian epic. The first four books of *Idylls of the King* were completed by 1859, but he continued to write new poems until the early 1870s, and the final version was not published until 1885. From the perspective of Tennyson's earlier poetry, the remarkable thing about the *Idylls* is the extent to which the heart is absent. References are relatively few, and the kind of poetic concentration on the heart seen in *In Memoriam* and *Maud* is conspicuously lacking. *Idylls of the King* is concerned with the public, epic mode, not the lyrical first-person meditations on feeling of the earlier poems, and so spares little time for the vagaries of the individual heart. Those characters associated with it, like Pelleas and his 'helpless heart' (*Pelleas and Ettarre*, 123), or Elaine's 'heart's sad secret' (*Lancelot and Elaine*, 831), are pathetic or doomed lovers, who might be described as misplaced within the world of these poems. Significantly, the one notable heart-centred incident in *Idylls of the King* occurs when the Holy Grail appears to Percivale's sister:

> [A]nd then
> Streamed through my cell a cold and silver beam,
> And down the long beam stole the Holy Grail,
> Rose-red with beatings in it, as if alive, (*The Holy Grail*, 115–18)

As the container of Christ's blood (which may be why the beatings are 'in' it) the Grail itself is an organic vessel, immaterial and material at once. Percivale's sister is a nun whose 'heart is pure as snow' (97), and so her account might also be read in the tradition of visions of the Sacred Heart. This 'Holy Thing' (124) is symbolically central to the *Idylls*, but its influence is harmful, for it is the source and goal of the quest which will destroy the fellowship of the Round Table. Only Galahad can see it uncovered, and it is questionable whether the intensity of his vision becomes pathological. The Grail pursues and haunts him:

> Fainter by day, but always in the night
> Blood-red, and sliding down the blackened marsh
> Blood-red, and on the naked mountain top
> Blood-red, and in the sleeping mere below
> Blood-red. And in the strength of this I rode, (472–6)

The pathetic fallacy here (unusual in these poems), and the memory of the opening lines of *Maud* in 'blood-red', heighten the sense of near-insanity. Galahad's movements are in counterpoint to the stasis of the initial repetitions. The second clause in each line refers ambiguously both to him and the Grail; it is unclear whether he or it is 'sliding', for example, as though it possesses and is indistinguishable from him. Tennyson's poem suggests that the Grail incites men to bloody fighting (Galahad's succeeding lines describe how he clashed with pagan hordes), disorder, and madness, rather than to peace and sympathy. In the form of the Grail, then, the heart is vital to the poem. But for the knights, fallen men who are not pure at heart, and so use their hearts in love and desire with disastrous consequences for the stability of Arthur's state, it is an unachievable and distanced vision.

The Holy Grail was published in 1869, at the start of a decade when religious doubt was to become predominant in literature and culture—though less in the form of the agonized accounts of the 1840s and 1850s than as a secure and unapologetic agnosticism.[1]

---

[1] The term 'agnostic' was invented by Huxley in 1870, and popularized by Leslie Stephen in *An Agnostic's Apology*, first published 1876. See Lance St John Butler, *Victorian*

The failed, disruptive religious quest in Tennyson's poem mirrors contemporary problems with confident belief and trust, particularly in the light of scientific debates over evolution, a marked feature from the late 1850s onwards. With the slow decline of widespread expressions of passionate faith, whether in religion, politics, or literature, this Conclusion argues, one strand of the discourse of the heart faded in intensity. Another strand, that which linked poetry and physiology, also became partly discredited due to the increasing specialization of medical research, which began to confine itself to observable results and detailed description, rather than conjecture. Rather than writing for a large audience encompassing both lay and professional readers, later authors directed their works specifically towards medical students. In 1879 J. Milner Fothergill looked back on the past decades of cardiological research with nostalgia:

> Much that lies outside mere physical signs, has been forgotten. The works of Hope and Latham, full of philosophical consid-erations of the greatest value, have given place to works more devoted to the consideration of diagnosis, and the requirements of the examination table.[2]

In the Introduction, I noted that the heart's prominence in Victorian literature might be less a sign of dominance than of imminent decline, as the heart seems gradually to fade in significance throughout the century. Medical literature and comments such as Fothergill's support this view. Although there are numerous publications on the heart pre-1870, and the number of articles in medical journals on cardiac disease and related topics considerably outstrips those on any other part of the body in this period, the heart was in effect fighting a losing battle against the dominance of the nerves and, by the end of the century, the brain. While pioneering work on the heart did continue (notably by the great physiologist Michael

Doubt: Literary and Cultural Discourses (Hemel Hempstead: Harvester Wheatsheaf, 1990), especially pp. 86–7.

[2] J. Milner Fothergill, *The Heart and its Diseases, with their Treatment*, 2nd edn. (London: H. K. Lewis, 1879), 31–2. On Hope and Latham, see below.

Foster and his student Walter Gaskell), the nervous system and the relatively new discourse of psychology were taking over from heart, blood, and circulation as the focus of exciting new research; and as the locus of interaction between literature and medicine in the form of the 'sensation novel'. The 1850s had seen the publication of poetry designed to move and excite the reader in physical terms. But by 1869 Barrett Browning was dead, Arnold had stopped writing poetry, and the spasmodic school and their followers were largely forgotten. The main controversy over affective literature had shifted firmly to the novel.

This is not to say that important poetry on or of the heart was not published after mid-century. The poetry of Swinburne and, in America, Walt Whitman pushed 'sensational' poetry to its furthest limits, as with very different intentions and ends did the poems of Christina Rossetti and Gerard Manley Hopkins. Yet in the extremity of their heart-based poetry there is a kind of despair of affect, to varying degrees a sense of self-absorption and incapacity to touch the reader. This Conclusion briefly examines how these poets can be located, in terms of their use of the heart, in the aftermath of the traditions described in previous chapters. In all these writers, either the heart is more violent and passionate than in earlier poetry, or it is more cold and alienated (and it can also be both in the same poem) in what could be read as the dying throes of its significance. Rebelling against or reworking earlier writings on the heart, these poets also recognize that an image used so commonly will eventually lose its power to surprise or interest the reader. In order to do so, they have to go further than their predecessors.

Walt Whitman's *Leaves of Grass* was first published in 1855, but was not initially well known—and was certainly not well received—in England. Early reviews were short and hostile, admitting Whitman's poetic power but horrified by his open invocations of sexuality and his concentration on the body. It was not until the late 1860s and after that Whitman attracted significant critical comment, notably from W. M. Rossetti, Edward Dowden in the *Westminster Review* (1871), and Robert Louis Stevenson in the *New Quarterly*

Magazine (1878). Whitman's poems deliberately and provocatively broke with previous bounds of poetic form and content. As Richard Dellamora argues: 'Whitman's embodied, at times explicitly sexual, poetry, provides a new standard ... for writers interested in producing a poetry closer to somatic experience.'[3] Nowhere is this more obvious than in the poem known as 'Trickle Drops', the fifteenth section of *Calamus* (1860):

Trickle drops! my blue veins leaving!
O drops of me! trickle, slow drops,
Candid from me falling, drip, bleeding drops,
From wounds made to free you whence you were prison'd,
From my face, from my forehead and lips,
From my breast, from within where I was conceal'd,
      press forth red drops, confession drops,
Stain every page, stain every song I sing, every word I say, bloody drops,
Let them know your scarlet heat, let them glisten,
Saturate them with yourself all ashamed and wet,
Glow upon all I have written or shall write, bleeding drops,
Let it all be seen in your light, blushing drops.[4]

Comparison of this poem to Frederick Faber's 'The Confessional', cited in Chapter 4 (which, like a number of Whitman's poems in *Calamus*, stages itself as a self-lacerating poem about love for another man), highlights the extent to which Whitman is working within an established tradition, and provides a measure for how far he exceeds it. Both poems deal with shameful heartfelt revelation, imaged as an exposure of the heart's interior to the gaze of another, though Whitman does not address the poem to one person but to all his readers. Both also self-consciously abandon masculine reserve and self-control, albeit that Faber does so within the confines of a religious tradition of private confession. Whitman's tone is, however, very different. The relatively few critics who discuss *Calamus* XV

---

[3] Richard Dellamora, *Masculine Desire: The Sexual Politics of Victorian Aestheticism* (Chapel Hill: University of North Carolina Press, 1990), 45.

[4] Walt Whitman, *Leaves of Grass*, ed. Jerome Loving (Oxford: Oxford University Press, 1990 (1891–2 edn.)), 104.

tend to agree with the verdict of James Miller, who describes it as 'an anguished confessional poem—indeed the opposite of celebratory'.[5] M. Jimmie Killingsworth argues that 'the poet sees himself martyred like Christ, bleeding to death'.[6] Roman Catholicism and extreme Evangelicalism did focus on Christ's blood and wounds, and Whitman's imagery is reminiscent of some hymns—the chorus of an 1862 hymn by Faber, for instance, runs, 'He bleeds, | My Saviour bleeds! | Bleeds!'[7] Killingsworth's repeated assertion, however, fails to explain the presence of 'pages' and 'songs'. Whitman is Christlike in that he is a poet, like the hero of Barrett Browning's 'A Vision of Poets', Smith's 'A Life-Drama', and numerous others, and therefore can be portrayed as a sacrificial martyr.

In the light of earlier poems in the same tradition, Whitman's version seems self-evidently a positive and even potentially celebratory invocation of the trope of writing from the heart. He is unabashedly open and deliberate about summoning forth his blood, which is, as 'drops of *me*' suggest, the representative part of himself. He demands to be read through and in his blood, more confidently than Aurora Leigh, or any other fictional or real poets of the time.[8] Writing in blood could be perceived as analogous to sexual release, which was one reason why Victorian writers perceived it as shameful. But in this poem, critical focus on the word 'ashamed' seems to have obscured the ambiguity of where this shame lies. If 'all ashamed and wet' applies to 'yourself' (i.e. the drops of blood, which Whitman is addressing), it contrasts strangely with 'Let them know your scarlet heat', because this phrase implies boldness and openness. In this case,

[5] James E. Miller, Jr, 'Trickle Drops', in J. R. LeMaster and Donald D. Kummings (eds.), *Walt Whitman: An Encyclopedia* (New York: Garland, 1998), 96.

[6] M. Jimmie Killingsworth, *Whitman's Poetry of the Body: Sexuality, Politics and the Text* (Chapel Hill: University of North Carolina Press, 1989), 123, 128.

[7] Frederick Faber, 'Blood is the price of heaven', in *Hymns* (London: Richardson, 1862), 85.

[8] Whitman had definitely read *Maud* and 'A Life-Drama', and as a journalist, reviewer, and published poet it seems unlikely that he would not have known of *Aurora Leigh*, which was widely reviewed on both sides of the Atlantic. For details of Whitman's literary interests see LeMaster and Kummings and Jerome Loving, *Walt Whitman: The Song of Himself* (Berkeley and Los Angeles: University of California Press, 1999).

shame then becomes, like a blush, an almost pleasurable indicator of desire. On the other hand, 'ashamed' might apply to 'them', the pages. This then suggests that it is the poems, the texts themselves, which shrink from this rush of blood. The *poet* welcomes it. The series of commands become more forceful and frequent as the poem progresses, and syntax and metre become more rapid and excited as the lines are extended, urging on this release. Whitman delights in the flows of his body, he seeks further exposure rather than trying or even pretending to try to restrain it. A more excessive depiction of bloody writing and self-revealing can scarcely be imagined.

Swinburne read Whitman's poetry in 1859, and was one of his first English champions. 'O strong-winged soul with prophetic | Lips hot with the blood-beats of song' was his description of him in an 1871 tribute, 'To Walt Whitman in America'. [9] Swinburne's Whitman speaks in pulsations, his heart in his mouth as he declaims his verse. Swinburne's imagery of heart, blood, and body was also influenced by Barrett Browning's depiction of the poet's passionate heart (he described her as one of the greatest women that ever lived), and he admired 'Empedocles on Etna', which he owned in the first edition as a schoolboy.[10] He was also familiar with the spasmodic poets, particularly Sydney Dobell's 'Balder', and Margot Louis notes that he was well read in the works of High Churchmen such as Newman and Trench.[11] *Poems and Ballads* (1866) makes its debts evident throughout, but again evinces a determination to go beyond any previous poet. As several recent critics have observed, the physicality of Swinburne's imagery and his emphasis on sensation and emotion contribute to the affective power of his poetry: it literally 'gets under

---

[9] *The Complete Works of Algernon Charles Swinburne*, ed. Edmund Gosse and Thomas J. Wise, 20 vols. (London: William Heinemann, 1925–7), ii. 184. All further references are to this edition and will be given in the text.

[10] On Barrett Browning see Swinburne to John Nichol, 11 Feb. 1857, *The Swinburne Letters*, ed. Cecil Y. Lang, 6 vols. (New Haven: Yale University Press, 1959), i. 10. On Arnold, see 'Matthew Arnold's New Poems' (1867), in *Essays and Studies*, 3rd edn. (London: Chatto & Windus, 1888), 123–83 (p. 126).

[11] Margot Louis, *Swinburne and his Gods: The Roots and Growth of an Agnostic Poetry* (Kingston: Queen's University Press, 1990), 9–10.

the skin', not least because of Swinburne's mastery of formal shocks and starts.[12] He twists the language of the heart into a fantasy of sado-masochistic desire in which the body becomes porous, open, dissolved, and uses rhythm to represent the hypnotic palpitation of the heartbeat. Where earlier lovers feared that their wayward hearts would destroy their identity and sense of self, here they are totally 'undone', in body and spirit.

In 'Laus Veneris', blood fills the palace of Venus ('Her little chambers drip with flower-like red' (i. 150)) in terms which suggest that the palace itself is like the interior of the body. The lovers trapped here are reduced to blood, nerves, and bones, yet in dissolution they are somehow still conscious of sensation:

> There is the knight Adonis that was slain;
> With flesh and blood she chains him for a chain;
>   The body and the spirit in her ears
> Cry, for her lips divide him vein by vein. (i. 151)

Desire acts inside the body rather than on the exterior: kisses are like the anatomist's probe, splitting the physical self into constituent parts, and awakening each part to painful sensation. Swinburne's poetic bodies, unlike those in earlier poetry, do not make physiological sense. They are nightmares of detached organs, localized feelings, burning, swooning, and aching blends of 'body' and 'spirit'. Swinburne often seems more concerned with the interior of the body than its visible surface. The speaker of this poem nostalgically recalls the old days of manly war:

> When all the fighting face is grown aflame
>   For pleasure, and the pulse that stuns the ears,
> And the heart's gladness of the goodly game. (i. 154)

This is reminiscent of the tradition of nationalistic poetry, resembling Hemans or the later Crimean war poets. But the glad heart and loud,

---

[12] See Kathy Psomiades, *Beauty's Body: Femininity and Representation in British Aestheticism* (Stanford, Calif.: Stanford University Press, 1997), 76 and Catherine Maxwell, 'Swinburne: Style, Sympathy and Sadomasochism', *Journal of Pre-Raphaelite Studies*, 12 (2003), 86–96.

firm pulse here (represented in the alliteration of hard consonants, 'p' and 'g') have been superseded in the present of the poem by trickling blood, deliquescence, passivity, as seen in the soft flowing alliteration of 'runs round the roots of time like rain' (i. 150).

In common with Whitman's poetry, much of Swinburne's writing rejects the discipline of masculinity. Imagining the body in 'feminine' terms is one way of conveying this. His speaker feels how in the presence of Venus:

> Each pore doth yearn, and the dried blood thereof
> Gasps by sick fits, my heart swims heavily,
> There is a feverish famine in my veins. (i. 152)

Like Tennyson's 'Eleanore', this deliberately recalls Sappho. The uneven stresses here and slow spondees ('dried blood', 'sick fits') weigh down these lines, like the heavy heart, and contrast with the more regular, rapid rhythm of the last line, as the circulation speeds up. It is not the speaker himself but his blood that yearns, that takes over agency. 'Veins' is a key word in Swinburne's poetry and is obsessively repeated. This may be partly because of its rhyming connotations ('pain', 'slain', 'chain', for instance), but it also means that a central focus of sensation and agency in the body, the heart, is replaced with a body sensitive at all points and feeling through and in every part. Even in terms of man's relation to God, Swinburne removes the direct associations with God's heart and writes instead: 'Our lives are as pulses or pores of his manifold body and breath' ('Hymn of Man', ii. 160). God has a heart, but men are merely transient and unstable 'thoughts passing through it, the veins that fulfil it with blood' (ii. 161). When the heart *is* described it is devoid of feeling:

> My heart swims blind in a sea
>   That stuns me; swims to and fro,
> And gathers to windward and lee
>   Lamentation, and mourning, and woe.
>
> A broken, an emptied boat,
>   Sea saps it, winds blow apart,

> Sick and adrift and afloat,
> The barren waif of a heart. ('Satia Te Sanguine', i. 219)

The heart becomes increasingly distanced throughout these stanzas, moving from 'my heart' and 'me', to 'it'. In Swinburne's world of perverse desire, sexuality, and questioning of Christianity, the heart is 'at sea', displaced and purposeless. Such fluctuations 'to and fro' are also evident in his rhythms, which tend to alternate between speed and languor, avoiding a too secure pulse. 'Thy mouth makes beat my blood in feverish rhymes' (i. 141), Swinburne writes in 'A Ballad of Life'. He seems to use the heart's systolic/diastolic movements as an analogy for the interchange of desire and suffering: the active pulse interchanged with the passive, or the violent actions of the heart alternating with its surrender.

Christina Rossetti knew Swinburne from the 1860s onwards, and he dedicated an 1883 volume of poetry to her.[13] Through her brothers, they moved in the same circle of Pre-Raphaelite artists and writers. In some ways, Rossetti's envisioning of a poetics of the body, in which its forces are used, unfolded, poured out, and spent, chimes with that of *Poems and Ballads*. Yet the ferocious religious faith of her poetry sets it apart both from Swinburne and from the women's poetry discussed in Chapter 3; in many ways she is more of an heir to the Tractarian writers of Chapter 4. The heart in her poems negotiates between love and faith. Unlike the release of Whitman's 'Trickle Drops', or Swinburne's fervent yet unsustainable moments of desire, its exposure and self-revelation are fiercely policed. Just as it seems that her poetic speaker is becoming a more outspoken advocate of the desiring heart than in any other previous poem, the voice is silenced and contained, the heart's energies shut down.

In 'The heart knoweth its own bitterness' ('When all the over-work of life'), Rossetti writes:

> You scratch my surface with your pin;
> You stroke me smooth with hushing breath;—

---

[13] Rikky Rooksby, *A. C. Swinburne: A Poet's Life* (Aldershot: Scolar, 1997), 67.

> Nay pierce, nay probe, nay dig within,
>   Probe my quick core and sound my depth.[14]

The body and the heart are revealed only by active and anatomical investigation of what lies within. Indeed, 'probe' and 'sound' are almost medical terms of investigation. Browning's Count Guido in *The Ring and the Book* tells his torturers that their surface wounds are nothing compared to the agony of mind and soul caused by his marriage: 'And in and out my heart, the play o' the probe | Four years have I been operated on.'[15] Rossetti's 'quick core' is a version of the living heart, oceanic in its untold depths. 'How should I spend my heart on you, | My heart, that so outweighs you all?' (39–40), the poem continues, perhaps hinting at the 'spending' of the self in sex. Rossetti takes an image that is generally negative, that of the heavy heart, and perversely turns it into a means of claiming superiority. 'I long to pour myself, my soul' (26), she writes, but:

> Your vessels are by much too strait;
>   Were I to pour you could not hold,
> Bear with me: I must bear to wait
>   A fountain sealed thro' heat and cold. (41–4)

Her commands are simultaneously agonized and arrogant, dismissive yet entreating, and her demands are represented as excessive. They will only be fulfilled in heaven—hence the heart's bitterness on earth, for it has not been touched 'to the core'. Even the punctuation here seems to clamp down on release, using colons and full stops rather than commas; there is little sense of fluency. Her language deliberately recalls the Psalms: 'I am poured out like water, and all my bones are out of joint: my heart is like wax; it is melted in the midst of my bowels' (22: 14). This is the psalm that is read most explicitly as a premonition of the Crucifixion, and which begins with

---

[14] Lines 33–6. *Christina Rossetti: The Complete Poems*, ed. R. W. Crump, introd. and notes by Betty Flowers (Harmondsworth: Penguin, 2001). All further references given in the text.

[15] *The Ring and the Book*, V. 28–9, ed. Richard D. Altick (Harmondsworth: Penguin, 1971).

the words Christ spoke on the cross. To see Rossetti as a Christlike figure, yearning for expression and release, suggests that this poem could be read not simply as addressed to a human lover but to any earthly 'you', and perhaps particularly to the readers or arbiters of poetry—that is, this trapped desire is also a desire for free poetic expression. Language such as 'Ready to spend and be spent for your sake' ('Monna Innominata', 9.14), for instance, strongly recalls Barrett Browning's speaker vowing his life to poetry in 'A Vision of Poets'.

Whatever the nature of these desires, the sole location where the heart's longings may be quenched, Rossetti argues, is in heaven:

> I lift my heart to Thy Heart,
>   Thy Heart sole resting-place for mine:
> Shall Thy Heart crave for my heart,
>   And shall not mine crave back for Thine?
> ('Because Thy Love hath sought me', 5–8)

The pleading tone of this poem contrasts with the disturbing assertion of 'The Heart Knoweth its Own Bitterness'. Rossetti's questions are delicate, almost rhetorical, yet her subtlety is unbalanced by the powerful implications of desire in 'crave'. She provides an excuse for the speaker's desire by picturing it as a response to God's feeling. God will quicken the heart disillusioned with man, a theme returned to in 'Twice' and 'A Better Resurrection'. This is by no means a new trope in Victorian poetry. Adelaide Procter similarly writes, in 'A Parting':

> I thank you that the heart I cast away
>   On such as you, though broken, bruised and crushed,
> Now that its fiery throbbing is all hushed,
>   Upon a worthier altar I can lay.[16]

As in several of Rossetti's poems, Procter appears to address a lover who has rejected her. Pain and loss are turned into a (religious)

---

[16] Adelaide Procter, *Legends and Lyrics, together with A Chapter of Verses*, introd. Charles Dickens (London: Oxford University Press, 1914), 128.

victory. God's love is not entirely different from that of man, but it seems, here and in Rossetti, less passionate, on a lower key, and so perhaps inviting a different kind of poetic.

Rossetti's poems focus more on the pain that comes before the happy resurrection than on that resurrection itself, on the moments when the heart is broken, frozen, or silenced. The anxiety that the heart is not worthy of God and may be rejected by him is often acute in these poems. In 'What Would I Give?' she writes:

> What would I give for a heart of flesh to warm me thro',
> Instead of this heart of stone ice-cold whatever I do;
> Hard and cold and small, of all hearts the worst of all. (1–3)

Leighton observes: '[I]n many of Rossetti's later poems ... love shatters at a touch and leaves to the poet an unspecific object buried at the heart, too complex to be named, too distant to be recalled, yet cold and central'.[17] But this object is not just 'at' the heart, it *is* the heart. That is the full horror of such moments. The almost chatty tone in 'What Would I Give?' contrasts with the terrible alienation described, the sense that the heart is completely unresponsive to the speaker's efforts. 'Whatever I do' despairs of being able to effect salvation, and invokes a powerful sense of distancing, darkness at the core. In Psalm 4 the reader is told to 'Stand in awe, and sin not: commune with your own heart upon your bed, and be still' (4). The command to 'be still', as it relates to Rossetti's poetic heart, is one that must be wrestled with and obeyed even in the act of speaking out:

> Then cried I to my heart: If thou wilt, break,
> But be thou still; no moaning will I make,
> Nor ask man's help, nor kneel that he may bless.
> So I kept silence in my haughtiness, ('Sonnet from the Psalms', 4–7)

This poem recalls Tractarian adjurations to keep the heart quiet, though 'haughtiness' induces some doubt about how far this poem

---

[17] Angela Leighton, *Victorian Women Poets: Writing against the Heart* (Hemel Hempstead: Harvester Wheatsheaf, 1992), 146.

subscribes to notions of modest reserve. The heart is 'thou', but the speaking and actions are performed by an 'I'. It may break, but 'I' will go on. This is scarcely a hopeful conclusion. In Rossetti's poems, the heart generally ends up dead, often entombed within a living body. The forms of her poems themselves encapsulate this, in that they counter her extreme or passionate declarations with regularity and firm end-rhymes. They are complex and controlled patterns, but seem designed less to soothe than to hold down. She is the true heir of Keble, and conscious of his influence; but the feelings which he contains in his poems without apparent care are infinitely more forceful, disruptive, and painful to ignore here.

The final poet whose writings of the 1870s and 1880s are highly significant with respect to the heart is of course Hopkins. Hopkins met Rossetti in 1864, and was deeply interested in her poetry. He also (reluctantly) confessed that he felt an affinity with Whitman.[18] His engagement with the heart seems part of a general rather than a specific concern with the division between the physical—the heart 'all naked and bleeding'—and the spiritual.[19] Lesley Higgins remarks (on the 'terrible sonnets') that Hopkins's poetry stages the speaker's 'intimate confrontations with his own debased and debasing somatic reality'.[20] The heart brings out the ambiguity of this confrontation because it is at once a physical organ, flawed and wayward, and a part responsive to the presence of the Divine:

> Ah, touched in your bower of bone,
> Are you! turned for an exquisite smart,

---

[18] On Hopkins and Rossetti, see Margaret Johnson, *Gerard Manley Hopkins and Tractarian Poetry* (Aldershot: Ashgate, 1997), 8. 'I always knew in my heart Walt Whitman's mind to be more like my own than any other man's living. As he is a very great scoundrel this is not a pleasant confession.' Hopkins to Robert Bridges, 18 Oct. 1882, in *The Letters of Gerard Manley Hopkins to Robert Bridges*, ed. Claude Colleer Abbott (London: Oxford University Press, 1935), 155.

[19] *Sermons*, 102.

[20] Lesley Higgins, ' "Bone-House" and "Lovescape": Writing the Body in Hopkins's Canon', in Francis L. Fennell (ed.), *Rereading Hopkins: Selected New Essays*, English Literary Studies Monograph 69 (Melbourne: University of Victoria, 1996), 11–35 (p. 26).

> Have you! make words break from me here all alone,
> Do you!—mother of being in me, heart.
> O unteachably after evil, but uttering truth.
>
> ('The Wreck of the Deutschland', stanza 18)

The 'turning' of the heart is carried out in the syntax, as the sentences turn past the end of each line. 'Exquisite smart' recalls Swinburne's mingling of pain and pleasure, and describing the heart as a 'mother' genders it feminine. Hopkins seems to address the heart colloquially, with rueful affection but also sadness. If it is 'unteachable' it may be wilful: he cannot control its actions, which apparently stem from the human impulse towards evil. The heart in his poetry stands for the fallible self, which must be chided and put down by God.

This is particularly true of the 'terrible sonnets', on which Hopkins wrote to Bridges, 'if ever anything was written in blood one of these was':[21]

> I am gall, I am heartburn. God's most deep decree
> Bitter would have me taste: my taste was me;
> Bones built in me, flesh filled, blood brimmed the curse.
>
> ('I wake and feel the fell of dark', 9–11)

As in Swinburne and Whitman, the self consists of the physical body, but for Hopkins this is agonizing. He cannot find an identity outside physicality: he does not *feel* heartburn but *is* it. Daniel Harris has argued that this is related to Hopkins's inability, at this period, to feel the truth of the Incarnation; his poetry 'renders, in the most intimate terms possible, his experience of dis-Incarnation', the absence of Christ's presence in the body.[22] Of course, the organ in which religious feeling might be expected to inhere is the heart. Hopkins wrote to Bridges in 1879 that Christ 'seldom,

---

[21] 17 May 1885, Hopkins, ed. Abbott (1935), 219.
[22] Daniel Harris, *Inspirations Unbidden: The 'Terrible Sonnets' of Gerard Manley Hopkins* (Berkeley and Los Angeles: University of California Press, 1982), 55.

especially now, stirs my heart sensibly'.[23] Yet a later sonnet in the sequence begins 'My own heart let me have more pity on', perhaps indicating that the speaker accepts the impossibility of escaping from his 'sad self', and the untenable harshness of his attitude towards his own weakness. The heart's instinctive physical reactions can occasionally be unfeigned and positive, as in 'Carrion Comfort', 'my heart lo! lapped strength, stole joy, would laugh, cheer' (11) or 'The Windhover', 'My heart in hiding | Stirred' (7–8). But the heart is still 'in hiding', not confidently asserting its truthfulness or fidelity, and it is not clear whether these responses successfully meld the physical and the spiritual.

Heart, blood, pulse, and circulation do not cease to be vital in these writers. What these poets have in common, however, is that they are working at the extreme edges of the tradition of heart-centred poetry. Regardless of whether this extremism is associated with religion, love, or sexuality, it still creates tensions within the language of the heart. In terms of form as well as subject matter, Whitman and Hopkins strain conventional rhythms and inaugurate a break with the kind of steady metre which might hope to emulate the regular heartbeat. Swinburne, meanwhile, virtually does away with the shocking implications of the embodied heart by discussing blood, veins, and circulation so much that they cease to hold affective power and are pushed almost to the point of parody. John Morley's comment that 'his hunting of the same word to death is ceaseless' applies nicely here, and not merely to Swinburne.[24] Rossetti too defies conventions to write bold and shocking poetry (particularly from a woman writer) that incessantly invokes the heart. What she invokes, however, is its absence: her poems have a kind of hopeless cynicism about the heart's potential to be healed or saved. Although all these poets

[23] 15 Feb. 1879, Hopkins, ed. Abbott (1935), 66.
[24] Cited in Clyde K. Hyder (ed.), *Swinburne: The Critical Heritage* (London: Routledge and Kegan Paul, 1970), 27.

recognize the power of affect, there seems relatively little attempt to address the function of sympathy. Most of their poems seem self-enclosed, and if they do seek to create an effect, it is, it appears, no longer expected to be morally uplifting. The heart has been devalued, perhaps because its constant use in earlier poetry forced it to carry an unsustainable burden of significance, or perhaps because structures of feeling were changing in later nineteenth-century culture.

This is not to say that the heart vanishes from poetry post-1860, or that it ceases to be an important poetic image. The poetry discussed here is far from inclusive, and there are countless other Victorian and indeed twentieth-century poems, not to mention novels and other texts, that deploy and play with the language of the heart, pulses, and circulation. Literary men and women over fifty years after most of the poets discussed here had died continued to worry about their own hearts. Virginia Woolf suffered from a racing pulse for many years ('my eccentric pulse had passed the limits of reason and was insane') and her doctors informed her that 'the rhythm of her heart was wrong'.[25] Samuel Beckett lay awake suffering the palpitation of his 'old internal combustion heart', bubbling and 'pouncing' upon him: his recurring symptoms reappeared in his first novel, *Murphy* (1938), where the protagonist's 'irrational heart' has been 'inspected, palpated, auscultated, percussed, radiographed and cardiographed', without any solution to its unpredictable behaviour.[26] The heart, it seems, continued to defy neat scientific conclusions. It would be entirely possible, moreover, to read the rhythms of Woolf's and Beckett's works, as well as their content, in relation to pulse and heart imagery. Yet it would be difficult to set these works in the same all-encompassing culture of the heart evident in Victorian poetry—such

[25] Cited in Hermione Lee, *Virginia Woolf* (London: Vintage, 1997), 185, 454.
[26] Cited in James Knowlson, *Damned to Fame: The Life of Samuel Beckett* (London: Bloomsbury, 1996), 64, 180, 200. Samuel Beckett, *Murphy* (New York: Grove, 1957), 3.

a culture evidently still existed, but was arguably no longer a shaping force in literature to anything like the same degree. The heart remains a valued and valuable literary image, but by the twentieth century it seldom achieves the same force of conviction and assurance of cultural value that it possessed in mid-nineteenth-century poetry and poetics.

Bibliography

PRIMARY SOURCES

Abercrombie, John, 'Contributions to the Pathology of the Heart', *Transactions of the Medico-Chirurgical Society of Edinburgh* (1823), 48.

Allen, Matthew, *Essay on the Classification of the Insane* (London: John Taylor, 1837).

Ancell, Henry, *Course of Lectures on the Physiology and Pathology of the Blood*, Lecture XVIII, *Lancet* (1839–40), ii. 548–56.

Arnold, Matthew, *Matthew Arnold: A Critical Edition of the Major Works*, ed. Miriam Allott and R. H. Super (Oxford: Oxford University Press, 1986).

—— *The Complete Prose Works of Matthew Arnold*, ed. R. H. Super, 11 vols. (Ann Arbor: University of Michigan Press, 1960–77).

—— *Matthew Arnold: The Yale Manuscript*, ed. S. O. A. Ullmann (Ann Arbor: University of Michigan Press, 1989).

—— *The Letters of Matthew Arnold*, ed. Cecil Y. Lang, 6 vols. (Charlottesville: University Press of Virginia, 1996–2001).

Bailey, Philip, *Festus* (London: William Pickering, 1839).

—— *Festus*, 3rd edn. (London: William Pickering, 1848).

Balfour, George W., 'Clinical Lectures on Diseases of the Heart', *Edinburgh Medical Journal*, 19 (1873–4), 1057–87.

Beckett, Samuel, *Murphy* (New York: Grove, 1957).

Bigg, J. Stanyan, *Night and the Soul: A Dramatic Poem* (London: Groombridge, 1854).

—— *Alfred Staunton* (London: Blackwood, 1861).

Billing, Archibald, 'On the Auscultation and Treatment of Affections of the Heart', *Lancet* (1831–2), ii. 198–201.

—— *Practical Observations on Diseases of the Lungs and Heart* (London: S. Highley, 1852).

Bowden, John Edward, *The Life and Letters of Frederick William Faber* (London: Thomas Richardson, 1869).

Brimley, George, *Essays*, ed. William George Clark (Cambridge: Macmillan, 1858).

Browning, Elizabeth Barrett, *The Complete Works of Elizabeth Barrett Browning*, ed. Charlotte Porter and Helen A. Clarke, 6 vols. (New York: AMS Press, 1973).

——— *Casa Guidi Windows*, ed. Julia Markus (New York: Browning Institute, 1977).

——— *Aurora Leigh*, ed. Margaret Reynolds (Athens: Ohio University Press, 1992).

——— and Browning, Robert, *The Brownings' Correspondence*, ed. Philip Kelley and Scott Lewis, 13 vols. (Winfield, Kan.: Wedgstone Press, 1992–).

Browning, Robert, *Robert Browning: The Poems*, ed. John Pettigrew and Thomas Collins, 3 vols. (Harmondsworth: Penguin, 1981).

——— *The Ring and the Book*, ed. Richard D. Altick (Harmondsworth: Penguin, 1971).

Bryan, E. L., 'Observations on Dr Hope's Exposition of the Sounds, Impulse and Rhythm of the Heart', *Lancet* (1832–3), ii. 780–3.

——— Letter to editor, *Lancet* (1835–6), i. 501–2.

Buchanan, Robert, *A Look around Literature* (London: Ward & Downey, 1887).

Burgess, Thomas, *The Physiology or Mechanism of Blushing* (London: John Churchill, 1839).

Burns, Allan, *Observations on Some of the Most Frequent and Important Diseases of the Heart* (Edinburgh: James Muirhead, 1809).

Burrows, George Man, *On Disorders of the Cerebral Circulation; and on the Connection between Affections of the Brain and Diseases of the Heart* (Philadelphia: Lea and Blanchard, 1848).

Byron, George Gordon, *Lord Byron: The Complete Poetical Works*, ed. Jerome McGann, 7 vols. (Oxford: Clarendon Press, 1986).

Carlyle, Thomas, *Sartor Resartus* (London: Chapman and Hall, 1896).

Champneys, Basil, *Memoirs and Correspondence of Coventry Patmore*, 2 vols. (London: George Bell, 1901).

Clough, Arthur Hugh, *The Poems of Arthur Hugh Clough*, ed. F. L. Mulhauser, 2nd edn. (Oxford: Clarendon Press, 1974).

_____ *The Correspondence of Arthur Hugh Clough*, ed. F. L. Mulhauser, 2 vols. (Oxford: Clarendon Press, 1957).

Clutterbuck, Henry, *On the Proper Administration of Blood-Letting for the Prevention and Cure of Disease* (London: S. Highley, 1840).

Coleridge, J. T., *A Memoir of the Reverend John Keble* (Oxford: James Parker, 1869).

Coleridge, Samuel Taylor, *The Collected Works of Samuel Taylor Coleridge*, ed. Kathleen Coburn et al., 16 vols. (London: Routledge, 1971–2001).

_____ *Collected Letters of S. T. Coleridge*, ed. Earl Leslie Griggs, 6 vols. (Oxford: Clarendon Press, 1956).

Collins, Wilkie, *The Woman in White*, ed. John Sutherland (Oxford: Oxford University Press, 1996).

Conolly, John, Forbes, John, and Tweedie, Alexander (eds.), *The Cyclopaedia of Practical Medicine*, 3 vols. (London: Sherwood, Gilbert & Piper, 1833).

Corvisart, J. N., *A Treatise on the Diseases and Organic Lesions of the Heart and Great Vessels*, trans. C. H. Hebb (London: Underwood and Blacks, 1813).

Cowper, W., and Newton, J. *Olney Hymns* (London: [n.p.], 1779).

Dallas, E. S., *Poetics: An Essay on Poetry* (London: Smith, Elder, 1852).

Davies, Herbert, *Lectures on the Physical Diagnosis of the Diseases of the Lungs and Heart* (London: John Churchill, 1851).

Dickens, Charles, *Pickwick Papers*, ed. Mark Wormald (Harmondsworth: Penguin, 1999).

Dobell, Horace, *On Affections of the Heart and in its Neighbourhood: Cases, Aphorisms and Commentaries* (London: H. K. Lewis, 1872).

Dobell, Sydney, *Balder* (London: Smith, Elder, 1854).

_____ *Thoughts on Art, Philosophy and Religion*, introd. John Nichol (London: Smith, Elder, 1876).

Dowden, Edward, *Studies in Literature 1789–1877* (London: Kegan Paul, 1878).

'Dr Abernethy's Lectures on Sympathy of the Heart', *The Times*, 22 May 1827, p. 3.

Durrant, C. M., 'Functional Affections of the Heart', *British Medical Journal*, (1859), 3–4.

Eliot, George, *Scenes of Clerical Life*, ed. Graham Handley (London: J. M. Dent, 1994).

Eliot, George, *The Lifted Veil and Brother Jacob*, ed. Helen Small (Oxford: Oxford University Press, 1999).

———*Middlemarch*, ed. W. H. Harvey (Harmondsworth: Penguin, 1965).

Elliotson, John, *On the Recent Improvements in the Art of Distinguishing the Various Diseases of the Heart* (London: Longman, Rees, Orme, Brown and Green, 1830).

——— 'Clinical Lecture on Disease of the Heart', *Lancet* (1830–1), i. 487–95.

Ellison, Henry, *Madmoments: or First Verseattempts by a Bornnatural*, 2 vols. (London: Painter, 1839).

Elwood, Sarah, *Memoirs of the Literary Ladies of England*, 2 vols. (London: Henry Colburn, 1843).

'England's Heroes!' ([n.p.]: [n.p.], 1855).

Faber, Frederick, *The Cherwell Water-Lily and Other Poems* (London: J., G., F. and J. Rivington, 1840).

———*Hymns* (London: Richardson, 1862).

Feuerbach, Ludwig, *The Essence of Christianity*, trans. George Eliot, introd. Karl Barth (New York: Harper and Row, 1957).

Fichte, Johann, *The Destination of Man*, trans. Mrs Percy Sinnett (London: Chapman, Brothers, 1846).

Fitzgerald, Edward, *Letters and Literary Remains of Edward Fitzgerald*, ed. William Aldis Wright, 3 vols. (London: Macmillan, 1889).

Fletcher, John, *The Battle of the Alma: A National Ballad*, 2nd edn. (London: R. Theobald, 1855).

Fothergill, J. Milner, *The Heart and its Diseases, with their Treatment*, 2nd edn. (London: H. K. Lewis, 1879).

Furnivall, J. J., *The Diagnosis, Prevention and Treatment of Diseases of the Heart* (London: John Churchill, 1845).

Gaskell, Elizabeth, *Wives and Daughters*, ed. Pam Morris (Harmondsworth: Penguin, 1996).

Gilfillan, George, *Galleries of Literary Portraits*, 2 vols. (Edinburgh: James Hogg, 1856).

Graham, Thomas J., *On the Diseases of Females: A Treatise . . . Containing also an Account of the Symptoms and Treatments of Diseases of the Heart*, 7th edn. (London: Simpkin, Marshall, 1861).

Halford, George Britton, *The Actions and Sounds of the Heart: A Physiological Essay* (London: John Churchill, 1860).

Hallam, Arthur Henry, *The Writings of Arthur Hallam*, ed. T. H. Vail Motter (London: Oxford University Press, 1943).

_____ *The Letters of Arthur Henry Hallam*, ed. Jack Kolb (Columbus: Ohio State University Press, 1981).

Hallam, Henry (ed.), *Remains, in Verse and Prose, of Arthur Henry Hallam* (London: W. Nichol, 1834).

Harvey, William, *An Anatomical Disputation Concerning the Movement of the Heart and the Blood in Living Creatures*, trans. and introd. Gweneth Whitteridge (Oxford: Blackwell, 1976).

Hazlitt, William, *Collected Works of William Hazlitt*, ed. A. R. Waller and Arnold Glover, 12 vols. (London: J. M. Dent, 1902).

Hemans, Felicia, *The Works of Mrs Hemans, with a Memoir of her Life, by her Sister*, 7 vols. (Edinburgh: William Blackwood, 1839).

Holland, G. Calvert, *An Experimental Inquiry into the Laws which Regulate the Phenomena of Organic and Animal Life* (Edinburgh: MacLachlan and Stewart, 1829).

_____ *The Philosophy of the Moving Powers of the Blood* (London: John Churchill, 1844).

Holmes, Oliver Wendell, *The Writings of Oliver Wendell Holmes*, 13 vols. (London: Sampson Low, 1891).

Hope, James, *A Treatise on Diseases of the Heart and Great Vessels* (London: William Kidd, 1832).

Hopkins, Gerard Manley, *The Poems of Gerard Manley Hopkins*, ed. W. H. Gardner and N. H. MacKenzie, 4th edn. (Oxford: Oxford University Press, 1970).

_____ *The Letters of Gerard Manley Hopkins to Robert Bridges*, ed. Claude Colleer Abbott (London: Oxford University Press, 1935).

_____ *Further Letters of Gerard Manley Hopkins, Including his Correspondence with Coventry Patmore*, 2nd edn., ed. Claude Colleer Abbott (London: Oxford University Press, 1956).

_____ *The Sermons and Devotional Writings of Gerard Manley Hopkins*, ed. Christopher Devlin (London: Oxford University Press, 1959).

Horne, R. H., *The Poems of Geoffrey Chaucer, Modernized* (London: Whittaker, 1841).

Howitt, William, *Homes and Haunts of the Most Eminent British Poets*, 2 vols. (London: Richard Bentley, 1847).

Hughes, H. M., *A Clinical Introduction to the Practice of Auscultation* (London: Longman, Brown, Green and Longmans, 1845).

Hull, Robert, *Essays on Determination of Blood to the Head* (London: John Churchill, 1842).

'Inquest on Alla Arab', *The Times*, 25 Dec. 1841, p. 2.

'Inquest on Honoria O'Brien', *The Times*, 15 Jan. 1841, p. 5.

'Inquest on Sir. F. W. Slade', *The Times*, 15 Aug. 1863, p. 8.

'Inquest on Sir W. H. Pringle', *The Times*, 29 Dec. 1840, p. 7.

Jewsbury, Geraldine, *The Half-Sisters*, ed. Joanne Wilkes (Oxford: Oxford University Press, 1994).

Jolly, Emily (ed.), *Life and Letters of Sydney Dobell*, 2 vols. (London: Smith, Elder, 1878).

Jones, Ebenezer, *Studies of Sensation and Event*, ed. Richard Shepherd, with memorial notices by Sumner Jones and W. J. Linton (London: Pickering, 1879).

Jones, Ernest, *The Battle-Day, and Other Poems* (London: G. Routledge, 1855).

Kant, Immanuel, *Critique of Pure Reason*, trans. and ed. Paul Guyer and Allen W. Wood (Cambridge: Cambridge University Press, 1997).

Keats, John, *The Poems of John Keats*, ed. John Barnard, 3rd edn. (Harmondsworth: Penguin, 1988).

Keble, John, *The Christian Year, Lyra Innocentium and Other Poems* (Oxford: Oxford University Press, 1914).

——*Keble's Lectures on Poetry, 1832–1841*, trans. E. K. Francis, 2 vols. (Oxford: Clarendon Press, 1912).

Kingsley, Charles, *Literary and General Lectures and Essays* (London: Macmillan, 1890).

Knox, Dr, 'Physiological Observations on the Pulsations of the Heart, and on its Diurnal Revolution and Excitability', *Edinburgh Medical and Surgical Journal*, 47 (1837), 358–77.

Laennec, René, *A Treatise on the Diseases of the Chest and on Mediate Auscultation*, trans. John Forbes, 3rd edn., revised (London: Thomas & George Underwood, 1829).

Landon, Letitia, *The Poetical Works of L.E.L.*, ed. William B. Scott (London: Routledge, 1873).

Latham, Peter Mere, *Lectures on Subjects Connected with Clinical Medicine, Comprising Diseases of the Heart*, 2nd edn., 2 vols. (London: Longman, 1846).

_____ *The Collected Works of P. M. Latham*, ed. Robert Martin, 2 vols. (London: New Sydenham Society, 1878).

Law, Robert, 'Disease of the Brain Dependent on Disease of the Heart', *Dublin Journal of Medical Science*, 17 (1840), 181–210.

Leighton, Robert, *Records and Other Poems* (London: Kegan Paul, 1880).

Lewes, G. H., *The Physiology of Common Life*, 2 vols. (London: William Blackwood, 1859).

Lister, Anne, *No Priest But Love: The Journals of Anne Lister 1824–1826*, ed. Helena Whitbread (Otley: Smith, Settle, 1992).

Longfellow, Henry Wadsworth, *Poetical Works* (London: Oxford University Press, 1973 (first published 1904)).

Lord, Perceval Barton, *Popular Physiology* (London: John W. Parker, 1834).

Lowell, James Russell, *My Study Windows* (London: Sampson Low, 1871).

McCarthy, Justin, *A History of our Own Times*, 4 vols. (London: Chatto & Windus, 1879).

MacGregor, Helen, *Lays of the Crimea* (London: Longman, 1855).

Mackay, Charles, *Egeria, or The Spirit of Nature* (London: David Bogue, 1850).

Madden, R. R., *The Infirmities of Genius*, 2 vols. (London: Saunders and Otley, 1833).

Mann, R. J., *Tennyson's 'Maud' Vindicated: An Explanatory Essay* (London: Jarrold, 1856).

Manning, Henry, *The Divine Glory of the Sacred Heart* (London: Burns and Oates, 1873).

Markham, W. O., *Diseases of the Heart: Their Pathology, Diagnosis and Treatment*, 2nd edn. (London: John Churchill, 1860).

Marshall, John, *Practical Observations on Diseases of the Heart, Lungs, Stomach, Liver, Occasioned by Spinal Irritation* (Philadelphia: Haswell, Barrington and Haswell, 1837).

Marston, J. Westland, *Gerald: A Dramatic Poem, and Other Poems* (London: C. Mitchell, 1842).

Massey, Gerald, *War Waits*, 2nd edn. (London: David Bogue, 1855).

_____ 'Poetry: The Spasmodists', *North British Review*, 28 (1858), 231–50.

Massey, Gerald, 'Last Poems and Other Works of Mrs Browning', *North British Review*, 36 (1862), 514–34.

——*My Lyrical Life: Poems Old and New*, 2 vols. (London: Kegan Paul, Trench, 1889).

Meynell, Alice, *The Rhythm of Life and Other Essays* (London: Mathews and Lane, 1893).

Newman, Francis, *Phases of Faith*, introd. U. C. Knoepflmacher (Leicester: Leicester University Press, 1970).

Newman, John Henry, *Essays: Critical and Historical*, 2 vols (London: Basil Montagu Pickering, 1872).

Newnham, William, *The Reciprocal Influence of Body and Mind Considered* (London: J. Hatchard, 1842).

Odell, J., *An Essay on the Elements, Accents and Prosody of the English Language* (London: Lackington, Allen, 1806).

Paget, James, 'On the Cause of the Rhythmic Motion of the Heart', *Proceedings of the Royal Society of London*, 8 (1856–7), 473–88.

——'On the Chronometry of Life', *Proceedings of the Royal Institution*, 3 (1858–62), 117–24.

Paget, Stephen (ed.), *Memoirs and Letters of Sir James Paget*, 3rd edn. (London: Longmans, Green, 1901).

Paley, William, *Natural Theology*, 3rd edn. (London: R. Faulder, 1803).

Patmore, Coventry, *The Angel in the House: The Betrothal* (London: John W. Parker, 1854).

——*The Angel in the House: The Espousals* (London: John W. Parker, 1856).

——*Coventry Patmore's 'Essay on English Metrical Law': A Critical Edition with a Commentary*, ed. Mary Augustine Roth (Washington: Catholic University of America Press, 1961).

Pattison, Mark, *Memoirs* (London: Macmillan, 1885).

Philip, A. P. Wilson, 'Experiments Made with a View to Ascertain the Principle on which the Action of the Heart Depends, and the Relation which Subsists between that Organ and the Nervous System', *Philosophical Transactions of the Royal Society*, 105 (1815), 65–90.

——*An Experimental Inquiry into the Laws of the Vital Functions, with Some Observations on the Nature and Treatment of Internal Diseases* (London: Thomas and George Underwood, 1817).

Poe, Edgar Allan, *Collected Works*, ed. Thomas Ollive Mabbott, 3 vols. (Cambridge, Mass.: Harvard University Press, 1969).

Procter, Adelaide, *Legends and Lyrics, together with A Chaplet of Verses*, introd. Charles Dickens (London: Oxford University Press, 1914).

[Procter, Bryan], 'On English Poetry', *Edinburgh Review*, 42 (1825), 31–64.

Pusey, Edward Bouverie, *Parochial Sermons*, 2 vols. (Oxford: John Henry Parker, 1853).

—— *Spiritual Letters of E. B. Pusey*, ed. J. O. Johnston and W. C. E. Newbolt (London: Longmans, Green, 1898).

Richardson, Benjamin, *Diseases of Modern Life* (London: Macmillan, 1876).

Robertson, F. W., *Lectures and Addresses on Literary and Social Topics* (London: Smith, Elder, 1858).

Roe, Richard, *The Principles of Rhythm, Both in Speech and Music, and Especially as Exhibited in the Mechanism of English Verse* (Dublin: R. Graisbury, 1823).

Rossetti, Christina, *Christina Rossetti: The Complete Poems*, ed. Rebecca Crump, introd. and notes by Betty Flowers (Harmondsworth: Penguin, 2001).

—— *The Letters of Christina Rossetti, i: 1843–1873*, ed. Antony H. Harrison (Charlottesville: University of Virginia Press, 1997).

Rossetti, William Michael, *Selected Letters of William Michael Rossetti*, ed. Roger Peattie (University Park: Pennsylvania State University Press, 1990).

Ruskin, John, *The Works of John Ruskin*, ed. E. T. Cook and Alexander Wedderburn, 39 vols. (London: George Allen, 1909).

Sanderson, J. Burdon, *Handbook of the Sphygmograph* (London: Robert Hardwicke, 1867).

Searle, Henry, *A Treatise on the Tonic System of Treating Affections of the Stomach and Brain* (London: Richard and John E. Taylor, 1843).

Semple, Robert Hunter, *A Manual of the Diseases of the Heart: Their Pathology, Diagnosis, Prognosis and Treatment* (London: John Churchill, 1875).

Shairp, J. C., *John Keble: An Essay on the Author of the 'Christian Year'* (Edinburgh: Edmonston & Douglas, 1866).

Shakespeare, William, *William Shakespeare: The Complete Works*, ed. Stanley Wells and Gary Taylor (Oxford: Clarendon Press, 1986).

Shelley, Percy Bysshe, *The Complete Poetical Works of Percy Bysshe Shelley*, ed. Neville Rogers, 4 vols. (Oxford: Clarendon Press, 1972).

Smith, Alexander, *Poems* (London: David Bogue, 1853).

—— *Last Leaves: Sketches and Criticisms*, ed. Patrick Alexander (Edinburgh: Nimmo, 1868).

Spencer, Herbert, *First Principles* (London: Williams and Norgate, 1863).

—— *The Life and Letters of Herbert Spencer*, ed. David Duncan (London: Routledge/Thoemmes, 1996).

Steele, Joshua, *Prosodia Rationalis*, 2nd edn. (London: J. Nichols, 1779).

Stirling, James, *Jerrold, Tennyson and Macauley, with Other Critical Essays* (Edinburgh: Edmonston & Douglas, 1868).

Stodart, M. A., *Female Writers: Thoughts on their Proper Sphere, and on their Powers of Usefulness* (London: Seeley and Burnside, 1842).

Swan, Joseph, *An Essay on the Connection between the Action of the Heart and Arteries and the Functions of the Nervous System* (London: Longman, Rees, Orme, Brown and Green, 1829).

[Swayne, G. C.], 'Peace and War, I', *Blackwood's Edinburgh Magazine*, 76 (1854), 589–98.

Swinburne, Algernon Charles, *The Complete Works of Algernon Charles Swinburne*, ed. Edmund Gosse and T. J. Wise, 20 vols. (London: William Heinemann, 1925–7).

—— *Essays and Studies*, 3rd edn. (London: Chatto & Windus, 1888).

—— *The Swinburne Letters*, ed. Cecil Y. Lang, 6 vols. (New Haven: Yale University Press, 1959).

Tainsh, Edward, *A Study of the Works of Alfred Tennyson* (London: Chapman and Hall, 1868).

Taylor, Isaac, *Natural History of Enthusiasm* (London: Holdsworth & Ball, 1829).

Tennyson, Alfred, *The Poems of Tennyson*, ed. Christopher Ricks, 2nd edn., 3 vols. (Harlow: Longman, 1987).

—— *The Letters of Alfred Lord Tennyson*, ed. Cecil Y. Lang and Edgar F. Shannon, 3 vols. (Oxford: Clarendon Press, 1982).

—— *In Memoriam*, ed. Susan Shatto and Marion Shaw (Oxford: Clarendon Press, 1982).

—— *Tennyson's Maud: A Definitive Edition*, ed. Susan Shatto (London: Athlone Press, 1986).

Tennyson, Emily, *Lady Tennyson's Journal*, ed. James O. Hoge (Charlottesville: University of Virginia Press, 1981).

Tennyson, Hallam, *Alfred Lord Tennyson: A Memoir*, 2 vols. (London: Macmillan, 1897).

_____ (ed.), *Tennyson and his Friends* (London: Macmillan, 1911).

Trench, Richard Chenevix, *Poems, Collected and Arranged* (London: Macmillan, 1865).

Tyndall, John, *Fragments of Science*, 5th edn. (London: Longmans, Green, 1865).

Walshe, Walter Hayle, *A Practical Treatise on the Diseases of the Heart and Great Vessels* (London: Walton and Maberly, 1862).

Wardrop, James, *On the Nature and Treatment of Diseases of the Heart, with Some New Views on the Physiology of the Circulation* (London: John Churchill, 1837).

_____ *On the Nature and Treatment of Diseases of the Heart*, 2nd edn., revised (Edinburgh: Thomas Constable, 1859).

Warren, George, *A Commentary, with Practical Observations, on Disorders of the Head* (London: Longman et al., 1829).

Webster, John, 'On Insanity', *Medico-Chirurgical Transactions*, 26 (1843), 374–416.

Wesley, Charles, and Wesley, John, *A Rapture of Praise: Hymns of John and Charles Wesley*, selected by A. M. Allchin and H. A. Hodges (London: Hodder and Stoughton, 1966).

Wharton, Grace, and Wharton, Philip, *The Queens of Society* (London: James Hogg, 1861).

Wheatstone, Charles, *The Scientific Papers of Charles Wheatstone* (London: Taylor and Francis, 1879).

Whitman, Walt, *Leaves of Grass*, ed. Jerome Loving (Oxford: Oxford University Press, 1990).

Wilkinson, James John Garth, *The Human Body and its Connexion with Man* (London: Chapman and Hall, 1851).

Williams, Charles, *The Pathology and Diagnosis of Diseases of the Chest*, 4th edn. (London: John Churchill, 1840).

Williams, Isaac, 'On Reserve in Communicating Religious Knowledge' (Part 2), Tract 87, *Tracts for the Times 1838–1840* (London: J. G. & F. Rivington, 1840).

Williams, Jane, *The Literary Women of England* (London: Saunders, Otley, 1861).

Williams, John, *Practical Observations on Nervous and Sympathetic Palpitation of the Heart*, 2nd edn. (London: John Churchill, 1852).

Wilson, James, *On Spasm and Other Disorders, Termed Nervous, of the Muscular System* (London: John W. Parker, 1843).

Winslow, Forbes, *On the Preservation of the Health of Body and Mind* (London: Henry Renshaw, 1842).

Wordsworth, Christopher, *Thoughts on English Hymnody, or Preface to 'The Holy Year'* (London: Rivington, 1865).

Wordsworth, William, *The Prelude 1799, 1805, 1850*, ed. Jonathan Wu, M. H. Abrams, and Stephen Gill (New York: Norton, 1979).

—— *Selected Prose*, ed. John O. Hayden (Harmondsworth: Penguin, 1988).

—— and Coleridge, S. T., *Lyrical Ballads*, ed. R. L. Brett and A. R. Jones, 2nd edn. (London: Routledge, 1991).

Yonge, Charlotte M., *Musings over the 'Christian Year' and 'Lyra Innocentium'* (Oxford: James Parker, 1871).

SECONDARY SOURCES

Allen, Peter, *The Cambridge Apostles: The Early Years* (Cambridge: Cambridge University Press, 1978).

Armstrong, Isobel, *Language as Living Form in Nineteenth-Century Poetry* (Brighton: Harvester, 1982).

—— *Victorian Poetry: Poetry, Poetics and Politics* (London: Routledge, 1993).

—— 'Misrepresentation: Codes of Affect and Politics in Nineteenth-Century Women's Poetry', in Armstrong and Blain, 3–32.

—— *The Radical Aesthetic* (Oxford: Blackwell, 2000).

—— and Blain, Virginia (eds.), *Women's Poetry, Late Romantic to Late Victorian: Gender and Genre 1830–1900* (Houndmills: Macmillan, 1999).

Avery, Simon, and Stott, Rebecca, *Elizabeth Barrett Browning* (Harlow: Longman, 2003).

Aviram, Amittai, *Telling Rhythm: Body and Meaning in Poetry* (Ann Arbor: University of Michigan Press, 1994).

Baldry, P. E., *The Battle against Heart Disease* (Cambridge: Cambridge University Press, 1971).

Beer, Gillian, *Darwin's Plots: Evolutionary Narrative in Darwin, George Eliot and Nineteenth-Century Fiction* (London: Routledge, 1983).

_____ *Open Fields: Science in Cultural Encounter* (Oxford: Oxford University Press, 1996).

Beer, John, *Wordsworth and the Human Heart* (London: Macmillan, 1978).

Bennett, J. R., 'The Historical Abuse of Literature: Tennyson's *Maud: A Monodrama* and the Crimean War', *English Studies*, 62 (1981), 34–45.

Black, Max, *Models and Metaphors* (Ithaca, NY: Cornell University Press, 1962).

Blair, Kirstie, 'Touching Hearts: Queen Victoria and the Curative Properties of *In Memoriam*', *Tennyson Research Bulletin*, 7 (2001), 246–54.

_____ 'John Keble and the Rhythm of Faith', *Essays in Criticism*, 53 (2003), 129–51.

_____ 'Spasmodic Affections: Poetry, Pathology and the Spasmodic Hero', *Victorian Poetry*, 42 (2004), 473–90.

_____ (ed.), *John Keble in Context* (London: Anthem, 2004).

_____ 'Breaking Loose: Frederick Faber and the Failure of Reserve', forthcoming in *Victorian Poetry*, 44 (2006).

Bordo, Susan, *Unbearable Weight: Feminism, Western Culture and the Body* (Berkeley and Los Angeles: University of California Press, 1993).

Bradford, Charles Angell, *Heart Burial* (London: Allen & Unwin, 1933).

Brennan, Teresa, *The Transmission of Affect* (Ithaca, NY: Cornell University Press, 2004).

Briggs, Asa, *The Age of Improvement, 1783–1867*, 2nd edn. (Harlow: Longman, 2000).

Bristow, Joseph, 'Coventry Patmore and the Womanly Mission of the Mid-Victorian Poet', in Miller and Eli Adams, 118–40.

_____ (ed.), *The Cambridge Companion to Victorian Poetry* (Cambridge: Cambridge University Press, 2000).

Buckley, Jerome, *The Triumph of Time* (Cambridge, Mass.: Harvard University Press, 1966).

Butler, Lance St John, *Victorian Doubt: Literary and Cultural Discourses* (Hemel Hempstead: Harvester Wheatsheaf, 1990).

Bynum, W. F., Lawrence, C., and Nutton, V. (eds.), *The Emergence of Modern Cardiology* (London: Wellcome Institute, 1985).

Campbell, Matthew, *Rhythm and Will in Victorian Poetry* (Cambridge: Cambridge University Press, 1999).

Campbell, Nancie (ed.), *Tennyson in Lincoln*, 2 vols. (Lincoln: Tennyson Society, 1971).

Carlson, Eric (ed.), *Critical Essays on Edgar Allan Poe* (Boston: G. K. Hall, 1987).

Christ, Carol T., 'The Feminine Subject in Victorian Poetry', *ELH* 54 (1987), 385–403.

Cixous, Hélène, *'Coming to Writing' and Other Essays*, ed. Deborah Jenson, introd. Susan Suleiman, trans. Sarah Cornell et al. (Cambridge, Mass.: Harvard University Press, 1991).

Clarke, Eric O., 'Shelley's Heart: Sexual Politics and Cultural Value', *Yale Journal of Criticism*, 8 (1995), 187–208.

Coleman, William, and Holmes, Frederic L. (eds.), *The Investigative Enterprise: Experimental Physiology in Nineteenth-Century Medicine* (Berkeley and Los Angeles: University of California Press, 1988).

Colley, Anne C., *Tennyson and Madness* (Athens: University of Georgia Press, 1993).

Collins, Joseph J., 'Tennyson and the Spasmodics', *Victorian Newsletter*, 43 (1974), 24–8.

Corns, Alfred, *The Poem's Heartbeat: A Manual of Prosody* (Ashland, Ore.: Story Line Press, 1997).

Cosslett, Tess, *The 'Scientific Movement' and Victorian Literature* (Brighton: Harvester, 1982).

Csordas, Thomas. J. (ed.), *Embodiment and Experience: The Existential Ground of Culture and Self* (Cambridge: Cambridge University Press, 1995).

Culler, A. Dwight, *Imaginative Reason: The Poetry of Matthew Arnold* (New Haven: Yale University Press, 1966).

D'Amico, Diane, 'Christina Rossetti's *Christian Year*: Comfort for "the Weary Heart" ', *Victorian Newsletter*, 72 (1987), 36–42.

David, Deirdre, *Intellectual Women and Victorian Patriarchy: Harriet Martineau, Elizabeth Barrett Browning, George Eliot* (Houndmills: Macmillan, 1987).

Dellamora, Richard, *Masculine Desire: The Sexual Politics of Victorian Aestheticism* (Chapel Hill: University of North Carolina Press, 1990).

DeLaura, David, *Hebrew and Hellene in Victorian England: Newman, Arnold and Pater* (Austin: University of Texas Press, 1969).

Dereli, Cynthia, 'Tennyson's *Maud*: Ambiguity and the War Context', *Tennyson Research Bulletin*, 7 (1997), 1–6.

De Sousa, Ronald, *The Rationality of Emotion* (Cambridge, Mass.: MIT Press, 1987).

Doueihi, Mihad, *A Perverse History of the Human Heart* (Cambridge, Mass.: Harvard University Press, 1997).

Douglas-Fairhurst, Robert, *Victorian Afterlives: The Shaping of Influence in Nineteenth-Century Literature* (Oxford: Oxford University Press, 2002).

East, Terence, *The Story of Heart Disease* (London: William Dawson, 1958).

Erickson, Robert, *The Language of the Heart, 1600–1750* (Philadelphia: University of Pennsylvania Press, 1997).

Faas, Ekbert, *Retreat into the Mind: Victorian Poetry and the Rise of Psychiatry* (Princeton: Princeton University Press, 1988).

Feher, Michel, et al. (eds.), *Fragments for a History of the Human Body*, 3 vols. (New York: Zone, 1989).

Fennell, Francis L., *Rereading Hopkins: Selected New Essays*, English Literary Studies Monograph 69 (Melbourne: University of Victoria, 1996).

Fleming, P. R., *A Short History of Cardiology* (Amsterdam: Rodopi, 1997).

Flint, Kate, *The Woman Reader* (Oxford: Clarendon Press, 1993).

Frank, Robert G., 'The Telltale Heart: Physiological Instruments, Graphic Methods and Clinical Hopes, 1854–1914', in Coleman and Holmes, 211–90.

French, R. K., *The History of the Heart: Thoracic Physiology from Ancient to Modern Times* (Aberdeen: Equipress, 1979).

Fuchs, Thomas, *The Mechanization of the Heart: Harvey and Descartes*, trans. Marjorie Grene (Rochester, NY: University of Rochester Press, 2001).

Gallagher, Catherine, '*Daniel Deronda*: The Prostitute and the Jewish Question', in Veeser, 124–40.

Gauld, Alan, 'Elliotson, John (1791–1868)', *Dictionary of National Biography*: **www.oxforddnb.com/view/article/8671**, accessed 7 June 2005.

Geison, Gerald, *Michael Foster and the Cambridge School of Physiology: The Scientific Enterprise in Late Victorian Society* (Princeton: Princeton University Press, 1978).

Gliserman, Susan, 'Early Victorian Science Writers and Tennyson's *In Memoriam*: A Study in Cultural Exchange', *Victorian Studies*, 18 (1974–5), 277–308, 437–60.

Griffiths, Eric, *The Printed Voice of Victorian Poetry* (Oxford: Clarendon Press, 1989).

Harris, Daniel, *Inspirations Unbidden: The 'Terrible Sonnets' of Gerard Manley Hopkins* (Berkeley and Los Angeles: University of California Press, 1982).

Helmstadter, Richard, and Lightman, Bernard (eds.), *Victorian Faith in Crisis: Essays on Continuity and Change in Nineteenth-Century Religious Belief* (Houndmills: Macmillan, 1990).

Higgins, Lesley, ' "Bone-House" and "Lovescape": Writing the Body in Hopkins's Canon', in Fennell, 11–35.

Hillman, David, and Mazzio, Carla (eds.), *The Body in Parts: Fantasies of Corporeality in Early Modern Europe* (London: Routledge, 1997).

Hoelever, Diane, *Romantic Androgyny: The Women Within* (University Park: Pennsylvania State University Press, 1990).

Honan, Park, *Matthew Arnold: A Life* (London: Weidenfeld & Nicolson, 1981).

Howell, Joel D., ' "Soldier's Heart": The Redefinition of Heart Disease and Speciality Formation in Early Twentieth-Century Great Britain', in Bynum, Lawrence, and Nutton, 34–52.

Hyder, Clyde K. (ed.), *Swinburne: The Critical Heritage* (London: Routledge and Kegan Paul, 1970).

Jacobus, Mary, Keller, Evelyn Fox, and Shuttleworth, Sally (eds.), *Body/Politics: Women and the Discourses of Science* (London: Routledge, 1990).

Jacyna, L. S., *Philosophic Whigs: Medicine, Science and Citizenship in Edinburgh, 1789–1848* (London: Routledge, 1994).

Jäger, Eric, *The Book of the Heart* (Chicago: University of Chicago Press, 2000).

Jalland, Pat, *Death in the Victorian Family* (Oxford: Oxford University Press, 1996).

James, William, *The Varieties of Religious Experience*, introd. Reinhold Niebuhr (New York: Simon & Schuster, 1997).

Jasper, David (ed.), *The Interpretation of Belief: Coleridge, Schleiermacher and Romanticism* (London: Macmillan, 1986).

Jay, Elisabeth, *The Religion of the Heart: Anglican Evangelicalism and the Nineteenth-Century Novel* (Oxford: Clarendon Press, 1979).

Johnson, Margaret, *Gerard Manley Hopkins and Tractarian Poetry* (Aldershot: Ashgate, 1997).

Johnson, Mark, *The Body in the Mind: The Bodily Basis of Meaning, Imagination and Reason* (Chicago: University of Chicago Press, 1987).

Jordan, Elaine, *Alfred Tennyson* (Cambridge: Cambridge University Press, 1988).

Joseph, Gerhard, *Tennyson and the Text: The Weaver's Shuttle* (Cambridge: Cambridge University Press, 1992).

Jump, John (ed.), *Tennyson: The Critical Heritage* (London: Routledge, 1967).

Keele, Kenneth D., 'The Application of the Physics of Sound to 19th-Century Cardiology: With Particular Reference to the Part Played by C. J. B. Williams and James Hope', *Clio Medica*, 8 (1973), 191–221.

Killingsworth, M. Jimmie, *Whitman's Poetry of the Body: Sexuality, Politics and the Text* (Chapel Hill: University of North Carolina Press, 1989).

Kincaid, James R., *Tennyson's Major Poems: The Comic and Ironic Patterns* (New Haven: Yale University Press, 1975).

Kline, Daniel, ' "For rigorous teachers seized my youth": Thomas Arnold, John Keble, and the Juvenilia of Arthur Hugh Clough and Matthew Arnold', in Blair, 143–58.

Knowlson, James, *Damned to Fame: The Life of Samuel Beckett* (London: Bloomsbury, 1996).

Lawford, Cynthia, 'Bijoux beyond Possession: The Prima Donnas of L.E.L.'s Album Poems', in Armstrong and Blain, 102–14.

—— 'Diary', *London Review of Books*, 21 Sept. 2000, 36–7.

Lawrence, Christopher, 'Moderns and Ancients: The "New Cardiology" in Britain 1880–1930', in Bynum, Lawrence, and Nutton, 1–33.

Lee, Hermione, *Virginia Woolf* (London: Vintage, 1997).

Lee, Ruth Webb, *A History of Valentines* (London: Batsford, 1953).

Le Goff, Jacques, 'Head or Heart? The Political Use of Bodily Metaphors in the Middle Ages', in Feher, iii. 12–27.

Leibowitz, J. O., *The History of Coronary Heart Disease* (London: Wellcome Institute, 1970).

Leighton, Angela, ' "Because man made the laws": The Fallen Woman and the Woman Poet', *Victorian Poetry*, 27 (1989), 109–29.

—— *Victorian Women Poets: Writing against the Heart* (Hemel Hempstead: Harvester Wheatsheaf, 1992).

—— (ed.), *Victorian Women Poets: A Critical Reader* (Oxford: Blackwell, 1996).

Leighton, Angela, and Reynolds, Margaret (eds.), *Victorian Women Poets: An Anthology* (Oxford: Blackwell, 1995).

LeMaster, J. R., and Kummings, Donald D. (eds.), *Walt Whitman: An Encyclopedia* (New York: Garland, 1998).

Levine, George (ed.), *One Culture: Essays in Science and Literature* (Madison: University of Wisconsin Press, 1987).

Logan, Peter, *Nerves and Narratives: A Cultural History of Hysteria in Nineteenth-Century British Prose* (Berkeley and Los Angeles: University of California Press, 1997).

Lootens, Tricia, *Lost Saints: Silence, Gender and Victorian Literary Canonization* (Charlottesville: University Press of Virginia, 1996).

Louis, Margot, 'Enlarging the Heart: L.E.L.'s "The Improvisatrice", Hemans's "Properzia Rossi" and Barrett Browning's *Aurora Leigh*', *Victorian Literature and Culture*, 26 (1998), 1–19.

——— *Swinburne and his Gods: The Roots and Growth of an Agnostic Poetry* (Kingston: Queen's University Press, 1990).

Loving, Jerome, *Walt Whitman: The Song of Himself* (Berkeley and Los Angeles: University of California Press, 1999).

Lüderitz, Berndt, *History of the Disorders of Cardiac Rhythm* (New York: Futura, 1995).

Lyon, M. L., and Barbalet, J. M., 'Society's Body: Emotion and the "Somatization" of Social Theory', in Csordas, 48–68.

Lystra, Karen, *Searching the Heart: Women, Men and Romantic Love in Nineteenth-Century America* (Oxford: Oxford University Press, 1989).

McGann, Jerome, *The Poetics of Sensibility* (Oxford: Clarendon Press, 1996).

Markley, A. A., *Stateliest Measures: Tennyson and the Literature of Greece and Rome* (Toronto: University of Toronto Press, 2004).

Martin, Robert Bernard, *Tennyson: The Unquiet Heart* (Oxford: Clarendon Press, 1980).

Mattes, Eleanor, *In Memoriam: The Way of a Soul* (New York: Exposition Press, 1951).

Matthews, Samantha, *Poetical Remains: Poets' Graves, Bodies and Books in the Nineteenth Century* (Oxford: Oxford University Press, 2004).

Maxwell, Catherine, 'Swinburne: Style, Sympathy and Sadomasochism', *Journal of Pre-Raphaelite Studies*, 12 (2003), 86–96.

Mee, Jon, *Romanticism, Enthusiasm and Regulation: Poetics and the Policing of Culture in the Romantic Period* (Oxford: Oxford University Press, 2003).

Mellor, Anne K., *Romanticism and Gender* (London: Routledge, 1993).

Michie, Helena, *The Flesh Made Word: Female Figures and Women's Bodies* (Oxford: Oxford University Press, 1987).

Miller, Andrew, and Eli Adams, James (eds.), *Sexualities in Victorian Britain* (Bloomington: Indiana University Press, 1996).

Miller, J. Hillis, *Topographies* (Stanford, Calif.: Stanford University Press, 1995).

Moretti, Franco, *Signs Taken for Wonders: Essays in the Sociology of Literary Forms*, trans. Susan Fischer et al., 2nd edn. (London: Verso, 1988).

Morgan, A. D., 'Some Forms of Undiagnosed Coronary Disease in Nineteenth-Century England', *Medical History*, 12 (1968), 344–58.

Nelson, Claudia, 'Sex and the Single Boy: Ideals of Manliness and Sexuality in Victorian Literature for Boys', *Victorian Studies*, 32 (1989), 525–50.

Nussbaum, Martha, *Upheavals of Thought: The Intelligence of Emotions* (Cambridge: Cambridge University Press, 2001).

Omond, T. S., *English Metrists* (Oxford: Clarendon Press, 1921).

O'Neill, James Norman, 'Anthem for Doomed Youth: An Interdisciplinary Study of Tennyson's *Maud* and the Crimean War', *Tennyson Research Bulletin*, 5 (1990), 166–82.

Oppenheim, Janet, *'Shattered Nerves': Doctors, Patients and Depression in Victorian England* (Oxford: Oxford University Press, 1991).

Oram, William A., 'Arnold's "Scholar-Gipsy" and the Crisis of the 1852 *Poems*', *Modern Language Quarterly*, 45 (1984), 144–62.

Peltason, Timothy, *Reading 'In Memoriam'* (Princeton: Princeton University Press, 1985).

Peterson, Linda H., 'Rewriting "A History of the Lyre": Letitia Landon, Elizabeth Barrett Browning and the (Re)construction of the Nineteenth-Century Woman Poet', in Armstrong and Blain, 115–34.

Peterson, M. Jeanne, *The Medical Profession in Mid-Victorian London* (Berkeley and Los Angeles: University of California Press, 1978).

Piette, Adam, 'Sound-Repetitions and Sense, or How to Hear Tennyson', *Swiss Papers in English Language and Literature*, 7 (1994), 157–70.

Pilloud, Severine, and Louis-Courvoisier, Micheline, 'The Intimate Experience of the Body in the Eighteenth Century: Between Interiority and Exteriority', *Medical History*, 47 (2003), 451–72.

Pinch, Adela, *Strange Fits of Passion: Epistemologies of Emotion, Hume to Austen* (Stanford, Calif.: Stanford University Press, 1996).

Platizky, Roger S., *A Blueprint of his Dissent: Madness and Method in Tennyson's Poetry* (London: AUP, 1989).

Prickett, Stephen, *Romanticism and Religion: The Tradition of Coleridge and Wordsworth in the Victorian Church* (Cambridge: Cambridge University Press, 1976).

Priestley, J. B., *Victoria's Heyday* (London: Heinemann, 1972).

Prins, Yopie, 'Victorian Meters', in Bristow, 89–113.

Psomiades, Kathy, *Beauty's Body: Femininity and Representation in British Aestheticism* (Stanford, Calif.: Stanford University Press, 1997).

Rader, Ralph W., *Tennyson's 'Maud': The Biographical Genesis* (Berkeley and Los Angeles: University of California Press, 1963).

Raven, James, Small, Helen, and Tadmor, Naomi (eds.), *The Practice and Representation of Reading in England* (Cambridge: Cambridge University Press, 1996).

Reddy, William, *The Navigation of Feeling: A Framework for the History of the Emotions* (Cambridge: Cambridge University Press, 2001).

Reynolds, Margaret, *Fragments of an Elegy: Tennyson Reading Sappho* (Lincoln: Tennyson Society, 2001).

Reynolds, Matthew, *The Realms of Verse: English Poetry in a Time of Nation-Building* (Oxford: Oxford University Press, 2001).

Richard, Claude, 'The Heart of Poe and the Rhythmics of the Poems', in Carlson, 195–206.

Ricks, Christopher, *Keats and Embarrassment* (Oxford: Clarendon Press, 1974).

—— 'Tennyson Inheriting the Earth', in Hallam Tennyson (1981), 66–104.

—— *Tennyson*, 2nd edn. (London: Macmillan, 1989).

Rooksby, Rikky, *A. C. Swinburne: A Poet's Life* (Aldershot: Scolar, 1997).

Ross, Marlon B, *The Contours of Masculine Desire: Romanticism and the Rise of Women's Poetry* (Oxford: Oxford University Press, 1989).

Rousseau, G. S., 'Medicine and Literature: The State of the Field', *Isis*, 72 (1981), 406–24.

Rudy, Jason, 'Rhythmic Intimacy, Spasmodic Epistemology', *Victorian Poetry*, 42 (2004), 451–72.

Russett, Cynthia Eagle, *Sexual Science: The Victorian Construction of Womanhood* (Cambridge, Mass.: Harvard University Press, 1989).

Rylance, Rick, *Victorian Psychology and British Culture 1850–1880* (Oxford: Oxford University Press, 2001).

Sachs, Curt, *Rhythm and Tempo* (London: J. M. Dent, 1953).

Sacks, Peter, *The English Elegy* (Baltimore: Johns Hopkins University Press, 1985).

Saintsbury, George, *A History of English Prosody*, 2nd edn., 3 vols. (London: Macmillan, 1923).

Shannon, Edgar F., *Tennyson and the Reviewers* (Cambridge, Mass.: Harvard University Press, 1952).

Shapiro, Karl, and Beum, Robert, *A Prosody Handbook* (New York: Harper and Row, 1975).

Shaw, W. David, *Tennyson's Style* (Ithaca, NY: Cornell University Press, 1976).

Shires, Linda, '*Maud*, Masculinity and Poetic Identity', *Criticism*, 29 (1987), 269–90.

Shuttleworth, Sally, 'Female Circulation: Medical Discourse and Popular Advertising in the Mid-Victorian Era', in Jacobus, Keller, and Shuttleworth, 47–68.

—— *Charlotte Brontë and Victorian Psychology* (Cambridge: Cambridge University Press, 1996).

Sinfield, Alan, *The Language of Tennyson's 'In Memoriam'* (Oxford: Blackwell, 1971).

Skerrit, P. W., 'Anxiety and the Heart: A Historical Review', *Psychological Medicine*, 13 (1983), 17–24.

Slinn, E. Warwick, *Victorian Poetry as Cultural Critique: The Politics of Performative Language* (Charlottesville: University of Virginia Press, 2003).

Small, Helen, 'A Pulse of 124: Charles Dickens and a Pathology of the Mid-Victorian Reading Public', in Raven, Small, and Tadmor, 263–90.

Sontag, Susan, *AIDS and its Metaphors* (New York: Farrar, Strauss and Giroux, 1989).

Stedman, Gesa, *Stemming the Torrent: Expression and Control in the Victorian Discourses on Emotions, 1830–1872* (Aldershot: Ashgate, 2002).

Stevens, Scott Manning, 'Sacred Heart and Secular Brain', in Hillman and Mazzio, 263–84.

Tamke, Susan, *Make a Joyful Noise unto the Lord: Hymns as a Reflection of Victorian Social Attitudes* (Athens: Ohio University Press, 1978).

Taylor, Dennis, *Hardy's Metres and Victorian Prosody* (Oxford: Clarendon Press, 1988).

Tennyson, Hallam (ed.), *Studies in Tennyson* (London: Macmillan, 1981).

Tinker, C. B., and Lowry, H. F., *The Poetry of Matthew Arnold: A Commentary* (London: Oxford University Press, 1940).

Todd, Janet, *Sensibility: An Introduction* (London: Methuen, 1976).

Trotter, David, 'Hidden Ground Within: Matthew Arnold's Lyric and Elegiac Poetry', *ELH* 44 (1977), 526–53.

——*Circulation : Defoe, Dickens and the Economies of the Novel* (London: Macmillan, 1988).

Tucker, Herbert, *Tennyson and the Doom of Romanticism* (Cambridge, Mass.: Harvard University Press, 1988).

——'Glandular Omnism and Beyond: The Victorian Spasmodic Epic', *Victorian Poetry*, 42 (2004), 429–50.

Turner, Frank, 'The Victorian Crisis of Faith and the Faith that was Lost', in Helmstadter and Lightman, 9–38.

Veeser, H. Aram (ed.), *The New Historicism Reader* (London: Routledge, 1994).

Vinken, Pierre, *The Shape of the Heart*, trans. Kenneth Ellison Davis (Amsterdam: Elsevier Press, 2000).

Vrettos, Athena, *Somatic Fictions: Imagining Illness in Victorian Culture* (Stanford, Calif.: Stanford University Press, 1995).

Waddington, Patrick (ed.), *Theirs But to Do and Die: The Poetry of the Charge of the Light Brigade at Balaklava, 25th October 1854* (Nottingham: Astra, 1995).

Warren, Alba H., *English Poetic Theory, 1825–1865* (Princeton: Princeton University Press, 1950).

Watson, J. R., *The English Hymn: A Critical and Historical Study* (Oxford: Clarendon Press, 1997).

Weinstein, Mark A., *William Edmonstoune Aytoun and the Spasmodic Controversy* (New Haven: Yale University Press, 1968).

Wheeler, Michael, 'Tennyson, Newman and the Question of Authority', in Jasper, 185–201.

_____ *Death and the Future Life in Victorian Literature and Theology* (Cambridge: Cambridge University Press, 1990).

Williams, Margaret, *The Society of the Sacred Heart: History of a Spirit 1800–1975* (London: Darton, Longman and Todd, 1978).

Willius, Frederick A., and Dry, Thomas, *A History of the Heart and the Circulation* (Philadelphia: W. B. Saunders, 1948).

_____ and Keys, Thomas (eds.), *Cardiac Classics* (London: Henry Kipton, 1941).

Wood, Jane, *Passion and Pathology in Victorian Fiction* (Oxford: Oxford University Press, 2001).

Youngson, A. J., *The Scientific Revolution in Victorian Medicine* (London: Croom Helm, 1979).

Zonana, Joyce, 'The Embodied Muse: Elizabeth Barrett Browning's *Aurora Leigh* and Feminist Poetics', in Leighton (1996), 53–74.

Index